Wildlife
& THE LAW

previous books by the author

Wildlife Detective (Argyll 2007)
The Thin Green Line (Argyll 2009)
A Lone Furrow (Argyll 2011)

Wildlife
& THE LAW

a field guide to recognising,
reporting and investigating
wildlife crime in Scotland

ALAN STEWART

Alan Stewart

Nov 2012

ARGYLL✢PUBLISHING

Argyll Publishing
Glendaruel
Argyll PA22 3AE
Scotland
www.argyllpublishing.co.uk

The Partnership for Action Against Wildlife Crime
Scotland, otherwise known as PAW Scotland, is
delighted to part-fund the publication of this latest book
by Alan Stewart. The PAW Scotland partnership consists
of a large variety of partners including police, land
managers, conservationists, Scottish Natural Heritage and
the Scottish Government , working together to reduce
wildlife crime. This book will not only help to raise the
profile of wildlife crime with the general public, but will
also provide users with a concise guide in relation to
wildlife crime legislation.

British Library Cataloguing-in-Publication Data.
A catalogue record for this book is available from the
British Library.

ISBN 978 1 908931 15 3

Printing & Binding Bell & Bain Ltd, Glasgow

Contents

Acknowledgements

I AM extremely grateful to the following individuals and organisations for their help in the production of this guide. All are experts in their own field and I have regularly picked their brains on some of the more complex issues on which they have far more knowledge than I. If their advice has altered slightly in my interpretation I apologise and insist that any mistakes are mine.

British Association for Shooting and Conservation (Scotland)

Bruce, John	British Deer Society
Campbell, Steve	Science and Advice for Scottish Agriculture
Canning, Phil	Inspector, Bedfordshire Police
Charleston, Pete	Bat Conservation Trust
Cooper, Margaret E	Visiting lecturer, Faculty of Veterinary Medicine, University of Nairobi, Kenya
Cooper, Prof John E	Dept of Veterinary Medicine, University of Cambridge
Davidson, Brian	Association of Salmon Fishery Boards
Dignon, Hugh	Team Leader, Wildlife Management Branch, Scottish Govt
Drummond, Kevin QC	Sheriff, Borders Courts
Elliot, Bob	RSPB
Everitt, PC Charles	UK National Wildlife Crime Unit
Fleming, Kate	Crown Office and Procurator Fiscal Service
Hartley, Dr Gill	Science and Advice for Scottish Agriculture
Hunter, Karen	Wildlife Crime Policy Officer, the Scottish Govt
Hunter, Nevin	Inspector, UK National Wildlife Crime Unit
Hutchison, Ian	Scottish Badgers
McDonald, Kim	Guild of Taxidermists
McJannett, Shona	Crown Office and Procurator Fiscal Service
MacKinnon, PC Dave	Grampian Police
Morton, Keith	RSPB Scotland
Munro, Prof Ranald	Royal (Dick) School of Veterinary Studies
Murdoch, Catherine	Wildlife and Protected Areas, the Scottish Govt
O'May, PC Malcolm	Central Scotland Police
Patterson, Gordon	Forestry Commission Scotland
Pendry, Stephanie	TRAFFIC
Pritchard, Stewart	Scottish Natural Heritage
Ross, Dr Ben	Scottish Natural Heritage
Scott, James	Scottish Natural Heritage
Shedden, Dr Colin	British Association for Shooting and Conservation (Scotland)
Sharp, Elizabeth	Science and Advice for Scottish Agriculture
Thompson, Prof Des	Scottish Natural Heritage
Walker, Ian	Marine Scotland
Webster; Dr Lucy	Science and Advice for Scottish Agriculture

Foreword

IS IT NOT a shame that we need such a field guide? It implies that a lot of criminal activities occur in our countryside to the extent that we need to take special steps to recognise and record it, and then take appropriate action. We have field guides on birds, mammals, butterflies and other insects, and on many habitats and other features of nature, but that is because we enjoy recording what we see and learning more. Many of these guides have the further purpose to support national recording schemes which help us all better understand nature. But a field guide to legislation, and to tackling crime – that is something altogether different.

Crime is in many ways a symptom of failure in society. Whist this book rightly does not delve into the causes or perpetrators of wildlife crime, we need to accept two things about it. First, criminal activities happen, and possibly much more widely and closer to us than we care to acknowledge. Second, crime has far reaching implications for wildlife and for people who depend on or enjoy it. Scarce nesting birds whose eggs are robbed, badger setts which are destroyed, or dwindling populations with members shot, poisoned or otherwise destroyed all suffer. In some cases national populations have been put at risk – the extermination and subsequent return of ospreys to Scotland being a classic example.

When we read or hear a reference to wildlife crime we should be mindful that the victims are real. Many illegally-killed or captured animals suffer extreme pain; the poisoned corpse of a golden eagle is not just a statistic, it is the body of a once-wild and iconic bird which in all probability suffered a merciless death. There may be other victims, such as dependent young, which are unreported following the finding of a poached deer or a coursed brown hare. And *people* suffer, for most of us want to see wildlife thriving and feel it as our right to witness the best and wildest of nature. Put another way, a symptom of an unjust and criminal society would be regular and widespread encounters with a countryside diminished in what should be present because of crime. Examples of this already are the scarcity in areas where they should be common of the freshwater pearl mussel and hen harrier. Wildlife crime is a stain on our country's identity and values; it is not just an assault on nature.

In Scotland, we have worked hard to stamp out criminality, and there are important signs of improvement and success. Many laws have been passed by the UK and Scottish governments to tackle wildlife crime, and we now have some exemplars of legislation and good practice. Licensing systems have improved in effectiveness and transparency, and a lot of effort has been spent on sharing good practices to ensure the law works well. The Partnership for Action against Wildlife Crime in Scotland (PAW Scotland) is a splendid example of how government agencies, non-government organisations and other parties can work together against the forces of crime. The number of committees and groups working under this umbrella reflects the complex nature of wildlife crime and the many ways of rooting it out. Indeed the partnerships forged to root out wildlife crime represent a determined effort by government, the police, environmental bodies and land managers. We have come a long way with growing determination to make our environment safer and healthier.

So, why do we need this field guide? Well, for land and wildlife managers, it helps reinforce what can, and should, be done within the law. Gamekeepers, deerstalkers, farmers, crofters and anglers undertake much of their work under licence, and most do their utmost to abide by licence conditions. This is not easy, and some of the machinations of the law mean, for instance, that managers have to take extreme care in their pest control. People observing nature, be these researchers or licensed surveyors, have to be equally mindful of how they work within the law – not least in minimising disturbance. For the police, the guide will be invaluable as an *aide memoire* for good practice. And there are the occasions when we, members of the public, will suspect something untoward or witness criminal activities or their consequences. Here, we enter an unfamiliar world, and the three clear messages are to record what you see, immediately report it to the police, and not to tamper with any of the evidence. If you find a pile of freshwater pearl mussel shells by a river bank, an emaciated buzzard in a Larsen trap, or a hare killed by dogs, record – then report to the police.

That this book ranges over so much of our wildlife is rich testament to the experience, persistence and expertise of the author. Plants and animals, eggshells, horns, tusks and even bird skins all have starring roles here. No stone is left unturned as the author deploys his great breadth and depth of specialist knowledge. A retired, but still highly active, senior police officer, Alan Stewart adeptly takes you, the reader, through the uniquely complex world of tackling wildlife crime. On the journey we see the intricacies of the law and the myriad workings of nature.

In Scotland, nature defines much of what we love about our country, so let's do what we can to keep it in good health.

Des Thompson
Scottish Natural Heritage
August 2012

Introduction

IN SCOTLAND we have a wide range of legislation protecting an equally diverse range of species of animals, plants and, in some cases, habitat. Some of the legislation is very old, for instance the Agriculture (Scotland) Act 1948; some is very new, such as the Marine (Scotland) Act 2010 or the Spring Traps Approval (Scotland) Order 2011; and legislation such as the Nature Conservation (Scotland) Act 2004 and the Wildlife and Natural Environment (Scotland) Act 2011 have updated various older statutes. In some cases the updates have been quite dramatic, for example the nineteenth century game laws have been repealed and all poaching is now covered by the Wildlife and Countryside Act 1981; and the new provisions within that act that which cover vicarious liability.

Some of this legislation is very complex, for example the Conservation (Natural Habitats etc) Regulations 1994, and even people who deal with this diverse legislation on a daily basis can be confused by it. So it is hardly surprising that people whose daily occupations are governed by the provisions of the law as to what they can and can't legally do are sometimes caught out. Nevertheless, ignorance of the law is not a valid excuse in court.

This field guide is a synopsis of wildlife crime attempting to make the law clearer and more explicit. It is intended to assist in preventing offences being committed, which of course should be the aim of every single person who values wildlife. But where prevention has failed, and infringements of wildlife law are encountered, this guide will help the reader recognise the offence, respond appropriately and effectively, be aware of how to preserve evidence and what assistance to expect after reporting the matter to the police. Where appropriate, I have cross-referenced (in brackets) the text to its origin in the legislation. This should be particularly helpful to police officers investigating, or about to investigate, a case. Apart from occasional use for emphasis, text in *italics* constitutes direct quotes from the legislation rather than my abbrieviations or interpretations. Mid-point in the guide (p142) is a FAQ secton for quick reference.

There is a separate chapter on cruelty to domestic and captive wild animals, a brief chapter on offences relating to dogs, and one on offences committed against Sites of Special Scientific Interest (SSSIs). These are all inextricably linked with the advances in specialised policing and prosecution.

Many wildlife and environmental crime officers (WECOs), in addition to investigating crimes against our wildlife, also assume an overview of cruelty and dog offences dealt with by their colleagues. A specialist unit with the Crown Office and Procurator Fiscal Service now deals with wildlife and environmental crime, and also has an overview of cruelty offences.

The book should assist a range of people including:

- Police officers, and the staff of other statutory or non-government organisations who have some responsibility in the investigation of wildlife crime
- Countryside rangers, foresters, badger groups, bat groups and the staff or members of similar organisations who, though not investigators, have a professional interest in wildlife issues
- Gamekeepers, farmers and pest controllers, who might use traps and snares or control 'pest' species in the course of their work
- Hill walkers, and others who take advantage of the countryside for recreation
- Property owners, developers or even householders who might have concerns with nesting birds or bat roosts

Since some of the chapters following relate to the capture and killing of animals and birds, it is important to appreciate that for the most part this is carried out legally. Even if some readers do not agree with shooting pheasants or grouse, the use of snares or traps or even the culling of deer as part of deer management, all of these are legitimate activities. Providing they stay within the law, those who participate in these activities are entitled to do so without interference. As part of agriculture, game management and sometimes conservation of rare species, some mammals and birds are controlled. Provided certain conditions are met or licences obtained, this is also legal. It is important that snares and traps should not be damaged or interfered with except in circumstances where they are clearly illegal and liable to catch a victim, though in doing so it should be recognised this may destroy evidence.

A warning to amateur detectives: it is advisable for members of the public witnessing a wildlife crime not to approach a suspect. Some offenders may be violent, particularly those involved in poaching and hare coursing. Approaching suspects is also likely to cause evidence to be removed or destroyed. It is usually much better to watch unseen and provide a detailed report to the police as soon as you can.

Lastly, despite the many years of being involved in the investigation of crime, and the significant number of years specialising in wildlife crime, I certainly don't profess to know it all. The interpretations are based on the knowledge I have gained over the years, and I'd be surprised if I've interpreted absolutely everything in this field guide with 100% accuracy. **For any legal purposes the contents of this book should be checked against current legislaton.** New editions are planned as the legislation evolves, so if you notice something that you know or believe to be incorrect – or you have any comments on how to improve the book – please let me know by email: alanstewart164@btinternet.com

1. Police Powers

THOUGH police officers have a wide range of powers of search without warrant, both from statutory law and common law, these powers – which in effect are an intrusion into someone's privacy – are rightly limited. They apply only to situations in which the officer has reasonable cause to believe that a person has committed a crime, that a person is in possession of items related to a crime or that there are items connected to a crime on any land (which in certain circumstances can include buildings or other places that are unlocked, though not a dwelling house.) Carrying out searches *without* reasonable cause is illegal and can subject the officer to criminal and/or disciplinary proceedings. This is clear to officers, though not necessarily to all members of the public, who sometimes feel that little is being done when in fact there is insufficient evidence to justify a search. The following, as well as being an aide memoire to officers, gives the layperson an indication of the parameters and the limitations of powers given to the police.

Under the Wildlife and Countryside Act 1981

Of the various pieces of wildlife legislation, the most widely-used is the Wildlife and Countryside Act 1981. It has been updated by various other pieces of legislation since 1981, most notably the Nature Conservation (Scotland) Act 2004 and the Wildlife and Natural Environment (Scotland) Act 2011.

In many wildlife investigations, joint enquiries with the police and other organisations are to be commended. They are often more successful because of the amalgamation of expertise plus the police power of arrest or detention. It is likely, therefore, when police officers are searching either under the terms of a search warrant or simply under their relevant statutory powers, they may have with them personnel from at least one other organisation. Any non-police personnel attending are there to assist or to advise, though invariably the police will be the lead organisation. The powers within the Wildlife and Countryside Act and the other legislation mentioned earlier cater for this situation.

Section 19 (1) – Police powers of arrest, search and seizure without a warrant

If a constable suspects with reasonable cause that any person is committing or has committed an offence under this Part (Part I of the WCA), the constable may, without warrant:

> (a) stop and search that person if the constable suspects that evidence of the commission of the offence is to be found on that person;
>
> (b) search for, search or examine any thing which that person may then be using or may have used, or may have or may have had in his possession if the constable suspects with reasonable cause that evidence of the commission of the offence is to be found in or on that thing;
>
> (c) arrest that person;
>
> (c) seize and detain for the purposes of proceedings under this Part any thing which may be evidence of the commission of the offence or may be liable to be forfeited under section 21.

The stop and search power is well tried and tested, and is no different under this Act than the same power under various other non wildlife-related legislation.

The power of search without warrant is more extensive under this Act than in most other legislation. Prior to 2004 the wording gave power to 'search or examine any thing that the person may be using ... or on that thing.' This limited searches virtually to items in possession of a suspect. It did not allow the search *for* items, nor did it cover anything outwith the present tense. It was only after strong representation by police wildlife crime officers to the legislators within the then Scottish Executive that they agreed that change was necessary. As can be seen, the changes have made a substantial difference.

In many cases subsection (1) needs to be read in conjunction with subsection (2).

Powers of arrest have been expanded by the Criminal Justice (Scotland) Act 2003. An unconditional power of arrest is available for all offences under Part I of the Wildlife and Countryside Act, 1981. Courts also have the power to imprison a person convicted of any Part I offence, therefore a detention by a police officer under Section 14 of the Criminal Procedure (Scotland) Act 1995, would be an option in relation to a suspect.

Section 19 (2) – Power to search land without a warrant

If a constable suspects with reasonable cause that any person is committing or has committed an offence under this Part, he may, for the purpose of exercising the powers conferred by subsection (1), enter any land other than a dwelling or lockfast premises.

This would appear to allow a police officer, if he or she can justify the action taken, to search *or search for* any thing (which is not defined and would appear able to be taken at literal value as any 'thing' from a needle to a haystack) and in order to do so, enter any unlocked premises (apart from a dwelling) or unlocked vehicle in order to carry out this search. Because of the scarcity of case law, a search may well be challenged by a defence solicitor, however if the search immediately follows the obtaining of the evidence or information which creates the reasonable suspicion of a crime in the first place, the Crown position is much stronger. If a search is pre-planned and there are sufficient grounds to obtain a search warrant, this should be sought. In many cases the search warrant may only be made out to cover the requirement to search premises or vehicles, with the prosecutor relying on the powers under this section to search land without warrant.

In practical terms, evidence sufficient to satisfy a procurator fiscal to seek a search warrant, and of course a sheriff to grant one, may not be available. In that case the degree of intrusion may be taken into consideration by a court. Intrusion on to a large tract of land for a search is likely to be less of a legal challenge in a court than intrusion into an unlocked shed or vehicle. Each case has to be treated on its own merits.

Section 19 (3) – Search under warrant

If a justice of the peace is satisfied by evidence on oath that there are reasonable grounds for suspecting that an offence under this Part has been committed and that evidence of the offence may be found on any premises, he may grant a warrant to any constable to enter those premises, if necessary using reasonable force, and search them for the purpose of obtaining that evidence.

In the application of this subsection to Scotland, the reference to a justice of the peace includes a reference to the sheriff.

As full a description as possible of land and places to be searched should be included in the warrant request, as should a detailed list of items sought, sections of statutes believed contravened and details of persons other than police officers who will be involved. (see section on Search Warrants p21)

Section 19 (4) – Duration of warrant

A warrant under subsection (3) continues in force until the purpose for which the entry is required has been satisfied or, if earlier, the expiry of such period as the warrant may specify

Section 19 (5) – Produce evidence of authority
A constable authorised by virtue of this section to enter any land must, if required to do so by the occupier or anyone acting on the occupier's behalf, produce evidence of the constable's authority.

Section 19 (6) – Take other persons or equipment to land
A constable who enters any land in the exercise of a power conferred by this section –
> (a) may –
>> (i) be accompanied by any other persons, and
>> (ii) take any machinery, other equipment or materials on to the land,
>> for the purpose of assisting the constable in the exercise of that power,
> (b) may take samples of any articles or substances found there and remove the samples from the land.

Depending on the purpose of the search, police may request staff from one or more agencies to accompany them. These may be staff from Scottish Government Rural Payment Inspections Directorate (SGRPID), SNH, RSPB, SSPCA or Defra Animal Health Veterinary Laboratory Agency (AHVLA). Their purpose is to advise or to assist in the search of land. Apart from staff from statutory bodies, they should not be participating in a search of premises or vehicles unless requested to do so by a police officer and under that officer's direct supervision.

Section 19 (7) – Extended powers subject to terms of warrant
A power specified in subsection (6)(a) or (b) which is exercisable under a warrant is subject to the terms of the warrant.

Section 19 (8) – Leaving land secure
A constable leaving any land which has been entered in exercise of a power conferred by Section 19(2) or by a warrant under Section 19(3), being either unoccupied land or land from which the occupier is temporarily absent, must leave it as effectively secured against unauthorised entry as the constable found it.

SGRPID staff has powers without warrant under the Food and Environment Protection Act 1985, (FEPA), to carry out inspections in relation to the use and storage of pesticides. To carry out these inspections, they may enter land or buildings other than dwellings, using force if necessary. SGRPID staff may also make application for a search warrant under FEPA. Since SGRPID powers relate to inspections of the storage and use of pesticides, police officers should not piggy-back on their powers for a criminal investigation. In this case powers under Section 19 of the WCA should be used, or application should be made for a search warrant

Under other legislation with powers identical to those of the Wildlife and Countryside Act 1981:

The following three statutes have police powers identical to those under the Wildlife and Countryside Act 1981:

> Protection of Badgers Act 1972 (the section setting out police powers is section 11).
>
> Conservation (Natural Habitats etc) Regulations 1994 (the regulation setting out police powers is regulation 101).
>
> Nature Conservation (Scotland) Act 2004 (the section setting out police powers is section 43).

Under wildlife legislation not already covered (in date order):

> **Agriculture (Scotland) Act, 1948**: No statutory powers under the Act
>
> **Pests Act 1954**: No statutory powers under the Act
>
> **Wild Mammals (Protection) Act, 1996**: see Offences against mammals (cruelty) p94
>
> **Deer (Scotland) Act, 1996**: see Poaching – Deer p161
>
> **Control of Trade in Endangered Species (Enforcement) Regulations, 1997**: see chapter Illegal trade in endangered species (COTES) p136
>
> **Protection of Wild Mammals (Scotland) Act 2002**: See Offences against wild mammals (hunting) p89
>
> **Conservation of Salmon (Prohibition of Sale) (Scotland) Regulations 2002**: No statutory power under the Regulations
>
> **Criminal Justice (Scotland) Act 2003 (Section 77, Schedule 1, Schedule 2 and Schedule 3 only)**: The provisions of this Act strengthened the enforcement provisions and provided for custodial sentences within the Wildlife and Countryside Act 1981
>
> **Criminal Justice Act 2003 (Section 307 only)**: This section of the Act provides a power of arrest under COTES
>
> **Salmon and Freshwater Fisheries (Consolidation) (Scotland) Act 2003**: see Poaching – Fish p168
>
> **Environmental Protection (Restriction on Use of Lead Shot) (Scotland) (No.2) Regulations 2004**: No statutory powers under the Regulations
>
> **Possession of Pesticides (Scotland) Order 2005**: No statutory powers under the Order

Animal Health and Welfare (Scotland) Act 2006: See Cruelty to domestic and captive wild animals p191

Aquaculture and Fisheries (Scotland) Act 2007: No statutory powers under the Act. Amends the 2003 Consolidated Act

Conservation (Natural Habitats etc) Amendment (Scotland) Regulations 2007: No statutory powers under these Regulations. Amends the Habitats Regs1994

Freshwater Fish Conservation (Prohibition on Fishing for Eels) (Scotland) Regulations 2008: No statutory powers under the Regulations

Snares (Scotland) Order 2010: No statutory powers under the Order. Amends the WCA 1981

Marine (Scotland) Act 2010: See Wild Mammals – Seals p100

Wildlife and Natural Environment (Scotland) Act 2011: No statutory powers within the Act itself. Amends other legislation

Spring Traps Approval (Scotland) Order, 2011: No statutory powers under the Order

Deer (Close Seasons) (Scotland) Order 2011: No statutory powers under the Order

Under search warrants

Since this book is not restricted to police officers, operational issues that are not generally in the public domain are not discussed. I hesitated about a section on search warrants, but have included it as there is obvious benefit in anyone not involved in the investigation and prosecution of crime (of any kind, not just wildlife crime) to see the rigorous and transparent procedure required before a search warrant is granted. It is certainly not the case that on a whim (or a 'fishing expedition' as it is often referred to) an officer can obtain a legal piece of paper that allows intrusion into another person's privacy.

Search warrants relating to wildlife and countryside law are subject to the same procedures and scrutiny as other search warrants. In particular the warrant must (1) be applied for in accordance with the Lord Advocates Guidance on warrant applications and (2) comply with, and stand up to, scrutiny of human rights.

All applications for wildlife and countryside search warrants must be submitted to the procurator fiscal in writing, and should be in accordance with the protocol between the Crown Office and Procurator Fiscal Service (COPFS) and the Association of Chief Police Officers in Scotland (ACPOS) in relation to search warrants. Locally the police will have arrangements with their procurator fiscal to apply for search warrants. WECOs should be aware of these arrangements and should also have a good working relationship with the specialist wildlife prosecutors, who may be the preferred option for a warrant request.

On 2 October 2000 the European Convention on Human Rights (ECHR) was incorporated into the law of Scotland. This development in Scots law has made search warrants in particular subject to Article 8 – the right to respect for private and family life, home etc. The High Court has clearly indicated that whatever the reasons for and effects of the conservatism of the past decisions of courts, ECHR will have a persuasive effect. If former case law is in conflict with the European Court then the European Court decision will be preferred.

When a search warrant under Wildlife and Countryside legislation is being considered for a series of buildings, egg thief's house or poacher's shed, besides the evidence to be secured, other matters must now be taken into account. Is the obtaining of a warrant proportionate to the evidence to be obtained? Is it necessary to execute the warrant forthwith; can it not wait until the daylight hours?

Applications for a search warrant:
The investigating police officer (after discussing the case with a wildlife crime officer) has to consider:

- are there reasonable grounds to suspect (a) an offence has been committed; and (b) evidence of that offence may be found at the target address?
- is it necessary and proportionate to seek a search warrant?
- are there no alternative ways of achieving the same objective?
- the statutory authority for the warrant to be stated accurately in the body of the warrant
- time limits as set out by statute

A written application should be made to the procurator fiscal by the appropriate method. The police officer who contacts the procurator fiscal will require to be fully briefed as to case facts and be familiar with wildlife matters. Importantly, the search must be for particular items, and those items specified on the application.

Before craving a warrant from a sheriff the procurator fiscal must be satisfied that the information that is the basis of the application is both reliable and sufficient. A single anonymous source would be insufficient. The standard is 'reasonable grounds to suspect'. This standard does not have to be as high as certainty or beyond reasonable doubt; equally, mere suspicion is not acceptable.

Search warrants comply with the requirements of law if they are signed, contain a description of the premises to be searched and are precisely dated. Officers should be alert to the peculiarities of some wildlife crime search warrants –

- Wildlife and Countryside Act 1981, Section 19(3) provides for the grant of a warrant to a constable, and under section 19(6), inserted by the Nature Conservation (Scotland) Act 2004, Sch 6, 16(d) the constable may be accompanied by another person or persons. Consider, if a search is for wild birds' eggs, should an RSPB or relevant museum member of staff be asked to accompany the police. As well as the necessary components stated above for a warrant to be deemed valid, perhaps the name of this person should also be included in the search warrant. The warrant continues in force until the purpose for which the entry is required has been satisfied or, if earlier, the expiry of such period as the warrant may specify.
- Salmon and Freshwater Fisheries (Consolidation) (Scotland) Act 2003, section 52(2)(b) provides for the grant of a warrant to a constable (or water bailiff) to be executed within one week of the grant. The warrant may specify the time or times in the day or night at which the warrant is to be executed.
- Some Acts relating to wildlife crime are silent on search warrants for premises, e.g. Wild Mammals (Protection) Act 1996. However, at Common Law the absence of statutory machinery to search does not prevent the procurator fiscal's right to apply for a search warrant before anyone has been charged. If an officer cannot find a search warrant section in the legislation the specialist or duty procurator fiscal should be contacted, who will draft a style. It should not be assumed because the legislation is silent on search of premises a lawful warrant cannot be obtained.

Execution of a search warrant:
After a warrant is granted by a sheriff and handed to the police for execution, it should be checked. If a defect is found, such as even a minor error, then the officer should immediately contact the procurator fiscal and not proceed with the warrant or alter it. To do so will undoubtedly result in any evidence obtained under the defective warrant being dismissed by the court.

It should be borne in mind that offenders who are involved in all aspect of wildlife crime prepare ahead. Frequently they envisage the possibility of the police interviewing them or searching their property. Often a poacher or egg thief will be familiar with wildlife legislation.

Although each search will depend on the premises and the items to be searched for, the following are useful legal tips:

- It is important that the search of premises under the authority of a warrant is done so (a) as soon as practical; (b) professionally; (c) in a systematic manner; (d) with consideration for human rights, and (e) with an awareness of health and safety issues.
- The search team must be properly briefed at the police station before the search is commenced and everyone aware of the contents of the search warrant. The time of day at which a search warrant is executed is always left to the discretion of the police. Preparing well and not rushing the search pay dividends.
- If anyone, other than a police officer or person named in the warrant is involved in the search, such as a laboratory or computer technician, then that person must at all times be under the direct supervision of a police officer.
- As a matter of good practice the officer, or officers, to whom the warrant has been issued should be in possession of it at the time of execution and he or she is required to show it to the householder or other occupant of the premises if asked to do so. They are not obliged to part with it to anyone for inspection, but the duty to exhibit the warrant on demand seems absolute.
- A written log of all items of substance found should be maintained by one police officer (productions officer) who will note (a) time item found, (b) where found, (c) persons finding, (d) any comment made by the suspect. This officer should also ensure that labels are attached and provisionally numbered, and most importantly, that the items are correctly stored and/or delivered for analysis and that no cross-contamination may occur. The normal police arrangements for the transmission of productions should be used. The productions officer should be aware of the correct packaging of items e.g. dead birds or other carcasses are placed in a paper or polythene bag and stored if possible in a fridge before a post mortem rather than in a freezer.
- What happens if suspect items are unexpectedly found which are not covered in the warrant? Seize them but ensure the full reasons for seizing are included in the police summary offence report/statements. This is the most pragmatic approach. The procurator fiscal can decide, in the light of the plethora of case law on this subject, if the item can be used in evidence. The general rule being, did the police act fairly and was the degree of invasion of privacy reasonable. However, if it is anticipated that items will be found other than those covered by

the search warrant, the warrant should be extended to cover them at the outset, or an additional warrant(s) obtained.

* A video, if available, should be used to illustrate and record the search of the locus. The search team prior to a trial should see the video in order that they can identify where in the premises particular items were found.
* If the suspect is in the premises he should, if compliant i.e. not aggressive or violent, be invited under caution to comment on items as they are found.
* The suspect should not be allowed to handle any item (possibility of negating value of any fingerprint evidence) and ensure if detained that he travels to the police station in a vehicle separate to the productions.
* Unless the suspect is being reported in custody, a report should be forwarded to the procurator fiscal confirming the warrant has been executed with reference being made as to forensic analysis being carried out or instructions sought.

Example of Search Warrant:
[see over]

IN THE SHERIFF COURT OF THE LOWLANDS AT EDINBURGH
THE PETITION OF THE PROCURATOR FISCAL
Date: 14 December, 2011

From information received by the Petitioner, there are reasonable grounds for suspecting that offences under Sections 1, 5 and 11 of the Wildlife and Countryside Act, 1981, as amended, have been committed and that evidence of the offence may be found on the premises of Ardmore Farm, Musselburgh, Lowlands, including Ardmore Farm Cottage, occupied by Tom Sawyer.

The Petitioner therefore craves the court to take the oath or solemn affirmation of John Brock, constable of Lowlands Police, to the effect foregoing and thereafter to grant Warrant to said John Brock and other constables of Lowlands Police, together with Stuart Milne, (SGRPID), and investigations officers of RSPB (Scotland) to enter upon and search said aforementioned premises for the purpose of obtaining that evidence, all in terms of Section 19 of said Act.

ACCORDING TO JUSTICE
Procurator Fiscal Depute

At_____ on _____

in the presence of _____

Sheriff of _____ COMPEARED the said John Brock, constable of Lowland Police, who being examined on oath or solemn affirmation depones that what is contained in the forgoing Petition is true.

_____ Deponent

_____ Sheriff

At_____ on _____

The Sheriff having considered the foregoing Petition and relative oath or solemn affirmation, grants Warrant as craved.

_____ Sheriff

2. Reporting Wildlife Crime to the Police

POLICE have a duty to investigate crime and all forces have an officer who co-ordinates the investigation into wildlife offences. Each force also has a number of wildlife crime officers specially trained to deal with wildlife offences in a manner consistent with legal prosecution procedure. This includes knowledge regarding relevant legislation, power to enter and search land, authority to seize evidence, requirements for corroboration (the requirement for corroboration is being reviewed by Lord Carloway and may change), safeguarding chains of evidence and forensic capabilities. Consequently, all suspected wildlife offences or related suspicious activity should be reported to the police. After the amalgamation of the eight Scottish police forces into one in April 2013 the basics for reporting, and the response given, will remain the same.

In any crime that is in progress or has just been committed, or where the suspect(s) is still in the vicinity, the police should be contacted (if possible) using '999'. In non-urgent cases the caller should contact their respective (or nearest) police call centre (when the eight forces are amalgamated it is likely that a single telephone number will direct the caller to the nearest police control centre). In most wildlife crime reports to the police, it is advisable to speak with a wildlife crime officer, though most call handlers in police control rooms now have sufficient knowledge to note and pass on details for investigation. Crimes against wildlife require more specialist investigative experience than than a beat officer nornally possesses, and in many cases they also need urgent attention. If a wildlife crime officer is not immediately available to respond, another officer may attend under his or her remote direction. Control rooms also have electronic guidance and mapping they can access to assist whichever officer is attending.

A witness may also want to report the circumstances of a wildlife crime to another agency, such as reporting a bird-related crime to the RSPB (who do not investigate crime but on many occasions are of valuable assistance to the police). This should be done after the report to the police.

Obtaining and preserving evidence

In some cases an offence may be in progress, in which case the police need to respond quickly. Depending on the location, for instance out on a hill or moor, or because of other ongoing serious incidents, this may not always be achievable. If the witness is unable to contact the police from the scene, or the police are unlikely to arrive before the suspect is gone, then details of the suspect should be memorised (or better still, noted). A description of age, build, height, hair colour and clothing worn are all details of great value in the investigation. Vehicle details, if available, are also extremely helpful, especially if a registration number can be noted, though it is important to note this accurately. Taking photographs or video footage will be a great help.

Bear in mind that if a suspect is aware that his crime has been witnessed, he is likely to take steps to eliminate evidence or to make its retrieval more difficult. Witnesses should not normally remove evidence, as it is much better left *in situ* for the police to photograph and recover, but there may be circumstances when the witness can helpfully recover evidence. An example might be the recovery of empty cartridge cases or any other item left behind by the suspect, *but only if the witness is sure that taking possession of the items is the only way to prevent the suspect picking them up and disposing of them.* Any item handled by the witness should if possible be picked up in a way that does not contaminate it with their fingerprints or DNA; in other words don't physically touch it, and if possible don't breathe, cough or sneeze on it.

The place where a bird or mammal has been deliberately killed, injured or illegally trapped is a crime scene, and great care should be taken not to tramp about and destroy an item dropped that may provide DNA, or stand on sole or tyre impressions that might be suitable for the police to photograph or cast in plaster.

Standard of proof

Be aware that in Scotland for a person to be convicted normally two sources of evidence are required. These may be two eye witnesses, which is the easiest form of corroboration. It could also be one eyewitness and some other form of corroboration, such as the finding of particular items in the suspect's possession or his admission of the crime. A case can also be built purely from circumstantial evidence, though this is by far the most difficult form of evidence to obtain. Police, fiscals and courts are often unfairly criticised, but the standard of proof in criminal cases in Scotland is proof beyond reasonable doubt, which, especially in wildlife cases, is often difficult to achieve. Some poaching cases and the intentional or reckless taking or destruction of birds' eggs are an exception to this rule, with the statute allowing conviction on the evidence of one credible witness.

Single witness evidence under the Wildlife and Countryside Act 1981 – S. 19A WCA

In Scotland, section 19A of the Wildlife and Countryside Act 1981, as amended by the Wildlife and Natural Environment (Scotland) Act 2011, permits the conviction of an accused person on the evidence of one witness in the following circumstances:

- An offence under section 1(1)(a) in relation to a grouse, partridge, pheasant or ptarmigan included in Part I of Schedule 2. This is the intentional or reckless killing, injuring or taking of these species.
- An offence under section 1(1)(c). This is the taking or destruction of an egg of any wild bird.
- An offence under section 6(1) in relation to a grouse, partridge or pheasant included in Part 1A of Schedule 3. This is the selling or offering or exposing for sale, possession or transport for sale, or publishing or causing to be published any advertisement likely to be understood as conveying that he buys or sells, or intends to buy or sell, live specimens of these species, their eggs or parts thereof. This subsection replaces the provisions of the Game Acts and is to facilitate dealing with poaching activity. Note that exceptions (listed under subsection 6(1A)) allow trade by authorised persons. (See Poaching and legally taking, killing or trading in 'game' and quarry species, p178)
- An offence under section 6(2) in relation to a grouse, partridge, pheasant or ptarmigan included in Part IIA of Schedule 3. This is the selling or offering or exposing for sale, possession or transport for sale, or publishing or causing to be published any advertisement likely to be understood as conveying that he buys or sells, or intends to buy or dead specimens of these species. Again this subsection replaces the provisions of the Game Acts and is in part to facilitate dealing with poaching activity, and in part to allow the sale of 'game' birds throughout the year. Note that exceptions (listed under subsection 6(5B) and 6(6)) allow this trade by authorised persons provided the birds have been killed outside the close season. (See Poaching, and legally taking, killing or trading in 'game' and quarry species, p178)
- An offence under section 10A(1). This is the intentional or reckless killing injuring or taking of brown hares or mountain hares during the respective close season unless the activity is permitted by section 10B
- An offence under section 11G(1). This is the intentional or reckless

killing injuring or taking of brown hares, mountain hares or rabbits unless the activity is permitted by section 11H.

- An offence under section 11I(1). This is the possession or control of live or dead brown hares, mountain hares or rabbits killed or taken in contravention of sections 10A or 11G, or their parts or derivatives; their sale, offer for sale or exposure for sale, or their possession or transport for sale; or the publishing or causing to be published any advertisement likely to be understood as conveying that he buys or sells, or intends to buy or sell any of these things.

If you are a witness

If you are a witness to an incident, the police will note a statement from you. This will be a statement of facts and circumstances to which you could speak if the matter proceeds to court. You may have expertise in a particular field, in which case evidence of your opinion might be noted. Examples might be the fact that you have regularly witnessed hare coursing incidents and the circumstances in the case being investigated, even though no hare was seen being chased, were exactly the same as in previous incidents where hares had been chased or caught; or, being an experienced ornithologist, that in an investigation where a sand martin colony had been destroyed in, say, early June, that a high proportion of the nest burrows would contain eggs or chicks. You will also be asked to sign labels attached to any items you have found or have witnessed the police officer taking as physical or documentary evidence in the case.

As a witness, in due course you may want to know how the investigation is progressing. Obtain a case reference number or details of the investigating officer so that you can follow the case up. The police are notoriously bad at updating complainers or witnesses (I included myself in that category when a serving officer). This is not because they don't want to: simply that they are usually very busy with other things, and updates unfortunately slide to the bottom of the pile. Most are now contactable by email or mobile phone, which is far easier than trying to make contact with officers who work different shift patterns.

Depending on either the complexity of the case or the difficulty in obtaining evidence, it might take some time before the officer can firstly identify a suspect, and secondly, know if there is going to be sufficient evidence to submit a case to the procurator fiscal. Wildlife crime investigations are among the most difficult of all. That does not mean that the police are not trying their best to obtain evidence, but it simply isn't always available.

Under most of the wildlife legislation, a case can be brought to court at any time not exceeding six months from which sufficient evidence is received by the procurator fiscal, but not more than three years from the date of the commission of the offence. If evidence does not become available during the initial few months of the enquiry the investigation may be set aside, but can be re-opened if new evidence emerges later. Some statutes still stipulate that the case must be before the court not more than six months from the date of the commission of the offence. This is also the case where no 'time bar' or time stipulation is given.

The police act as investigators on behalf of the procurator fiscal, who is the public prosecutor in Scotland. The police electronically submit the case in summary form to the procurator fiscal. A specialsit unit of prosecutors, with advice where required from senior Crown Counsel, consider and prose-cute most cases that relate to wildlife, environmental and animal cruelty offences in Scotland. These prosecutors will be in regular communication with WECOs (and members of other reporting agencies) over these specialist cases, but it is ultimately the prosecutor's decision whether or not to take the case to court. This decision is based on sufficiency of evidence and public interest.

If the decision is taken to prosecute, in due course the case is called in court at a 'pleading diet', at which time the accused may plead guilty and be dealt with. If the accused pleads not guilty a trial date is set, with a date identified for an intermediate diet roughly two weeks before the trial date. This intermediate diet gives another opportunity for a guilty plea to be entered; in fact at any time right up to and even during a trial an accused person can enter a plea of guilty.

If a case proceeds to trial, some or all witnesses will be required to give evidence. In some cases there is an agreement on parts of the evidence between the prosecutor and the defence, thus limiting the number of witnesses required. An example could be that an accused person does not deny committing a particular act, but denies that the act committed constituted an offence. In that case, only witnesses that, in the Crown's view, can prove that the act was an offence might be called to give evidence.

There are three verdicts in Scottish courts: guilty, not guilty and not proven. The not proven verdict is often quoted as meaning 'we know you did it but sufficient proof is lacking.' Whether or not this is really the case, the result is the same as not guilty: an acquittal.

3. Traps and Snares

A PROFESSIONAL, responsible and humane approach should be the ultimate aim of all of those who use traps and snares. It should be appreciated that the species being trapped and snared may not be considered pests to all who witness their capture. For example, stoats may be harmful to game management interests, but beneficial to farmers controlling rats, mice and rabbits. It could also be argued that rooks, while they take some ground-nesting birds' eggs, and grain flattened by bad weather in advance of harvest-time, may well balance this by the number of insects and grubs that they take that are harmful to agriculture. There are people who don't like artificial control of species but they are more likely to accept it if they see that pest control is being carried out professionally.

Informational signs on cage traps and Larsen traps are often helpful, letting any passer-by know the reason that whichever legitimate member of the crow family is being targeted; for example that carrion crows have been taking wild bird's eggs or chicks, or that rooks and jackdaws have been taking feed set out for partridges or pheasants (and of course benefiting some other small birds). Signs are sometimes dual purpose, also displaying the police code and police contact number for the farm or estate that must be displayed when the trap is in use. Similar signs are sometimes helpful if used in conjunction with tunnel traps, the sign being hidden under a stone where it does not draw attention to the trap, but can be seen when the stone is lifted, often the prelude to accessing and damaging a trap. The local police wildlife crime officer should be able to help with wording for these signs.

General licences – please note!

General licences, issued annually by Scottish Natural Heritage, facilitate derogations from legislation to allow the legal use of some bird traps. It should be noted that licence conditions may well change from year to year and the wording of the licences should always be consulted to ensure that actions carried out against 'pest' species of birds are legal. It should also be noted that the conditions of use of the licence may well be different from the conditions of use of licences in other constituent countries of the UK.

The general licences produced by Scottish Natural Heritage are constantly evolving and are unlikely to be exactly the same in 2013 (and beyond) compared to the 2012 general licences detailed at the end of this book. It is likely in 2013 that they will be made clearer and more easily understood. In licences 1 to 4 there may be changes to the conditions relating to methods of killing and taking birds, and clarification of permitted types of traps, their use and design together with reporting requirements. For example, in these four licences there may be conditions grouped under headings such as 'Species that may be killed', 'Means of permitted killing and taking' and 'Design of traps'. Further species may be added for control purposes, for instance the ruddy duck and Canada goose, and the robin, house sparrow, blackbird plus swallow nests may be added to general licence 3 (to kill or take certain birds for preserving public health and safety). This is in response to individual applications made by supermarkets and pest control companies where birds have occasionally entered food shops and food preparation facilities and are posing a threat to public health.

To see how the 2013 general licences differ from those from 2012 consult the licensing pages of the Scottish Natural Heritage website at http://www.snh.gov.uk/protecting-scotlands-nature/species-licensing/bird-licensing/general/

Multi-catch cage traps

Multi-catch cage traps may be used to control certain wild birds under the terms of one or more of four general licences issued annually by Scottish Natural Heritage (see Annual General Licences p213). The traps are normally made of a large wooden framework roughly 12' by 8' by 6' high, with wire netting sides and top. The entrance for the birds intended to be caught is of two types. Firstly, there may be a wire netting funnel going down into the centre of the trap – in the manner of a lobster pot – through which the birds can enter, but have great difficulty accessing to escape. These are referred to as 'funnel traps'. The second method involves a 'V' shape in the centre of the trap with what looks like either a ladder or letterbox lying horizontally at the bottom of the 'V' through which the birds enter. Appropriately these traps are referred to as 'ladder' or 'letterbox' traps. Both types have a door so that the user can enter to despatch the birds caught. Cage traps are normally used from about late January/early February until about June, which is consistent with the time that birds would be sitting on eggs or have small chicks. They are also used from time to time for catching rooks or jackdaws in summer.

One or more captive bird may legally be used to lure others of the same species in to the trap provided it is given sufficient food, water, shelter and a suitable perch. These captive birds, often referred to as decoys or call birds, may by law only be carrion crow, hooded crow, jackdaw, rook, jay or magpie.

(Note that a jay may only be taken under the terms of Licence 1, which is the licence for the protection of wild birds. It may only be used as a decoy in a multi-catch crow trap under Licence 1 and never in a Larsen trap). The traps must be checked at least once at intervals of not more than 24 hours. When they are not in use a door or panel *must be taken off the trap and removed from the site or padlocked securely to the cage.* In this condition they do not need to display a tag or sign, though at all other times this is required. It is worth noting that failure to disable to trap in this manner is the most common offence committed in relation to these traps.

Those who operate any type of bird trap should begin from the base-line that *all* wild birds are protected by the law. Further, to trap a wild bird is illegal. The general licences allow derogation from the law in certain circumstances. An operator relying on the use of a licence does not require to apply for or even possess the licence, but must act only within its conditions. Firstly, the trap operator must be the owner or occupier of the land on which the trapping is taking place, or a person authorised by the owner or occupier. This may be a gamekeeper or farm worker, a pest controller, or even, in rare cases, the owner or tenant of a garden.

The licences only allow the killing or taking of certain birds, and only for the reasons outlined on the licences. (The licence allows various methods of control, including by shooting, though we are only dealing here with the use of a multi-catch cage trap). Arguably the main condition on all of these licences is that the operator has read and understood the licence on which he is relying. Consequently it is up to the operator to justify his use of the licence.

Licence 1, often referred to as the 'gamekeeper's licence', allows the killing or taking of certain birds for the purpose of the conservation of wild birds. This could allow, for example, a gamekeeper to control carrion crows that are taking gamebirds' or waders' eggs, or the owner or tenant of a garden to control magpies if there is genuine evidence that they are taking the eggs or chicks of garden birds, not simply that he may not like magpies. The licence can only be relied on in circumstances where the authorised person is satisfied that appropriate non-lethal methods of control such as scaring or proofing are either ineffective or impracticable. This means, for example, that if a scarecrow or suspended CDs have been tried and are ineffective, or if the 'pest' species cannot be excluded by some means from the 'victim' species, then the 'pest' species may be controlled.

There is no definition of a cage trap in any of the general licences, being referred to as 'any other cage trap' as opposed to a Larsen trap, which *is* defined. The fact that in the conditions of the licences one or more decoy birds may be kept within the trap without the necessity of a separate compartment, and a door or panel must be taken off the trap when it is not in use, seem indicators that a 'cage trap' is the well-known large wood and netting structure normally associated with catching permitted birds in multi-numbers. Until there is a definition of 'cage trap', or a list of traps considered to fall into this category, the benefit of doubt may need to be given to any accused person.

The birds that may legally be caught in a multi-catch cage trap using Licence 1 are great black-backed gull, carrion crow, hooded crow, rook, jackdaw, magpie and jay. However the list of birds that may be used as decoys is smaller, omitting the great black-backed gull.

Further conditions imposed on operators of multi-catch cage traps relying on Licence 1, when the trap is in use, are:

- The operator must not have been convicted after 1 January 2008 (unless admonished, the subject of an absolute discharge or the conviction is spent) of an offence under the Wildlife and Countryside Act 1981; the Conservation (Natural Habitats etc) Regulations 1994; the Protection of Badgers Act 1992; the Protection of Wild Mammals (Scotland) Act 2002; the Animal Health and Welfare (Scotland) Act 2006 or the Protection of Animals (Scotland) Act 1912, all as amended. (It should be borne in mind that such a conviction not only prohibits the person from trapping any of the species listed on the licence, but from shooting them as well).
- The operator must display a tag or a sign on the trap while it is in use that shows the code number issued by the police in the area in which the trap is set, and also the contact telephone number that the police have given. As an example a tag or sign in Tayside may carry information along the following lines: Police code: Tay 198. Police contact: 07808 899113. If a cage trap is not in use, *and has been disabled as per the relevant condition*, there is no need for this tag or sign to be displayed.
- The trap must be inspected, except where severe weather prohibits, at least once every day at intervals of not more than 24 hours.
- This inspection must be sufficient to determine whether there are any live or dead birds in the trap. This does not mean that the trap must be physically visited. It may be that a trap can be inspected by the use of binoculars or a telescope. In many cases the distance involved would need to be short, as many cage traps have undergrowth that may hide a bird, or a shelter of a type that would not permit the person inspecting to see a bird hidden within.

- In the case of decoy birds, (there is no condition that only one bird may be used) they must be provided with adequate food, water, shelter and a suitable perch. They shall also have protection from the prevailing wind. In addition to invalidating the legal use of the trap and attracting offences under the Wildlife and Countryside Act 1981, failure to comply with this condition is likely to attract additional offences under the Animal Health and Welfare (Scotland) Act 2006.
- Any bird not of the species listed on the licence should immediately be released unharmed.
- Any dead or sickly birds must be removed immediately from the trap
- Any birds killed shall be destroyed humanely, taking all reasonable precautions to ensure this is by a single, swift, action.
- When the cage trap is not in use, it must be immobilised (dictionary definition – made unable to move or work) and made incapable of use in such a way that the immobilisation could not be reversed without considerable forethought or considerable difficulty. *Doors or panels of cage traps must be removed from the site or, if not removed from the site, must be taken off the trap and secured by a locked padlock.* Though 'doors or panels' are mentioned in the plural, the principle behind this condition is that a door or panel must be completely taken off the trap to ensure that birds entering are able to exit. The door or panel taken off can either be completely removed from the site or securely padlocked to the trap. This safeguards the operator against any person maliciously closing the door.

Note that lesser black-backed gulls, since their numbers are in decline, were removed from licences 1 and 2 in January 2011.

Licence 2, often referred to as the farmer's licence, is for the purpose of the prevention of *serious* damage to livestock, foodstuffs for livestock, crops, vegetables and fruit.

An authorised person, under the same conditions as licence 1, may control great black-backed gull, carrion crow, hooded crow, jackdaw, jay, magpie, rook, collared dove, feral pigeon (though not rock dove) and wood pigeon. Jays may not be controlled under the terms of this licence, and only the corvids in this list may be used as decoy birds.

The same conditions as in licence 1 apply, and it is up to the operator to justify the use of the licence.

There have at times been issues if a pigeon is found in a multi-catch cage trap, which may well attract a bird of prey such as a goshawk or sparrowhawk. Nevertheless it would be perfectly legal to bait a trap with grain to attract rooks, jackdaws or feral pigeons, though no pigeon decoy is permitted. In most cases a trap baited with grain and used for feral pigeons will be used in the proximity to, or even inside, buildings. The operator might worry that the first pigeon caught could be seen as a decoy. It should be borne in mind that an 'attempt to kill, injure or take' a bird of prey must be proved beyond reasonable doubt to have been carried out intentionally or recklessly, or that a trap has been 'used for the purpose of killing or taking' a bird other than the legal target list. To dispel any concern that such a trap used to control feral pigeons is reported to and investigated by the police as an illegal trap, it might be an idea to advise the local WECO of its use in advance.

Licence 3 is for the purpose of preserving public health and safety and for the purpose of preventing the spread of disease.
An authorised person may control great black-backed gull, lesser black-backed gull, herring gull, carrion crow, hooded crow, jackdaw, magpie, rook, collared dove, feral pigeon (though not rock dove), and woodpigeon. The control of jays is again excluded and only the listed corvids may be used as decoy birds.

The same conditions as in licence 1 apply, and it is up to the operator to justify the use of the licence.

This licence is most likely to be used by pest controllers, often acting on behalf of Local Authorities. In many cases it is likely to be used in urban situations, nevertheless the advice given under Licence 2 on contacting the police if pigeons are the target is still worthwhile. The local wildlife crime officer is as good a contact for a pest controller to make as for a gamekeeper, landowner or farmer.

Gull species, in particular herring gulls with chicks, are often controlled as they occasionally attack humans. Since these problems are most likely to be occurring in a populated area, and since many people do not like seeing gull chicks killed or taken for the purpose of being destroyed, it is usually better to prevent this situation happening. Where there is evidence of these attacks, the matter should be dealt with the following year at the egg stage, even if this means more than one visit to deal with a subsequent clutch of eggs. It is a lot less distressing for witnesses and likely to lead to fewer complaints. Pricking, oiling or destroying eggs of relevant species is permitted, and the pest controller, normally reacting to a complaint (or a number of complaints) should have no difficulty in justifying his actions.

It should be noted that where any action is taken against the lesser black-backed gull or herring gull, the operator must, as soon as the action is completed or by 31 January of the following year at the latest, submit a report to Scottish Natural Heritage, Licensing Team, Great Glen House, Leachkin

Road, Inverness, IV3 8NW. The report should detail the number of such birds, or their eggs, killed, taken or destroyed in each month, the reason why such action was taken in each month, the methods of control used and the locations of any such actions.

In licence 4, which is for the purpose of preserving air safety, there is an extensive list of birds that may be controlled within or outwith the perimeters of airports or aerodromes (though only those airports that adhere to the guidelines set out in the Civil Aviation Authority document CAP 772). The action may only be used by owners or managers of airports and aerodromes or persons authorised by them or their deputies.

The birds that may be controlled are: greylag goose; Canada goose; mallard; curlew; oyster catcher; lapwing; black-headed gull; common gull; great black-backed gull; herring gull; lesser black-backed gull; feral pigeon (this includes racing pigeons which have settled or become resident in or around an airport, but does not include wild rock dove); woodpigeon; stock dove; carrion crow; hooded crow; jackdaw; magpie; rook; starling. A multi-catch cage trap would not be used against species of this list, since shooting is likely to be a better option, but when a cage is used, only the listed corvids may be used as decoy birds.

The same conditions as in licence 1 apply, and it is up to the operator to justify the use of the licence.

Three points to conclude:
- It is an offence under the Animal By-Products (Scotland) Regulations 2003 to use dead domestic livestock, including poultry, as bait or feeding in a cage trap (or in any trap for that matter). Wild game or deer are perfectly legitimate for use.
- Traps are sometimes vandalised or decoy birds released. There may be very rare, but urgent, occasions when a member of the public is justified in releasing a non-target bird, and some minor damage caused to a padlocked trap in doing so. This must only be done as a last resort, with a call to the police being the first option. Unjustified interference with legally-set cages is an offence. Operators of traps vandalised or where the call bird or birds caught are released, should report this to their local WECO.
- In the case of a non-target species, for instance a buzzard, being caught in a trap that seems not to have been checked for some time, the investigating officer might consider having the bird checked by a

vet before release in case it is suffering from starvation or dehydration. However unless there are obvious injuries, the best course of action may be simply to release the bird. The stress of taking it to a vet might do the bird harm, it may well have dependent chicks, and it is likely to find water and food once released. It is also being released to territory that it knows, which might be more difficult to accomplish at a later date.

Larsen traps

This part should be read in conjunction with Licence 1 above.

Larsen traps are defined in general licences 1 to 4 as *portable cage traps which have a closed compartment for confining a live bird as a decoy and one or more spring activated trap-doors which are either top or side mounted.* Normally these traps have three compartments; one for the decoy and a further two in which a corvid attracted by the decoy can be caught. They work on the principle that the bird attracted to the trap enters and stands on a split perch which is holding open the spring door of one of the compartments. The perch gives way and the spring door shuts, trapping the bird unharmed inside that compartment. A second corvid can be caught by the same method in the other compartment. Another variety of trap is circular, with the call bird in a compartment in the centre and several catching compartments round the perimeter. These traps work best at nesting time with territorial birds such as crow and magpie. These birds defend their territory and come to the trap to investigate an intruding bird of the same species.

Generally, keeping a bird confined in a cage, such as a Larsen trap, where it is unable to fully stretch its wings would be an offence under Section 8(1) of the Wildlife and Countryside Act, 1981. In order to use a corvid (other than a raven or chough, which are fully protected) as a 'decoy' bird in a Larsen trap, the four annual general licences derogate from these dimensional requirements *provided the operator abides by the terms and conditions.* Failure to do so would attract prosecution for offences under the Wildlife and Countryside Act and the Animal Health and Welfare (Scotland) Act 2006.

As detailed under Licence 1 above, the licences give authorised persons the right to use a Larsen trap to control crows, jackdaws and magpies, but only if they are causing any of problems set out in the general licence, and the operator is satisfied that appropriate non-lethal methods of control such as scaring or proofing are either ineffective or impracticable.

The conditions of use are identical to those in Licence 1 under multi-catch cage traps except for the following:

- In the case of a Larsen trap, only one decoy bird may be used, and it must be removed from the trap when not in use. In the Larsen trap there must be a separate compartment for the decoy bird
- When any Larsen trap is not in use, access doors must be secured with a padlock, or it must be removed from the site and stored in such a manner as to prevent its accidental use.

It is also important to realise that there are subtle differences with which birds can be used as decoy birds in Larsen traps under the different general licences. These are:

Licences 1, 3 and 4 – carrion crow, hooded crow or magpie.

Licence 2 – carrion crow, hooded crow, magpie or jackdaw.

Note that only under Licence 2 can a jackdaw be used, and at no time can a rook or jay be used. Though probably used by a gamekeeper, the use of a jackdaw in a Larsen trap to deal with jackdaws taking game bird feed would not be under the Licence 1, the 'Gamekeeper's Licence', but under Licence 2, the 'Farmer's Licence,' though of course the trap could still be used legally by a gamekeeper.

Many birds of prey will readily enter legally-set Larsen traps or multi-catch crow cage traps. In most cases the operator releases the birds, with some stating that particular buzzards are caught and released several times. It is easy for a passer-by to release a bird of prey caught in a Larsen trap, or if it is the only occupant of an unlocked multi-catch cage trap, but it is a different story if a buzzard is in a crow cage along with several carrion crows. It should be borne in mind that without proof that an operator is deliberately trying to catch birds of prey, he or she must be given the benefit of the doubt. It would be completely wrong for a passer-by to release all of the birds in a crow cage trap so that a bird of prey can escape. Instead, the witness should either make contact with the trap operator or with the police wildlife crime officer. The telephone number of the police wildlife crime officer should be on the tag or sign on the trap, and the police should be advised of the location of the trap and the code number on the tag or sign. This should be, for example, in a format similar to TAY 135 (Tayside), GRA 23 (Grampian) or CSP 75 (Central Scotland), representing the police force area in which the trap is sited. The officer can then determine the operator's details from the code number and either visit the trap or make contact with the operator. (see Frequently asked questions p143)

If there are birds – or indeed baits – in a set Larsen or crow cage trap, and there is no tag or sign, an offence is being committed and the police should be informed. Anything done to alter the situation before the police arrive, and not corroborated, may mean that a prosecution would be less likely.

There is no offence of 'failing to comply with the conditions of a general licence'. The general licence allows certain actions to be taken that would not otherwise be legal. For example if a Larsen trap or a crow cage is not being checked and a bird trapped inside dies (whether that be a decoy bird or a bird that has subsequently entered), likely charges could arise from the use of a trap for the purposes of killing or taking any wild bird (s. 5 WCA); intentional or reckless killing of the bird (s. 1 WCA); causing unnecessary suffering to a wild bird which is under the control of man on a temporary or permanent basis (s.19 Animal Health and Welfare (Scotland) Act 2006) or all three.

As another example, if a cage trap is set without a tag displayed bearing a code and contact telephone number issued by the police, the offence is likely to be the use of a trap for the purposes of killing or taking any wild bird (s. 5 WCA). If this is the only offence, there is a possibility that a procurator fiscal might not instigate proceedings, however experience has shown that with trap operators who are lax and sloppy in their work, a range of offences are often uncovered.

Spring-over traps

Since April 2008 the use of these traps has been made illegal by the wording of condition 19 of General Licences 1 to 4 'This licence does not permit the use of any form of spring-over trap'.

Spring-over traps work on much the same principle as a Fenn trap. The bait is attached to a plate, which when set is hooked under a catch. The victim pulling at the bait releases the catch and a net attached to a metal hoop, like the design of a landing net for salmon or a large butterfly net, springs over the top of the bird. The bird may be caught unharmed though there is real potential for it to be killed or injured if hit by the metal hoop. The offence involved would be to set in position an article of such a nature and so placed as to be likely to cause bodily injury to any wild bird coming in contact therewith (s. 5(1)(a) WCA), or alternatively to use a net for the purpose of killing or taking any wild bird (s 5(1)(b) WCA).

A variation of these traps may legally be used by bird ringers. SNH can issue a licence under WCA s. 16(1)(a), (b) and (c), not to the British Trust for Ornithology but to all persons who are trained and accredited by the BTO as ringers. A licence of this type is possible under the terms of WCA s. 16(5)(b) which states a licence may be issued to 'persons of a class', the class in this case being BTO ringers. Adherence to BTO permit conditions is a fundamental licence condition that thereby turns the BTO into a quasi-licensing authority as regards practical day-to-day operation of the ringing scheme. This scheme is government-funded, UK-wide, via the Joint Nature Conservancy Council.

'Clam', 'Butterfly' or 'Larsen-mate' traps

It is unfortunate that there is no description of a 'cage trap' in any of the general licences. It is simply referred to as 'any other cage trap' as opposed to a Larsen trap, which *is* defined. This has allowed the sometimes doubtful use of another small cage trap which is sold commercially as a 'Larsen Mate', though sometimes referred to as a 'clam' or 'butterfly' trap because of its action, or home-made variations of this trap. The trap consists of two halves of a wire mesh box, cut at an angle along a long axis. The two halves are hinged along a side. Typically, two strong springs attached between the two halves of the box operate to close the trap. Normally when set, a length of wooden dowling or plastic pipe cut into two, keeps the two halves apart, and thus acts a trigger mechanism. The trap requires a bait to draw the bird in. When a bird attempts to land on this 'split' perch or knocks the dowling, the dowling halves separate, causing the two box sections to spring together, trapping the bird. However, if the opening between the two halves is forced wide enough, it is also possible to place bait on the hinge section of the trap, which is now above ground level in the manner of the central part of the letter W. Any medium to heavy bird landing on top of the bait will probably provide enough weight to push the hinge down slightly and initiate closure of the trap.

There are concerns that some of these traps – particularly home-made versions with excessively strong springs and jagged edges – are likely to injure birds, especially larger birds such as a buzzard that may well be attracted to them. They may also close over the head of a mammal, and the creature will be unable to prise the trap open to escape. In preparation for the 2012 general licence, Scottish Natural Heritage (SNH) consulted on what action should be taken in relation to this trap. The SNH statement on the consultation conclusions reads:

> 'Taking all of the views provided in this consultation in to account, SNH believe that in future, it would be desirable that 'approved' traps are clearly defined in the General Licences and that, as with spring traps, specifications may require to be developed and included. We would suggest the industry promote a code of practice that addresses these design issues and additionally promotes its use only at a time and manner likely to be effective on the target

species. With this in mind we intend to gather together representatives of key stakeholder groups early in 2012 to take this work forward. This course of action will mean that a degree of the perceived deficiencies in the General Licences will persist into 2012. It is important to make sure that we do get this right.'

This statement appears to acknowledge that the use of the 'clam-type' trap could still be illegal. Though no case has been tested in court, it may well breach section 5(1) of the Wildlife and Countryside Act 1981 (set in position or use an article (trap) that . . . (is) likely to cause bodily injury to any wild bird coming in contact therewith. It may also be an offence under section 19 of the Animal Health and Welfare (Scotland) Act 2006 if a mammal is caught and escapes with the trap round its neck.

As it happened, I was part of the stakeholder group meeting, which took place on 31 May 2012. It was acknowledged that some of these traps may have excessively strong springs or jagged edges. It seems likely that modifications will be made to the trap and trials conducted to make its use less likely to contravene the Wildlife and Countryside Act or the Animal Health and Welfare Act, rather in the manner of the advent of the Larsen trap. Police officers dealing with complaints of the use of these traps may wish to consult the specialist wildlife prosecutors before preferring charges, though if there is evidence the trap is being used to catch protected birds it would be a clear offence.

Trapping live birds for the illegal cage-bird trade
see Taking live birds from the wild p76

Live-catch mammal traps
Live-catch mammal traps basically work on the same principle as the crow cage trap: that the target mammal is enticed into a cage by a bait. The cage is invariably rectangular, and the target animal usually stands on a treadle which releases a drop-down door. Another variety, to trap grey squirrels, entices the squirrel to push open two one-way doors angled away from it to get to the bait inside. The doors close, preventing its exit. This selection of traps, used for foxes (usually in an urban setting as rural foxes are usually too wily to enter them), feral cats, rabbits, mink and grey squirrels, are humane provided they are checked regularly.

With live-catch mammal traps there is nothing set down in legislation about the checking intervals; the over-riding principle is the welfare of the trapped animal. It seems reasonable to apply the same maximum intervals between checks as in the general licences and in relation to snares: at least one check at intervals of not more than 24 hours. This is the time scale that a court may well take into consideration. In a practical sense (apart from the squirrel trap with the two one-way doors), once the trap has been sprung it cannot catch another target animal until it has been re-set, so frequent checks are likely to result in the catching of more target mammals.

Any protected mammal must be released unharmed as soon as it is discovered. Particular care should be taken with any cat that might be a pure wildcat. While it benefits the overall wildcat population to have hybrids removed, it is an offence to kill a pure wildcat. Many gamekeepers have a copy of a guide to the identification of a wildcat, and those who may be likely to catch a wildcat should obtain one. *Highland Tiger's* http://www.highland tiger.com/science_wildcatID.asp website gives a downloadable identification chart, and *The Scottish Wildcat Association's* http://www.scottishwildcats.co.uk/ identify.html gives some good identification tips.

Be aware of the law in relation to hedgehogs (whose numbers, incidentally, have fallen dramatically in recent years). A hedgehog has part-protection, and while there is no offence in shooting a hedgehog (though a strange thing for any normal person to do), the mammal is on Schedule 6 of the Wildlife and Countryside Act 1981. Schedule 6 lists species that may not be killed by certain methods. This refers back to Section 11 of the 1981 Act, which states that a trap (undefined) or indeed a snare, are methods that may not be used for the purpose of killing or taking any wild animal included in Schedule 6.

While it could be argued that the trap was not set deliberately for a hedgehog, anyone with knowledge of wildlife and their ecology will know if hedgehogs are likely to be in the area, and if so, that they would be attracted to most baits in a trap. Err on the safe side and release the hedgehog.

One trap that is slightly different from the usual rectangular wire live-catch mammal trap is the drop-trap for rabbits. Hedgehogs are also likely to be caught in this trap. Since these traps are only used sporadically, it is wise to have them padlocked shut when not in use. The design of a 'box' or 'drop' trap is a wooden or metal box buried in the ground beside a netted fence. A wooden or metal tunnel runs over the top of the box, which allows the rabbits through the netted fence by using the tunnel. The underside of the tunnel is part of a treadle, which can be locked in an inactive position either by a padlock or by a large stone placed so that the treadle will not tilt. Rabbits are allowed to become accustomed to passing safely through the tunnel, though every so often the padlock or stone are removed for a few nights, allowing the trap to operate. The weight of the rabbit passing over the treadle makes it tip like a see-saw and the rabbit slips sideways off it into the box.

Traps that are padlocked are relatively safe from interference, but it only takes one inquisitive person to remove the large stone to make the trap 'live' and rabbits begin to be caught. Because the operator is not using the trap he is not checking it and assumes everything is in order. In the meantime the trapped rabbits die of starvation. If this is reported to the police, an investigation is begun, with suspicion probably falling on the operator. He is then at risk, at the very least, of being taken to a police station for interview. If there is evidence that he has not secured the drop-traps after use he is liable to be charged under the Animal Health and Welfare (Scotland) Act 2006 (s. 19). Trap operators should anticipate problems and avoid them. Traps that are padlocked are much less likely to result in this type of unwelcome suspicion and inquisition.

The most likely method of abuse of live-catch traps (though thankfully not too common) is failing to check them regularly, resulting in the captive animal being deprived of food or water for an unduly long period, or exposed to extreme weather. These offences may be difficult to prove unless the trap has been under observation for some time, in which case the observer would need to rescue or release the animal before it became ill due to the time spent in the trap. If the animal is extremely ill or dead (as opposed to simply being thin), then proof of an animal welfare offence is made much easier.

Rabbits, in particular, can lose condition very rapidly, but proof would need to be obtained that the loss of condition of the animal was due to an excessive period in the trap and not due for example to a period of extreme weather when food would be difficult to obtain. Unwell live animals may need to be examined by a vet, and dead specimens should be taken to a Scottish Agricultural College vet lab, from 1st October 2012 to come under the Scottish Rural College (SRUC).

The investigating officer should treat the trap and its surroundings like a crime scene and carry out a scene of crime investigation. With a metal trap the possibility of DNA from the operator should be borne in mind, though wet weather may have reduced this possibility. Any mammal released from a trap where there is likely to be a report submitted to the procurator fiscal should be photographed first along with a completed production label if possible.

The use of a rabbit box trap or rabbit cage trap on land where the operator does not have permission for its use would be a poaching offence (s.11G of the WCA).

Tunnel traps

Tunnel traps, which include bridge traps (often referred to as rail traps), are efficient methods of controlling small mammalian pest species. Operators of these traps should be aware of where the law originates that allows their use, and of the various restrictions imposed. If the law is understood then the tunnel trap operator should have no worries about falling foul of it.

The law permitting the use of these traps is the Spring Traps Approval (Scotland) Order 2011. A number of traps over the years have been tried and tested by the then MAFF experts, and more have been tested in recent years on behalf of the Scottish Government. If the trap on test appears to immediately kill the target mammal it is given approval to be used.

A summary of the traps listed on the Order and which may legally be used in Scotland, *provided there is compliance with the Agriculture (Scotland) Act 1948 and the Animal Health and Welfare (Scotland) Act 2006*, are:

BMI Magnum 55 – rats and mice

BMI Magnum 110 – grey squirrels, stoats, weasels, edible dormice, rats and mice

BMI Magnum 116 – in addition to the 110 list, mink and rabbits

DOC 150 – grey squirrels, stoats, weasels, edible dormice and rats

DOC 200 – in addition to the DOC 150 list, mink

DOC 250 – in addition to the DOC 150 list, mink

Fenn Mk I, II, IV and VI; Solway Nos. 4 and 6; Springer Nos. 4 and 6 – discussed below

Fenn rabbit trap Mk I – rabbits

Fuller – grey squirrels

Imbra Mk I and II – grey squirrels, rabbits, stoats, weasels, edible dormice, rats and mice

Juby – grey squirrels, rabbits, stoats, weasels, edible dormice, rats and mice

Kania 2000 – grey squirrels, mink, stoats, weasels, edible dormice, rats and mice

Kania 2500 – grey squirrels, mink, rabbits, stoats, weasels, edible dormice, rats and mice

Lloyd – grey squirrels, stoats, weasels, edible dormice, rats and mice

Nooski – rats

Nooski mouse trap – mice

Sawyer – grey squirrels, stoats, weasels, edible dormice, rats and mice

Skinns – grey squirrels

VS Squirrel trap – grey squirrels

WCS Collarum – foxes (Note that this is a spring-operated snare. While the conditions of use of a snare as outlined under the Wildlife and Countryside Act 1981 cannot be applied to it, the same conditions governing its use are contained within the schedule to the Spring Traps Approval (Scotland) Order 2011. Further, the original Collarum traps could not be said to be free-running. Recommendations to modify the trap have been agreed by the trap's manufacturer, and are now incorporated into the design. It is the responsibility of users of this trap to ensure it is free-running).

WCS Tube – grey squirrels, stoats, weasels, edible dormice and rats

Wise 110, 160, 200 and 250 – rats

Since by far the most common traps currently in use are the Fenn (Mk I, II, IV and VI), the Springer No 4 and 6 and the Solway No 4 and 6 this section will be restricted to them.

So far as the Fenn Mk I, II and IV, the Springer No 4 and the Solway No 4 are concerned, the Order states that *the traps shall be used only for the purpose of killing or taking grey squirrels, stoats, weasels, edible dormice, rats and mice. They must be set in a natural or artificial tunnel which is suitable for minimising the chances of capturing, killing or injuring non-target species whilst not compromising the killing or taking of target species.* The inclusion of edible dormice (*Glis glis*) is most likely because they are non-native, as opposed to the native hazel dormouse (*Muscardinus avellanarius*), which is on Schedule 2 of the Habitats Regulations as a European Protected Species. The UK range of the edible dormouse, at least in the meantime, seems restricted to southern England. No guideline as to the maximum size of the access hole to the tunnel is given in the Order, but in the design of the tunnel, particularly the entrance, the operator must minimise (dictionary definition – reduce to the lowest possible degree or amount) the chance of catching non-target species. An unsuitable tunnel would be one which permits access to species larger that the largest that may legally be caught: the grey squirrel.

This is a difficult area in which to be prescriptive, but the tunnel should not, *so far as is possible*, allow access to non-target mammals such as hedgehogs, rabbits, etc. Even when a genuine attempt has been made to restrict tunnel entrances by stones or other natural items, there will always be an odd occasion when a non-target mammal will manage to squeeze in. It may be a young hedgehog, a young rabbit or a mink, but these should be only very occasional by-catch, otherwise the trap should be removed or the entrance altered. Gridweld mesh end(s), or a wooden end to the tunnel with a hole in the centre, are much better and much less likely to result in by-catch.

If a genuine effort is made to comply with the law then, even if a red squirrel or pine marten is caught, the law may not necessarily be broken unless it would be reasonable to conclude that the operator should have known that he would be *likely* to trap such a protected animal. The part of the description of what is permitted in the use of the traps is interesting with the new (2011) inclusion of the phrase *whilst not compromising the killing or taking of target species*. Does this now mean that if both grey squirrels and red squirrels are in the same woodland a trap (particularly a bridge or rail trap which is more likely to take red squirrels than those set in dark tunnels) can be used even though it may take an occasional red squirrel? Might this be in conflict with Section 11(2) of the WCA states that it is an offence *if any person sets in position any of the following articles, being an article which is of such a nature and so placed as to be **likely** to cause bodily injury to any wild animal included in Schedule 6 which comes into contact therewith, that is to say, any trap or snare (etc)?* Schedule 6 includes the badger, wildcat, hedgehog, and red squirrel. This is as yet untested in court.

In respect of the heavier and more substantial Fenn Mk VI, the Springer No 6 and the Solway No 6, mink and rabbits may legally be caught in addition to the species on the list that may legally be caught using the Mk IV/No 4 versions. The trapping of rabbits in the open is an offence under section 50A(1) of the Agriculture (Scotland) Act 1948, therefore a trap set for a rabbit must be in a rabbit burrow.

The most common method of abuse with tunnel traps is their use in tunnels where the access is considerably greater that the approved use allows. Examples are stone-built tunnels with no attempt to restrict access, wooden tunnels with no ends fitted and no attempt to restrict access, or simply a couple of twigs stuck in the ground at the tunnel entrance that a hedgehog, cat or other larger mammal could easily bulldoze aside. Section 50(1)(b) of the Agriculture (Scotland) Act 1948, which states *'for the purpose of killing or taking animals, he uses, or knowingly permits the use of, an approved trap in circumstances for which it is not approved'* might be the most relevant offence.

From time to time traps which must by law be set in tunnels are found set in the open. These may be for rats, on a run used by a rat or in a grain store, or for birds on the ground beside a bait or on top of a pole in the manner of a pole trap. *These traps must not be used outwith a tunnel or for the purpose of catching birds.* The offences are not committed under the Spring Traps Approval (Scotland) Order, which simply approves certain traps for use; the offence committed, if set for a rat in the manner indicated, would be the use of a spring trap for the purpose of killing or taking animals in circumstances for which it is not approved (s. 50(1)(b) Agriculture (Scotland) Act 1948).

With the example relating to taking a wild bird, there may be an offence under the same section, though it is not clear in the Act whether 'animals' assumes its generic meaning of any living organism apart from bacteria and plants, since earlier in the Act it mentions 'animals and birds.' In any event there would be one or more of the following offences committed: intentionally or recklessly killing, injuring or taking a wild bird (s. 1 WCA); attempting to do so (s. 18 WCA); or using a trap to kill or take any wild bird. (s. 5 WCA) (see Offences against wild birds – bird of prey persecution – Fenn-type traps p65)

There is a clear power (s. 19 WCA) without warrant for a police officer to enter and search land if a crime is being committed against wild birds, however there is not always the same power available when a crime is being committed against a mammal. For enforcement purposes with tunnel trap investigations it would seem reasonable to assume that a tunnel trap set illegally is either:

- Set in the open for birds, in which case the power to enter and search land without warrant would be under section 19 of the Wildlife and Countryside Act 1981; or
- Set in a place that is likely to catch a protected species of mammal, in which case the same power of entry and search applies.

Gin traps

There are no circumstances in which these traps can legally be used. It is not an offence to possess a gin trap, though it is an offence to possess one with intent to use it. (s. 50(1)(d) Agriculture (Scotland) Act 1948)

There will seldom now be instances where gin traps are used to catch rabbits. Nevertheless their use *when legal* was to place the trap, with the jaws end first, in the entrance to a rabbit burrow. The plate was lightly covered with fine earth, making the trap almost invisible. A chain was attached to the trap and the holding peg was hammered into the ground outside the burrow. When the rabbit emerged it stood on the plate, activating the trap, and invariably was caught by one or both front legs. Part of the reason that the gin trap was banned is that it is a leg-hold trap which does not kill its victim but holds it by the leg, causing substantial pain and injuries.

It must be said that gin trap offences are now extremely uncommon, nevertheless there have been occasional instances when gin traps – either the rabbit gin trap or the larger fox gin trap – have been used at fox dens (use non- approved trap or possess for that purpose – s. 50(1)(b) Agriculture (Scotland) Act 1948, or possibly deliberately crushing a wild mammal – s. 1 Wild Mammals (Protection) Act 1996). Rabbit gin traps are likely to be used just inside the entrances to the den to catch cubs. Fox gin traps are likely be used just outside the den to catch an adult fox, though adult foxes are wily creatures and are extremely difficult to catch by this method.

Gin traps have also been used to catch foxes by using them in a 'pool trap' situation also sometimes known as a 'drowning set'. In this type of incident, a bait, often a long-dead cat or something equally strong smelling, is set out in water about 3 feet or so from the bank. To get to the bait a fox will wade out, to be caught by a gin trap that the operator has set underwater midway between the bank and the bait.

Gin traps may also be found to be used, in the same way as Fenn traps, covered over with fine earth, grass moss or leaves, to catch mammals, particularly cats. The catching of a cat, which is a domestic animal, can include an animal welfare offence (s.19 Animal Health and Welfare (Scotland) Act 2006). The police power without warrant to enter land to search for a gin trap offence is not always straightforward and needs to be considered as follows:

- Known or reasonably suspected that a bird has been caught. – Power under the Wildlife and Countryside Act (s. 19 WCA) to enter and search land, which allows the gathering of evidence, and by visiting the locus, the chance to relieve suffering.
- Known or reasonably suspected that a mammal caught is *on Schedule 5 or 6 of the WCA, or Schedule 2 or 3 of the Habitats Regs*. – Power under either legislation (s. 19 or reg. 101 respectively) to enter and search land, which allows the gathering of evidence, and by visiting the locus, the chance to relieve suffering.
- Known or reasonably suspected that a mammal has been caught, though species, or even if it is a wild or domestic mammal, not known. – Power under the Animal Health and Welfare (Scotland) Act 2006 to enter land to relieve the suffering of an animal, *though not to gather evidence for a prosecution if a warrant can be obtained*. However at paragraph 4(3) of Schedule 1 to the 2006 Act a constable may enter premises (the 2006 Act always mentions premises, though bearing in mind *PF Peebles v Andrew Crawford Struthers* – see p196 – it is likely that this would include land) and search for, examine and seize any animal (including the carcass of an animal), equipment, document or other thing tending to provide evidence of the commission of, or participation in a *'relevant offence'*, and do so without warrant if it appears that delay would frustrate the purpose for which the search is to be carried out. (At Paragraph 4(5) of the 2006 Act a *'relevant offence'* is
  - an offence under sections 19 to 23 o an offence under section 24 (causing unnecessary suffering; mutilations; cruel operations;

administration of poisons; animal fights)
- an offence under section 24 (ensuring welfare of animals)
- an offence under section 29 (abandonment of animals)
- an offence under section 40 (11) (breaching a disqualification order)
- Known that a gin trap has been set, but has not caught anything. – A bit more thought required, though animal welfare must be paramount. Consider if there is reasonable cause to believe that the gin trap has been set for a bird or one of the protected mammals already discussed, or from the knowledge available if it is to trap one of those. If so follow the course of action appropriate to the species, as the offence would be an attempt to kill or injure, which carries the same powers. If nothing further is known about the species intended (or likely) to be trapped, then use the powers under the Animal Health and Welfare Act to enter land to relieve suffering – in other words to remove the trap to prevent an animal being caught. If required, a warrant can be applied for to gather evidence for a prosecution.

During the investigation, officers should consider who might have a motive to set the gin trap, particularly if the target species is known. When taking a gin trap as a production, bear in mind that like Fenn traps set in tunnels, a wooden peg is made and fitted to the gin trap by the person using it. The pin and the way the pin is secured to the trap often give them a degree of uniqueness. If there is a suspect, gin traps with similar fittings may be found in a shed, store or vehicle used by the suspect.

Offences under the WCA, Habitats Regulations and the Animal Health and Welfare (Scotland) Act are punishable by imprisonment, therefore a suspect could also be detained.

Deadfall trap

A deadfall trap is a device not commonly encountered in Scotland. Two flat slabs of rock are used; one slab lies flat on the ground, while the other is propped up at roughly a 45 degree angle to it, held up by a configuration of sticks. The sticks hold down a small piece of bait. It is designed to catch small pest species, which come along and pull at the bait, dislodging the sticks and causing the 45 degree slab to fall on top of them, potentially crushing them.

Since the traps are non-selective it is possible that they may catch non-target species which, if they are larger than the target species – for instance a wildcat or pine marten – they may be injured rather than killed. In general terms the use of these traps does not appear illegal, though there may be specific circumstances where they may be. As examples, if the traps were to be set in an area where pine martens, an animal in Schedule 5 to the Wildlife and Countryside Act 1981, are common and one was caught there may be an offence under that Act (s. 9(1)). The prosecution, however, would need to show that the person accused knew, or at least ought to have known, of the presence of pine martens and the likelihood of one being caught, thus making his actions reckless.

On a similar principle if a badger or hedgehog, both listed on Schedule 6 of the Wildlife and Countryside Act, were to be caught and injured or killed, then there may also be an offence committed against section 11(2) of the 1981 Act, as it an offence *'if any person sets in position (a trap) being an article which is of such a nature and so placed as to be likely to cause bodily injury to any wild animal included in Schedule 6 which comes into contact therewith; or uses for the purpose of killing or taking any such wild animal any such (trap) whether or not of such a nature or so placed as aforesaid'.*

Lastly there may be an offence under the Animal Health and Welfare (Scotland) Act 2006 (section 19) if the trap is not being checked regularly and an injured animal is left suffering. Though this legislation mainly deals with cruelty to domestic animals, once a wild animal is under the control of man it is covered by the Act.

Snares

Of the different methods of pest control, the use of snares is the most controversial, with several animal charities and conservation groups calling for a complete ban. Changes to legislation *may* be made in due course, but from a policing point of view officers uphold the law the way that it is, not the way that some might prefer it to be. This applies to all aspects of criminality. It is the responsibility of all who currently use snares to ensure that they abide strictly within the evolving law, and to minimise suffering to species caught.

Foxes, and to a lesser extent rabbits, are the species normally targeted. Snares may also be used against brown hares, and against mountain hares under licence from Scottish Natural Heritage. The principle of the use of the snare is to catch the target animal by the neck and hold it with minimum injury until, when the snare is checked, the animal can be despatched. Provided the captured animal cannot get tangled round any object near the snare, such as a tree or fence, then this is usually the case. If it becomes tangled then it is frequently choked to death. Generally a snare is made up of the wire snare, which invariably is of the manufactured variety; the eyelet through which the snare runs to form a loop; a 'stop' to prevent the snare closing too tightly; and, in the case of fox snares, a swivel. The swivel decreases the chance of the snare becoming kinked, lessening the chance of the animal being strangled, and also of the snare breaking. The mandatory use of the 'stop' first came under the provisions of the Snares (Scotland) Order 2010, though is now embedded in the Wildlife and Countryside Act at section 11(1A). The 'stop' takes the form of a'coiled piece of wire rather resembling a spring. This must be crimped tight, in the case of a fox snare, not less than 23 cm from the end, and in the case of a rabbit or hare snare, no less than 13 cm from the end. This prevents the snare closing beyond the crimp or 'stop', reduces the chance of animals being caught by a leg and minimises the chance of a captive animal being choked. Snares are usually fitted with a wooden or metal peg hammered in to the ground, and with a wire or wooden pin, often referred to as a tealer, to hold the snare the correct distance off the ground.

Generally speaking snares may no longer be secured to a fence (unless there is absolutely no risk of the animal becoming fully or partially suspended) or any other place where an animal caught is likely to be fully or partially suspended. They must no longer be attached to a drag, which in the past a fox has been able to move a short distance – or in some cases a considerable distance – from the point at which the snare was set, and must now be secured to a peg, a tree or similar solid object. Snares must also not be set anywhere that a victim is likely to drown.

Fox snares are sometimes set round or inside a 'stink pit' or 'midden', which is a fenced-off area in which dead animals and birds are dumped to create a 'stink' to draw foxes. Normally the fence is made of netting, with holes at appropriate places where foxes can enter to investigate the smells. Snares at these holes are likely to be illegal, but with 'middens' surrounded by brushwood to form a stockade, and gaps every so often to admit the fox, they are likely to be legal. (The reason I say 'likely' is that the legality depends on whether or not a captured fox is likely to be fully or partially suspended). Stink pits may be found in woodland or on open moorland. They are of particular benefit to snare operators on moorland where sheep graze for most of the year, making it difficult to use snares for fear of catching sheep.

Most operators of snares have now been on a course run by the British Association for Shooting and Conservation, the Game and Wildlife Conservation Trust or the Scottish Gamekeepers' Association. The course sets out the practical aspects of using snares to minimise by-catch while at the same time being effective against the target species. It was confirmed through the Snares (Training) (Scotland) (No 2) Order 2012 that these courses will be accepted by the Scottish Government as the level of training required under the Wildlife and Natural Environment (Scotland) Act 2011. In addition to courses run by these organisations, courses run by Borders College, Elmwood

College, the North Highland College, the Scottish Agricultural College or the colleges under Scotland's Rural College (SRUC) from 1 October 2012, and the Scottish Association for Country Sports will suffice as they are 'approved bodies' listed under Schedule to the Order. The level of training is also detailed on the Order. Those persons with a valid snaring training certificate issued after 1 May 2010 may apply to the chief constable of their area for a code number. This will allow them to use snares once the final part of the 2011 Act relating to snares has taken effect on 1 April 2013. In summary, after this date no-one should be using a snare unless they have a code number issued by the police.

Legal position prior to 1 April 2013

1. Snares must not be possessed, sold (s. 3C), or set or otherwise used if they are self-locking. (s. 11(1)(a) WCA)

A snare would generally be a self-locking snare if the action of the snare is designed to allow it to close smoothly but not to allow it to open easily without some modification, either manual or as a result of use. A snare originally free-running may become self-locking because of a particular kink, bend or broken strand in it that prevents it slackening slightly to allow a snared animal to breathe. It may be argued that a snare is self-locking if it is rusted, but a defence solicitor may equally argue that if the snare is rusted to the extent that it would be difficult to open, then it would be equally difficult to close on a fox's neck and that the animal would be able to withdraw its head before being captured.

An example of '*or otherwise uses*' could be as follows. A gamekeeper moves on and is replaced by another. The new gamekeeper finds one or more locking fox snares still in a set position and left behind by his predecessor. He begins to check them on a regular basis. He has not *set* them but he is *using* them. If one becomes knocked and needs re-set, then the user has gone beyond the stage of simply using the snare, but has set it.

2. It is an offence to set or otherwise use any type of snare other than a self-locking snare when it is of a nature or so placed as to be calculated to cause unnecessary suffering to any animal coming into contact with it. (s. 11(1)(aa) WCA)

A snare set without a stop would come in to this category.

Subsection 1A states that for the purposes of subsection (1)(aa), a snare which is of such a nature or so placed (or both) as to be calculated to cause unnecessary suffering to any animal coming into contact with it includes—

(a) *where the person who sets in position or otherwise uses the snare does so to catch any animal other than a fox, uses a snare which is not fitted with a stop which is capable of preventing the noose of the snare reducing in circumference to less than 13 centimetres;*

(b) *where the person who sets in position or otherwise uses the snare does so to catch a fox, uses a snare which is not fitted with a stop which is capable of preventing the noose of the snare reducing in circumference to less than 23 centimetres;*

(c) *a snare which is neither staked to the ground; nor attached to an object, in a manner which will prevent the snare being dragged by an animal caught by it; and*

(d) *a snare which is set in a place where an animal caught by the snare is likely to become fully or partially suspended; or drown.*

An example of the term *'calculated to cause unnecessary suffering'* might be to set a snare and then knock a fence post into the ground at such a distance from the snare that the animal caught would become tangled round the post and would be liable to be choked.

It is an offence to set a snare attached to an item that can be dragged. The dragging need not be of any particular distance to become illegal: the fox simply must not be able to drag the snare anchor. Snares in the past were often set attached to the centre of a log or even a fence post. Some foxes travelled a considerable distance with the drag before eventually becoming entangled. Attaching a snare to one end of a log, with the other end of the log attached to something solid, such as a tree, is likely to be looked upon as an extension of the snare rather than a drag and would appear to be legal.

A snare set on a log over a burn, on a fence where the captured animal can jump over or through and become fully or partially suspended, or on the edge of a steep bank are examples of where they must not be set.

These offences were originally made under the Snares (Scotland) Order 2010. They are now embedded in the Wildlife and Countryside Act 1981 through the provisions of the Wildlife and Natural Environment (Scotland) Act 2011.

3. It is an offence to set or use a snare of a nature or so placed that is likely to cause bodily injury to a Schedule 6 animal. (s. 11(2) WCA)

Animals on Schedule 6 of the Wildlife and Countryside Act 1981 are: badger, hedgehog and red squirrel. It would be highly unusual to design a snare for this purpose, but a snare set on a badger path immediately adjacent to extremely sharp objects may fall into this category. An example may be a farm implement with sharp edges or spikes. Placing a snare in this situation might also be an offence under the previous section. There would be no need that such an animal be actually caught, but evidence that it was present in the area and *likely* to be caught would need to be established from an expert. An offence under the Protection of Badgers Act 1992 (s. 1 and s. 11A – taking a badger or an attempt to do so) may also take place but an interesting comparison between the two pieces of legislation is that under the badger legislation proof is required that the action took place *wilfully*. In this case it may be necessary to prove that the person setting the snare knew that he was setting the snare on a badger path. Much would depend on proving the experience and knowledge of the person who set the snare. As an example it would be expected that a farmer or gamekeeper would know of badger setts on the land for which he is responsible, more so if he has undertaken the statutory snare training now required. In the 1981 Act, from the wording of section 11(2) it appears that there is some responsibility on the person setting the snare to be aware of what creatures may be using the track. For prosecution purposes this may be a better choice than the Protection of Badgers Act.

4. Set snares must be checked at least once at intervals of not more than 24 hours. During this inspection any animal caught must be released or removed, whether live or dead. In addition, if the person carrying out the check finds that the snare is no longer free running it must be removed or restored to a state in which it is free running. (s. 11B(1), (2) and (3) WCA).

This should be good practice in any case. A snare is 'free-running' if it is not self-locking; or it is not capable (whether because of rust, damage or other condition or matter) of locking; and, subject only to the restriction on such movement created by the stop which is fitted, the noose must be able at all times to become wider or tighten, and not be prevented from doing so due to any factor other than the stop.

5. A person commits an offence if he or she, without reasonable excuse, is on any land and sets or has possession of any snare without the permission of the owner or occupier of the land. (s. 11C(a) and (b) WCA)

Legal position after 1 April 2013
The following covers the requirements to use snares within the law from 1 April 2013, and the offences that flow from failure to comply. The relevant legislation is the Wildlife and Countryside Act 1981 as amended by the Wildlife and Natural Environment (Scotland) Act 2011.

It is an offence to set or otherwise use any self-locking snare (s. 11(1)(a)), or a snare which is either of such a nature or so placed (or both) as to be calculated to cause unnecessary suffering to any animal coming into contact with it (s. 11(1)(aa)).

A snare set without a stop would come in to the latter category. S. 11(1A) states that for the purposes of subsection (1)(aa), *'a snare which is of such a nature or so placed (or both) as to be calculated to cause unnecessary suffering to any animal coming into contact with it'* includes:

(a) *where the person who sets in position or otherwise uses the snare does so to catch any animal other than a fox, uses a snare which is not fitted with a stop which is capable of preventing the noose of the snare reducing in circumference to less than 13 centimetres;*

(b) *where the person who sets in position or otherwise uses the snare does so to catch a fox, uses a snare which is not fitted with a stop which is capable of preventing the noose of the snare reducing in circumference to less than 23 centimetres;*

(c) *a snare which is neither staked to the ground; nor attached to an object, in a manner which will prevent the snare being dragged by an animal caught by it; and*

(d) *a snare which is set in a place where an animal caught by the snare is likely to become fully or partially suspended; or drown.*

An example of the term *'calculated to cause unnecessary suffering'* might be to set a snare and then knock a fence post into the ground at such a distance from the snare that the animal caught would become tangled round the post and would be liable to be choked.

A snare must not be attached to an item that can be dragged. The dragging need not be of any particular distance to become illegal: the fox simply must not be able to drag the snare anchor. Snares in the past were often set attached to the centre of a log or even a fence post. Some foxes travelled a considerable distance with the drag before eventually becoming entangled. Attaching a snare to one end of a log, with the other end of the log attached to something solid, such as a tree, is likely to be looked upon as an extension of the snare rather than a drag and would appear to be legal.

A snare set on a log over a burn, on a fence where the captured animal can jump over or through and become fully or partially suspended, or on the edge of a steep bank are examples of where they must not be set.

An example of *'or otherwise uses'* could be as follows. A gamekeeper moves on and is replaced by another. The new gamekeeper finds one or more locking fox snares still in a set position that were left behind by his predecessor. He begins to check them on a regular basis. He has not *set* them but he is *using* them. If one becomes knocked and needs re-set, then the user has gone beyond the stage of simply using the snare, but has set it.

It is an offence to set or use a snare of such a nature or so placed that is likely to cause bodily injury to a Schedule 6 animal. (s. 11(2))

Animals on Schedule 6 of the Wildlife and Countryside Act 1981 are: badger, hedgehog and red squirrel. It would be highly unusual to design a snare for this purpose, but a snare set on a badger path immediately adjacent to extremely sharp objects may fall into this category. An example may be a farm implement with sharp edges or spikes. Placing a snare in this situation might also be an offence under the previous section. There would be no need that such an animal be actually caught, but evidence that it was present in the area and *likely* to be caught would need to be established from an expert. An offence under the Protection of Badgers Act 1992 (s. 1 and s. 11A – taking a badger or an attempt to do so) may also take place but an interesting comparison between the two pieces of legislation is that under the badger legislation proof is required that the action took place *wilfully*. In this case it may be necessary to prove that the person setting the snare knew that he was setting the snare on a badger path. Much would depend on proving the experience and knowledge of the person who set the snare. As an example it would be expected that a farmer or gamekeeper would know of badger setts on the land for which he is responsible, more so if he has undertaken the statutory snare training now required. In the 1981 Act, from the wording of section 11(2) it appears that there is some responsibility on the person setting the snare to be aware of what creatures may be using the track. For prosecution purposes this may be a better choice than the Protection of Badgers Act.

Without reasonable excuse, snares must not be possessed, sold, or offered or exposed for sale if they are capable of operating as self-locking. (s. 11(3C))

A snare would generally be a self-locking snare if the action of the snare is designed to allow it to close smoothly but not to allow it to open easily. This may be through some modification or as a result of use. A snare originally free-running may become self-locking because of a particular kink, bend or broken strand in it that prevents it slackening slightly to allow a snared animal to breathe. It may be argued that a snare is self-locking if it is rusted, but a defence solicitor may equally argue that if the snare is rusted to the extent that it would be difficult to open, then it would be equally difficult to close on a fox's neck and that the animal would be able to withdraw its head before being captured. Ultimately the test of this argument would be the court.

In relation to these snaring offences thus far, any person who knowingly causes or permits the offence to take place is also guilty of an offence. (s. 11(3E))

Snare identification tags (s. 11A)

The enabling Order bringing this part of the legislation into force is the Snares (Identificaton Numbers and Tags) (Scotland) Order 2012. Though this is effective from November 2012 it will not be enforced until 1 April 2013 to allow time for snare users to obtain their licences and tag numbers from the police. Each registration will cost £20 and a photo of the applicant, similar to that on a passport, must be provided. Any person who sets in position or otherwise uses a snare must ensure that he or she has been trained to a standard agreed by the Scottish Government, and has applied to and obtained from the police an identification number which must be displayed on a tag fitted to every snare used (s. 11A(1)). The tag must not be capable of being easily removed from the snare (s. 11A(2)(a)), remain readable (s. 11A(2)(b)), and display whether the snare is intended to catch (i) brown hares (BH) or rabbits (R), or (ii) foxes (F) (s. 11A(2)(c)).

Once a person has an identification number from one police force area, he may use it on snares in any other and need not apply for a further identification number from any other police force. (Bear in mind that from April 2013 the eight Scottish police forces will be merged into a single Scottish Police Service).

Checking of snares (s. 11B)

Any person who sets a snare in position must, while it remains in position, inspect it, or cause it to be inspected, at least once every day at intervals of no more than 24 hours for the following purposes (s. 11B(1)):

(a) to see whether any animal is caught by the snare; and

(b) to see whether the snare is free-running

Any person who, while carrying out such an inspection (s. 11B(2)):

(a) finds an animal caught by the snare, must during the course of the inspection release or remove the animal (whether it is alive or dead); and

(b) finds that the snare is not free-running must remove the snare or restore it to a state in which it is free-running.

For the purposes of this section a snare is 'free-running' if it is not self-locking, not capable (whether because of rust, damage or other condition or matter) of locking; and, subject only to the restriction on such movement created by the stop fitted, the noose of the snare is able at all times freely to become wider or tighten (and is not prevented from doing so because of rust, damage or other condition or matter other than the stop).

On land with snares without permission of the landowner (s. 11C)

Any person without reasonable excuse, while on any land has in his possession or sets any snare without the permission of the owner or occupier of the land, commits an offence.

Presumption of person setting snare (s. 11D)

The identification number which appears on a tag fitted on a snare is presumed in any proceedings to be the identification number of the person who set the snare in position

Record-keeping (s. 11E)

Any person with an identification number must keep a record of (s. 11E(1)):
* the location of every snare set in position by the person which remains in position;
* the location of every other snare set in position by the person within the past two years;
* the date on which each snare mentioned above was set;
* the date on which each snare mentioned above was removed;
* in relation to each animal caught in a snare mentioned above –
  (i) the type of animal; and
  (ii) the date it was found.

For these purposes the location of a snare is to be recorded (s. 11E(2)):
* by reference to a map; or
* by such other means (for example, by means of a description) capable of readily identifying the location.

Production of records to police (s. 11E(4))

A person who is requested to produce the above records to a police officer must do so within 21 days. Any person who, without reasonable excuse, fails to comply with any of the above is guilty of an offence (s. 11E(4)).

Snares set for mountain hares

Snares must not be set for mountain hares without a licence from Scottish Natural Heritage.

Mountain hares are listed in Schedule 3 of the Conservation (Natural Habitats, etc) Regulations, 1994, as animals which may not be taken or killed by certain methods. In addition to a mountain hare, a pine marten and polecat are included in this schedule. The wording which would preclude the snaring of white hares (reg. 41(3)(j)) Conservation (Natural Habitats etc) Regulations

1994) is the use of *traps which are non-selective according to their principle or their condition of use.*

There are legal arguments around this term, though it seems that a trap *does* include a snare, and that a snare is *non-selective*, therefore the snaring of mountain hares must be licensed. It would have been preferable in this legislation to have defined a trap as also including a snare (or otherwise if that is what the legislators intended). It is interesting that a sheriff in Inverness repelled a defence submission of 'no case to answer,' in which the defence argued that a snare was not a trap. It would also be much clearer, and afford better conservation measures for mountain hares, if killing them by *any* means was licensed through a general licence with certain conditions. The logic of creating an offence in setting a snare for a mountain hare when that snare can catch an animal other than the intended mountain hare *(non-selective according to its principle or conditions of use)* is difficult to comprehend, though it could be argued that the term might include lactating female mountain hares.

The snaring of European Protected Species
Mammals in Schedule 2 – wildcat and otter – are protected as European Protected Species in any case, so it would be an offence to deliberately or recklessly kill or injure them, or attempt to do so. This would include deliberately setting a snare for them or deliberately or recklessly catching them in a snare.

Snares deliberately set for deer – see Deer poaching p161

Though the updated legislation has most certainly reduced some previous slovenliness in snaring, the most common remaining abuses are those of failing to check snares at intervals of no more than 24 hours, and setting a snare where the captive animal can become fully or partially suspended. With snares set on fences or where the animal is likely to become fully or partially suspended it may be appropriate, with a snare which is set in such a position but has not caught an animal, for investigating officers to test with the snare how far it would stretch if it had an animal in it. If it would result in an offence being committed, a photograph or video of how far it would stretch is likely to improve a case submitted for prosecution.

4. Wild Birds

IT IS WORTH opening this chapter with the definition of a 'wild bird', since reference will be made at various points to this legal term. The definition is found at s. 27(1) of the Wildlife and Countryside Act 1981.

> *'Wild bird' means any bird of a species which is ordinarily resident in, or is a visitor to, any member State or the European territory of any member State in a wild state but does not include poultry. For the purposes of section 1 of the Act it does not include any bird which is shown to have been bred in captivity unless –*
>
> *(a) it has been lawfully released or allowed to escape from captivity as part of a re-population or re-introduction programme; or*
>
> *(b) it is a mallard, grey or red-legged partridge, common pheasant or red grouse which is no longer in captivity and is not in a place where it was reared.*

Birds at (a) above would include the white-tailed eagle and red kite.

Offences against wild birds are undoubtedly the most common wildlife offences dealt with by the police, and can be categorised as follows.

Bird of prey persecution

This can include the shooting, trapping and poisoning of birds of prey, or the intentional or reckless disturbance or interference at their nest site to prevent them nesting successfully. An insidious, though not illegal, practice noted by police, conservationists and hill walkers is that on at least one estate in Angus all the rowan, birch, alder and larch trees that have been growing up the sides of hill burns for many years had been cut down. The conclusion drawn was that these were roosting places for birds of prey and had been removed for that reason. If they ever get a chance, it will be decades before these trees can be naturally replaced.

Bird of prey persecution can comprise one or more of the following.

Illegal shooting:

Illegal shooting of birds of prey (s. 1(1) WCA) is likely to take place anywhere, though very often it takes place at a nest site since that is the easiest place to

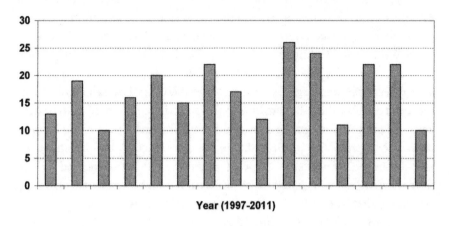

Confirmed bird of prey abuse incidents in Scotland

Year (1997-2011)

Source – Science and Advice for Scottish Agriculture

find a bird. Most frequently a sitting bird will be flushed off the nest and shot with a shotgun, the most common being hen harriers and peregrines. Even if the adult(s) are not shot, it is usually a simple matter to dispose of the eggs or chicks. There have also been numerous reports to the police of buzzards being shot at night, either being lamped while roosting or flushed from a wood on a moonlit night and shot by guns surrounding the wood. It is known that image intensifiers and extremely expensive thermal imaging are sometimes used to find and shoot the bird in darkness. Birds that roost communally, such as hen harriers, are sometimes shot coming in to their roost at dusk.

In the case of peregrines, evidence of an attempt to shoot the female can sometimes be seen in a bird flying with missing feathers on one wing, though of course if the feather damage is too severe the bird will be grounded. Evidence of shotgun pellets passing through a feather can be found in the form of a clean cut in the feathering on one (or even both) sides of the shaft. If the female has been killed and the season is not too late for egg-laying, the male may take an immature female as a new partner. A mature female present at the start of the nesting season, then an immature female later in the season may be an indication that the first female is dead. This does not necessarily mean that she has been the victim of a crime, but similar evidence over a number a years may build a picture that all is not right.

Reports are sometime made to the police of a pair of hen harriers being present and displaying in a particular area, then mysteriously disappearing. Displaying (skydancing) is a prelude to nesting, with the male carrying out this ritual over a chosen nesting area. The police must deal with evidence, not supposition. It could well be that one or both birds have been shot, but equally one or both may have died other than as a result of criminal activity or simply have moved elsewhere. The hen harrier is included on Schedule 1 of the Wildlife and Countryside Act 1981. The law protects a Schedule 1 bird against *intentional or reckless* disturbance *while it is building a nest or is in, on or near a nest containing eggs or chicks* (s. 1(5) WCA). Though it would be reprehensible conduct for someone to fire shots in the air, deliberately leave a vehicle or other item in the area, or otherwise disturb a pair of hen harriers during their *prelude* to nesting, this is not an offence if the birds have not actually begun to nest. This type of situation could be remedied by hen harriers being added to Schedule 1A (protection from harassment at all times). It is likely that, subject to Ministerial approval, there will soon be additions to the list of species on Schedule 1A.

Since firearms are the crux of this section, the safety of investigating officers and others who may be involved is paramount. A shotgun, rifle or air weapon may well need to be seized as a production. Before being put in a vehicle it must be checked to see if it is loaded, and if loaded, needs to be emptied in the presence of a witness, and the cartridges, bullets or pellets noted and labelled as productions. Many police officers will not have the practical experience to ensure that a weapon is empty and 'safe', and may need to call on the services of an authorised firearms officer or an experienced colleague to assist.

With birds or animals which have been shot, confirmation of shooting can usually be gained by x-ray providing a pellet, bullet or bullet fragments have remained within the body. X-rays are expensive, and officers might consider setting up an arrangement for discreet use of an x-ray device at an airport or prison. While this may not always be sufficient for court purposes, it is an excellent screening tool. If evidence of shooting is found, then a proper x-ray by a vet can be undertaken if the case is to be taken to court and the specialist prosecutor thinks this is necessary.

In some cases air weapon pellets and bullets can be matched to the weapon that fired them. It is imperative to ensure that the veterinary pathologist, when removing a pellet or bullet, handles it with extreme care and packs it in a medium such as tissue to protect it prior to examination by a ballistics expert.

Where possible, efforts should be made to recover cartridge cases and bullet cases from the scene of a shooting, as they may also be able to be matched to the weapon which fired them because of the often unique mark made by the firing pin. DNA testing will also be a consideration.

Where a bird or animal is to be examined by a vet with a view to finding injuries consistent with shooting, (unless there is a bullet or pellet visible by x-ray in the body) it is preferable that the carcass is not frozen beforehand. Freezing can change the texture of muscle tissue, and wounds to muscle tissue are therefore more difficult, or even impossible, to determine.

The illegal use of Fenn-type traps

These traps, normally used legally within tunnels, are sometimes deliberately used to catch birds of prey (and also crows) by being set in the open. If the bait is a dead mammal or bird, then all carrion-eating birds are like to be victims. The bait is likely to be set against a feature of the landscape, such as a rock, tree trunk or fence so the victim cannot approach it from behind. The trap will be set a few inches in front of the bait, usually with a shallow square the size of the trap being cut out of the ground so that, when set, the trap is flush with the ground. It is then lightly covered over with the vegetation that fits best into the surroundings. Invariably there will be some sort of lead-in built at each side of the trap so that the victim can only approach the bait over the top of the trap. The lead-in is also likely to be constructed of items that fit with the surroundings, usually branches. *This practice is never legal as traps must not be set in the open or set to catch birds.* (s. 5 WCA and s. 50 Agriculture (Scotland) Act 1948)

Pesticide abuse

Poisoned baits set out to kill wildlife are usually hare, rabbit, pheasant, pigeon, partridge or grouse. (s. 5 WCA). Rabbits and hares are usually gutted, with pesticide placed inside the body cavity. Often half of a hare is used rather than the whole carcass. Occasionally a rabbit is not gutted, and the pesticide placed on cuts on the inside of its back legs. With birds as baits, the breast is usually sliced open and pesticide placed on the open cuts. Depending on the pesticide used, traces in the form of light green, dark blue or even almost black crystals might be visible. With the use of insecticides, sometimes there are dead flies and/or beetles on the carcass. Less commonly, small birds such as starlings, pieces of venison, pieces of fish, sausage meat or bread have been used (though bread is much more likely to be used against rooks and gulls than birds of prey). In some cases dead birds, usually grouse or pigeons, may be used as poisoned baits to kill peregrine falcons. In these cases the baited bird is likely to be propped up with a stick or piece of wire under the head to look as if it is alive, with the pesticide inserted behind the head or neck. The peregrine swoops on the bait and 'kills' the bird by taking its head off, thus ingesting some of the bait. On rare occasions, usually found to be linked to pigeon fanciers, a tethered live racing pigeon may be contaminated with pesticide.

The victims of baits are usually found near to the bait, most often within 100 yards. There are exceptions to this and very occasionally a victim is found a greater distance away. The distance between bait and victim is not prescriptive and depends on the topography, the type of pesticide and the victim species. Birds such as a buzzard or golden eagle, which tend to gorge on a carcass, are more likely to be found near the bait than a bird that picks off morsels and carries them off to eat elsewhere, such as a red kite. Since some of the pesticides kill by muscle spasms, avian victims often have their feet clenched into a ball and/or their head thrown back.

Anyone suspecting that they have found a poisoned bait or a victim of poisoning should not touch it, since some of the pesticides are extremely toxic and can easily kill a human. Placing something over the bait should prevent any bird feeding from it, though this is less likely to be the case with a mammal. The police should be contacted immediately and the value of covering the bait should be assessed after it is known how long it will take the police to attend and whether or not the witness can await their arrival. The obvious downside is that any obvious interference will alert the person who set the bait, and the evidence is likely to be gone when the police arrive. Progress is being made on obtaining human DNA from poisoned baits at the Centre for Forensic Science section of the Department of Pure and Applied Chemistry at the University of Strathclyde. This would be a major prosecution (and prevention) tool in the war against wildlife crime.

A person commits an offence if he or she is in possession of any pesticide containing one or more prescribed active ingredient. (s. 15A WCA). Prescribed ingredients listed under the Possession of Pesticides (Scotland) Order 2005 are:

> Aldicarb; Alphachloralose; Aluminium phosphide; Bendiocarb; Carbofuran; Mevinphos; Sodium cyanide; Strychnine. If necessary other pesticides can be added by the Scottish Government.

A defence is provided if the person can show that the possession of the pesticide is for a lawful purpose.

For police officers investigating pesticide abuse cases every case is different and there is no prescriptive method of proceeding with an investigation. The first report may be of a suspected bait, a suspected victim or both. In many cases there tends to be a build up of intelligence beforehand about illegal activity in a particular area or farm or estate, sometimes with a named suspect. In other cases the first notification may be of considerable severity, such as a number of poisoned victims, or a high profile case such as a poisoned golden eagle, or a pet dog in an urban area.

It is important not to automatically assume that when a victim – for instance the most common one, a dead buzzard – is found on a farm or estate, that it must have been poisoned in that same area. It may well have been but this is not always the case. Victims *in rare cases* may be able to travel a mile or even more. Victims are frequently found on the boundary of two or more farms or estates, making the investigation even more difficult. This, of course, is sometimes because a bait has been deliberately placed near (or even over) the boundary.

Normally the beginning of a pesticide abuse investigation is the recovery of bait or a victim from a given location. When a report is received, and the witness is unable to take the police officer to the locus, it is important to obtain the exact location of the incident. A GPS reading or even a six figure map reference is a great start, *but it is also important to obtain landmarks*, which are invaluable to the officers when they get on to the ground. As full a description of the circumstances as possible should be obtained. This would include the reason that the caller thinks an item is a poisoned bait. In the case of a victim, an estimate of how long it has been dead or if it is a bird, might it have struck power lines or been electrocuted at an electricity pole where power is being drawn off or diverted via a transformer? This is a surprisingly common cause of electrocution in birds of prey, even kestrel-sized. In the case of a sparrowhawk, particularly a juvenile in brown plumage, could it have been killed by flying into something? All dead birds and animals are not necessarily baits or victims, and in many cases this can be established one way or the other by an experienced officer asking the correct questions. The answers to these questions should also determine the urgency with which the item may have to be recovered.

A witness should be discouraged from taking possession of the bait or victim and bringing it to the police station. Firstly its presence may well be uncorroborated, but more importantly the finder may be exposed to risk of injury or even death from contact with traces of pesticide. The advice should be that the item be photographed if possible, then covered with branches or whatever may be at the scene to lessen the risk of predation.

If the police officer concludes that the item is likely to be a bait or a poison victim, it must then be recovered, with corroboration, as a matter of urgency and a scene of crime examination carried out. As the recovery of the victim or bait is urgent (since both have the potential to claim further victims) a search warrant is not necessary at this stage. The recovery may be by two police officers or a police officer with corroboration from a person from another agency or, in cases where he or she is not thought involved or liable to tell the suspect, the owner or tenant of the land where the victim is found. *It is inadvisable to attend in uniform or in a marked car*, otherwise the person responsible, if he lives in the area, will realise very quickly that his crime has been discovered and any evidence that might incriminate him will quickly disappear. Again, procedure cannot be prescriptive, but at this stage often a reasonably brief and covert search in the near vicinity of the bait or victim will suffice. Events may dictate a different course, and it cannot be assumed by officers that they will not be committed to a thorough search or even the detention of a suspect though this was not envisaged at the outset of this search. Experience shows that baits are most likely to be found uphill of a victim and victims downhill of a bait.

It is worth mentioning at this point that, even before a bait or victim is examined by Science and Advice for Scottish Agriculture (SASA), there may be sufficient evidence to apply for a search warrant to progress the investigation further. Some of the most experienced police wildlife crime officers have now dealt with many poisoning investigations and the signs of pesticide abuse are frequently obvious to them. Factors that should be taken into consideration are:

1. Previous intelligence (which vindicates ensuring that all available intelligence is entered on the Scottish Intelligence Database)
2. The circumstances in which the victim is found. Has it clearly fallen from a tree? Is it in a pose, in death, typical of previously recovered poisoned victims, particularly birds?
3. Is there evidence of traces or granules of pesticides visible inside the beak, or has the bird vomited some bait and pesticide traces nearby?
4. Is there a suspected bait nearby?
5. If a suspected bait, are there pesticide traces or granules visible on the bait?
6. Are there, as might be the case with a bait laced with insecticide, dead insects in the bait?
7. Can SASA staff or an SAC vet give a verbal report, in advance of tests, that suggests there are pesticide traces or granules visible?

A quick x-ray at this stage to eliminate shooting as a cause of death might also be helpful. All of this should be enough to convince a specialist fiscal and subsequently a sheriff to grant a search warrant. Investigations with most success are usually those which proceed through the various stages rapidly without time being wasted.

In due course the item(s) will be forwarded to SASA at 1 Roddinglaw

Road, Edinburgh, for examination for pesticides. With fresher baits or victims, samples can also be taken by vets at any of Scotland's Rural College (SRUC – formerly SAC) vet labs and posted to SASA, *though officers should ensure the evidence chain is watertight, with all samples being labelled and signed.*

Unless there is a previous history where an individual has come to the attention of the police, and which should come to light through the checks carried out during any criminal investigation, the investigator may be starting from scratch. The officer should consider the elements of circumstantial evidence, which is basic police work. Who would have a motive? Who would have the ability? Was the act done intentionally or may it be the result of misuse rather than abuse? Has someone done something to cover his tracks or to throw the police off the scent? Who would have the opportunity to commit the crime? Is there any evidence of preparation? Many of these can be applied to begin to build a case against a suspect (or even to rule that person out), but of course the most essential – and difficult – element of all is to *identify* the suspect as the person responsible.

In rural situations, identifying the motive is important. Does it appear to be a farmer or shepherd trying to control foxes or crows? Is it a landowner, gamekeeper or part time gamekeeper trying to control crows, buzzards, peregrine falcons or other species? Might the incident be connected to pigeon fanciers? Is there a pigeon loft nearby? An officer should also keep in mind vicarious liability (s. 18A WCA), which may also be relevant (see Vicarious liability p72).

If pesticide abuse is confirmed by SASA, there may still be insufficient evidence to proceed further, or enquiries may simply have to be made with persons who *may* be suspects. This is a situation that often frustrates members of the public who know something of the incident but have much less knowledge of the level of evidence required for court purposes or the legal issues that might limit what the police can do. In best-case scenarios the investigating officer may have sufficient evidence to apply for a search warrant and continue the investigation to its next stage.

During a search of this nature under warrant it would be unusual for experienced staff of the Scottish Government Rural Payment Inspections Directorate (SGRPID) not to be involved, but the police would be entitled, if they so wish, to use the services of other non-government agencies.

When only a victim has been found, it is sometimes helpful to be aware of what the bait has been. Science and Advice for Scottish Agriculture (SASA) may be able to offer an idea from the stomach or gullet contents of the victim as to what the bait might have been. Officers should bear in mind the animal DNA facility now offered at SASA, where stomach contents can sometimes be subjected to DNA tests to reveal what species has been eaten. Will any such species be found in the buildings or vehicles during a search? If there are, this may be a relevant circumstantial link. Consider how the culprit would prepare the bait. Should you be looking for a knife which may be contaminated, or a spoon, syringe or even a twig. It is even worthwhile x-raying a bait as there may be a (slim) chance of finding a bullet inside that could be matched to a suspect's rifle. Might there be blood or feathers in the suspect's vehicle that could be matched through DNA?

Investigating officers should take possession of anything that seems relevant, bag them separately, and submit them to SASA. Consider how the bait would be transported to where it was recovered. Could it have been in a game bag or similar receptacle? Is there such an item that could be linked to the suspect? If so, seize it for examination by SASA. Were there vehicle tracks near the bait? Could there be a vehicle of that type that could be linked to the suspect? Baits may have been carried in the back of a vehicle; would the rear or footwells of the vehicle be worth taking sweepings from for traces of pesticide? Full scenes of crime examinations of 5 estate land rovers in a Tayside case in 2006 resulted in the recovery of two game bags, a sack and 4 knives with traces of pesticides, and 11 sets of sweepings from different parts of the 5 Land Rovers testing positive for either carbofuran, chloralose or in some cases both.

While traces of pesticide in vehicles may not be conclusive evidence, they may form another link in a circumstantial chain. What may be more conclusive are traces of pesticide on a suspect's clothing. SASA cannot carry out the necessary testing on clothing, so the garments will have to be vacuumed and the dust, especially from pockets, sent for submission. Using a different filter for each garment eliminates the risk of cross-contamination.

During a field search there may be only a few acres to be searched, or there may be thousands. The land may be woodland, agricultural land, moorland or a mixture of all three. The knack is in knowing where you are most likely to find something. To some extent the investigators can be guided by the motive, if that can be established. For instance if the motive is to protect lambs from foxes, start looking in the vicinity of the fields with lambs. If the motive appears to be to destroy peregrine falcons, look near to known nest sites. If the motive appears related to pheasant or partridge management, look near to release pens or feeding sites, especially in clearings. Birds which feed on a bait sometimes manage to fly to a tree, from which they then fall. Single trees are worth checking, or woodland edges. Look up the trees as well, as sometimes a dying bird gets stuck in branches. On moorland, baits are very often found near to land rover or quad bike tracks, often on ridges and invariably on bare ground where the bait can be seen by the bird targeted. Small baits have also been found on top of the posts of an electric deer fence. This is only a rough guide on where to start, though nothing beats experience.

Baits may have been set out for some considerable time or victims may have been long-dead, or even predated themselves. Nevertheless they are normally worth recovering and sending to SASA. Their evidential value will never be known unless they are taken and examined.

Ground searches work more effectively, with less time lost, when teams of two or three searchers are used. With a long line of searchers time is wasted searching, for instance, stands of long heather, or where the whole line has to stop while something is examined by one or more of the searchers. While it is accepted that a victim of poisoning may well be found in an area of long heather, generally this will not take the investigation much further forward evidentially and time is better spent looking for baits, which will be on more open ground. A large area can be covered much more quickly and effectively with groups of two or three searchers, with each of the groups being delegated to a particular segment of the land. Less time is wasted and irrelevant pieces of land can be ignored. Quad bikes, if available, can be used to access and search more remote parts of the land. If there is a regularly-used quad bike or Land Rover track baits may not be too far from it.

In dealing with pesticide abuse cases when some of the more dangerous pesticides, such as the carbamate-based pesticides, mevinphos (Phosdrin) or strychnine, have been used and where there was a potential for them to be found and handled by the public, which could result in their serious injury or death, consider the common law crime of culpable and reckless conduct.

Lastly, consider how a press release might help. Despite criticism from some raptor enthusiasts that press releases are not made for weeks – or even months – after an incident, there are on occasions a whole raft of valid reasons for not doing so, particularly the alerting of the suspect. Press releases are made if and when they might help progress the investigation. Nevertheless a press release *at the earliest possible stage*, might help enlighten those who know little about police investigations and think because they have not seen or heard anything in the media that the police and the specialist prosecutors are doing nothing to try to trace an offender and bring him to justice.

Schedule 1A and A1 – Harassment and damage to nest sites:
It is an offence to intentionally or recklessly harass a bird included in Schedule 1A of the Wildlife and Countryside Act 1981 *at any time*, not just when they are nesting. It is also an offence to intentionally or recklessly damage or destroy the nest or nest site of a bird in Schedule A1 at any time. These schedules, for

the time being at least, only include a white-tailed eagle, though it is likely that, subject to Ministerial approval, there will soon be additions to the list of species on these schedules.

Since many white-tailed eagles nest in trees, it is important during any forest operations not to work close to an active nest or to fell a tree with a nest. Forestry Commission Scotland have excellent guidelines relating to forest operations, which be downloaded at http://www.forestry.gov.uk/website/forest.nsf/byunique/infd-6vrjh2

Vicarious liability:
This provision, made under the Wildlife and Natural Environment (Scotland) Act 2011, is now part of the amended Wildlife and Countryside Act 1981. It affects anyone who has a legal right to kill or take wild birds on land, or agents or managers who have the delegated responsibility to exercise management or control of that right. This management or control might include the management of habitat for wild birds, the rearing of wild birds, the killing of wild birds and the management of predators of wild birds.

As an example, an owner, manager or agent is liable to be prosecuted if an employee commits the offence of:
* Intentionally or recklessly killing, injuring or taking a wild bird (a contravention of section 1(1) of the Act);
* Intentionally or recklessly disturbing a Schedule 1 bird while it is nesting (section 1(5)); harassing a bird in Schedule 1A (section 1(5B));
* Setting out an illegal trap or poisoned bait or using those to take or kill a wild bird (section 5(1)(a) or (b));
* Possessing a prescribed pesticide (section 15A(1); or
* Attempting, or having items capable of being used, to commit any of these offences (section18).

There is no requirement for the employee to be successfully prosecuted for the offence though for a successful prosecution of an employer, manager or agent, the Crown will require to prove who committed the alleged offence and the connection between that person and the employer, manager or agent.

Vicarious liability for certain offences by employee or agent:
This offence, introduced through the provisions of the Wildlife and Natural Environment (Scotland) Act 2011 and enforceable from 1 January 2012, comes under section 18A of the Wildlife and Countryside Act 1981. Vicarious liability takes effect when one person may be liable for the acts of another person, for example an employee or agent. In relation to wildlife crime it is applicable where, on or in relation to any land, a person (Person A, who may, for example,

be a gamekeeper,) commits *a relevant offence* while acting as the employee or agent of a person (Person B, who may, for example be a landowner or sporting agent) who either

> (a) has a legal right to kill or take a wild bird on or over that land; or
> (b) *manages or controls* the exercise of any such right.

Manages or controls the exercise of any such right includes in particular management or control of any of the following, (essentially, managing game birds for shooting) –

> (a) the operation or activity of killing or taking any such birds on or over that land;
> (b) the habitat of any such birds on that land;
> (c) the presence on or over that land of predators of any such birds;
> (d) the release of birds from captivity for the purpose of their being killed or taken on or over that land.

A relevant offence is –

> (a) an offence under –
>> (i) section 1(1), (5) or (5B);
>> (ii) section 5(1)(a) or (b); or
>> (iii) section 15A(1); and
> (b) an offence under section 18 committed in relation to any of the offences mentioned in paragraph (a)

An offence also takes place when, on or in relation to any land, a person (Person A, for example a contracted pest controller) commits a relevant offence while providing relevant services for a person (Person B, this time for example a person who leases a shoot.) The link between the perpetrator of the crime and the person with the shooting rights may be indirect through a third party. If another person (Person C, for example the owner of a pest control company) is providing or securing the provision of relevant services for Person B, Person B still may be liable.

Where there is evidence against Person A, Person B is also guilty of the offence and liable to be proceeded against and punished accordingly, *whether or not proceedings are also taken against Person A.*

It would be a valid defence of Person B to show that he or she did not know that the offence was being committed by Person A; *and* that Person B took all reasonable steps and exercised all due diligence to prevent the offence being committed.

This would appear to mean that if there is evidence against Person A, Person B needs to demonstrate that, firstly, he or she did not know Person A was committing the offence; *and*, secondly, he or she took all reasonable steps and exercised all due diligence to prevent the offence being committed. *Both* factors need to be demonstrated in order to provide a successful defence. Reasonable steps might include written guidelines and/or training courses for employees.

In summary, if a person falls within the definition of a (managerial) person to whom relevant services are provided either by an employee or someone simply acting on his or her behalf in the capacity of an agent, and that person (the agent) commits an offence, then that person in the managerial capacity may be liable for their actions. However the prosecution will still have to prove who carried out the offence, (even if that person is not prosecuted) and the link with the person who has the shooting rights.

Egg collecting

Nowadays this illegal 'hobby' is almost never carried out by schoolchildren; it is adults who are involved, coming from a wide range of social classes. If egg thieves can be stereotyped it is only that they are resourceful, determined and experts at the finding of birds nests. Invariably they target the rarer species of birds, and some egg thieves collect clutch after clutch from the same species, usually to show the varieties of markings on the eggs laid by different females. (s 1(1)(c) or 1(2)(b) WCA).

Egg thieves often return to the same area at the same time each year, providing an opportunity for police officers to be proactive in their efforts to catch them. Every year some are caught 'in the act', but by far the more successful strategies are identifying and searching suspects' houses or other places where there is intelligence that they store part of their egg collection, or stopping and searching their vehicles. Any person acting suspiciously in an area where it is known there are rare nesting birds should be reported to the police. 'Acting suspiciously' might include hitting bushes or beating heather or reeds with a stick to flush a bird off a nest, climbing trees or abseiling down known bird nesting cliffs. It is sometimes a practice of egg thieves to hide eggs and return for them later. If this practice is witnessed, or if a marker is left out on a moor, this should be communicated to the police.

The statutory defence existing prior to the Nature Conservation (Scotland) Act 2004 in relation to a charge of possessing wild birds, their eggs or specimens derived from wild birds was amended to differentiate between specimens which originated in Scotland and those which originated outwith Scotland. A person in possession of a bird's egg must be able to show that, if the specimen originated in Scotland, it was acquired without contravening the Protection of Birds Acts 1954 to 1967 or the Wildlife and Countryside Act 1981.

If the eggs originated outwith Scotland the person must show that the manner in which they were taken or otherwise acquired would not have breached the law of Scotland had the act occurred in Scotland.

This plugged a loophole in the law used by egg thieves who go abroad to collect eggs, taking advantage in some countries of a policing regime that may be less enthusiastic and knowledgeable than the police in the UK about the detection of wildlife crime.

A special exception is made in relation to eggs legally imported into Scotland in compliance with the Convention on International Trade in Endangered Species (CITES) as transposed into European law.

Though the *taking or possession* of wild birds' eggs is an offence under section 1 of the Wildlife and Countryside Act, the *sale* of wild birds' eggs comes under section 6(1). For an offence to have taken place regarding the *possession* of wild birds' eggs it must be shown by the eggs' owner that the eggs were taken after 1954, the year of the earlier Protection of Birds Act. Though the Wildlife and Countryside Act provides for this almost reverse burden of proof, taking account of human rights legislation, a case would have much more chance of succeeding if the Crown were able to *prove* that the eggs were taken after 1954. No such requirement in terms of a date needs to be shown regarding the *sale* of eggs, and it matters not whether the eggs were taken in 2012 or 1812.

During any wildlife-related search it is important for the investigating officer to list on the warrant application the sections of the Act believed contravened, and the items sought. In bird egg cases this may include:

- Wild birds' eggs or parts thereof
- Items capable of being used to commit the offence, which could include egg blowing equipment, climbing equipment, maps, GPS, storage equipment, binoculars, computers, films, photographs, video tapes, etc.
- Documentary evidence connected with the offence, which could include data cards, address books, diaries, notes, etc.

Since in many searches a high number of productions may be taken, one officer should be delegated to keep a log of what was found, where it was found, who found it and any comment made by the suspect. Advice can be obtained from a police search advisor (POLSA).

Many egg thieves photograph the eggs in the nest before they take them. In the case of eggs with a pattern, these are as unique as fingerprints and it may be possible to match up a clutch of eggs in a photograph to a clutch in a suspect's possession. Even though no eggs are found, there may be sufficient for a charge of taking eggs once all the evidence is examined. The taking of computers should be considered since that may be where data are kept.

Egg thieves are notorious for hiding small but very relevant items in obscure places. Items such as an egg blowing kit, which may simply be a small drill and a pipette or syringe, can easily be hidden either on the suspect or in a vehicle. Officers should carry out searches as if it were a search for drugs. Successful searches of vehicles have sometimes been by trained search personnel. On one occasion plastic tubs of eggs were found concealed between the car radiator and the grille, with the top panel that covered this space having been removed to hide the eggs, then screwed back into position so that the tubs were completely hidden. On other occasions, eggs have been found concealed in a flask with the internal parts removed, and in a cardboard whisky bottle tube.

In addition to the items listed as of interest during a search of premises, innocuous items in a vehicle such as toilet rolls, tissue paper or cotton wool may be there for wrapping eggs, and usually found in greater quantities than would be required for their normal use. A small fishing net may be there to scoop eggs from a ledge or cliff nest. Officers should look at each article found and try to assess its value to the suspect as an egg collecting, wrapping or transporting tool.

If charges are to be brought against the suspect, the investigating officer might consider the seizure of his car as an item capable of being used to commit the crime. If he has travelled some distance then this is likely to be valid. In any event a vehicle can be forfeit by the court.

Lastly, all police forces in the UK, and the RSPB Investigations Section, work closely to monitor known or suspected egg thieves through Operation Easter, initiated by Tayside Police in 1997. In tandem with increased sentencing powers for courts, this proactive and cohesive method of policing has made a dramatic reduction in the number of criminals still collecting eggs today, and has resulting in many thousands of eggs being recovered. Its success depends partly on good intelligence, and any information that indicates a person is collecting eggs, storing eggs for someone else or trading in wild bird eggs should be immediately passed to the police.

Taking live birds from the wild

The live-trapping of any wild bird is illegal (other than under licence, or the trapping of a few 'pest' species, or 'game' species which may be trapped in limited circumstances by legally permitted methods). This offence (s. 1(1); 1(2) or 5(1)(b) WCA) includes taking wild adult finches for the cage-bird trade; ringing small young in the nest and returning for them before they fledge, or taking young birds of prey (or their eggs) – particularly peregrines

– to launder into the falconry trade. On rare occasions birds may be taken and killed for taxidermy. Once the birds are trapped they become captive wild birds in terms of the Animal Health and Welfare (Scotland) Act 2006. Very often the trapping causes them injury or feather damage. In this case there may also be an offence under s. 19 of that Act. There may also be an offence if any of the birds is kept in a cage of a size that it cannot stand without touching the top, or be able to fully stretch its wings (s. 8 WCA).

The most common method of taking finches from the wild is by the use of mist nets set up in winter-time when birds are much more likely to be in flocks. The nets are sometimes set in clearings in woodland in order to catch birds as they fly across the clearing. Mist nets are strung between two fixed points, either poles (typically bamboo) or objects already at the site such as buildings or small trees. They are commercially manufactured and made of very fine mesh. Looked at broad-side on they are almost invisible when set, especially when placed against a dark background. Birds fly into the 'invisible' net and are caught. Often one or more call birds may be set out in cages to attract birds of that species. The trapper may well be hiding nearby and once birds are caught, he will remove them from the net and place them in small bags.

Note that mist nets are also one of the principal methods used to trap birds for legitimate bird ringing. The main source of illegal mist nets is their theft from legitimate ringing sites. Any unlicensed use of mist nets is illegal. SNH can issue a licence under WCA s.16(1)(a), (b) and (c), to any person who is trained and accredited by the BTO as a ringer. A licence of this type is possible under the terms of WCA s.16(5)(b) which states a licence may be issued to 'persons of a class', the class in this case being BTO ringers. If a net is being used legally the operator is likely to come forward and announce his or her presence and purpose to anyone near the net.

Clap nets are typically home made and thus come in a variety of shapes and sizes. They are usually operated on-site by the trapper, concealed near the trap, and essentially involve a net laid flat on the ground and designed to pivot along one long edge onto the adjacent piece of ground which has been baited to attract birds. A system of elasticated cords and short poles allows the trap to function. These are probably the least commonly encountered finch trap in the UK. Clap nets may also be operated on a rectangle of ground specially cleared to avoid entanglement. Feeding is put in the centre line of the rectangle and the nets are set at each side. When fired towards the centre line of the rectangle, the nets cross over each other trapping the birds underneath. This is a common method of bird trapping in Malta.

Smaller self-contained clap nets are also used, again covering a piece of baited ground. These are sometimes semi-circular when set and spring into a fully circular shape when set off. They may be triggered automatically by the feeding activity of the target birds but are usually set off by the trapper concealed close by, as the case with the more standard type of clap net.

Cages are used for songbird trapping both as actual traps and as containers to hold 'call' birds. All these cages are home-made and therefore variable in design and appearance. Call cages are usually small simple cages just large enough to contain a decoy bird that will attract target birds either by singing or by its mere presence. Call cages may be used in conjunction with any of the trapping methods described here.

More elaborate cage traps can be triggered by the target bird. The traditional trap of this sort is known as a 'chardonneret' (the French word for goldfinch). Some chardonneret traps incorporate a separate call bird compartment; some are merely trapping cages and may be used with one or more call cages placed nearby. Chardonneret traps usually have a roof entrance which is closed by a spring-loaded perch which functions when the target bird lands on it. The trap is baited with seed or other suitable food. Being automatic in operation they do not require the presence of an operator but will trap only one bird at a time so some degree of close monitoring is needed if the trapper wishes to take many birds.

Another method is the use of glue, often referred to as bird lime. This is a simple concept that involves making perches sticky so that birds using them adhere to the perch and are trapped. Traditionally the 'lime' was made from the sap of certain plants (e.g. holly) boiled and concentrated. Commercial non-hardening glues are also now used. Lime may be applied direct to the outer twigs of bushes and small trees in situ, or on pre-prepared twigs ('lime sticks') that are then attached to suitable vegetation. One method is to attach lime sticks to the top of long poles in such a way that the weight of the trapped bird dislodges the stick which then drops to the ground with the bird. This allows the trapping of birds (e.g. thrushes), which may not readily come on to lower perches. A further variation on liming is the use of a limed rope or long cord that is strung along the inside of a hedge or more open fence line.

Nearly all wild birds caught are fitted with a leg ring which has been stretched to get it over the foot, then crimped tight again. With some rings the tampering is obvious, but with others confirmation is required by an expert. When placed in an aviary, birds taken from the wild are frightened and fly back and forward in the cage, sometimes damaging their feathers and sometimes causing the cere (the soft area just above the upper mandible) to become damaged as they hit against the cage. They are as likely to be on the floor as on perches and will react to the presence of anyone, especially a stranger, entering the aviary by flying frantically around the cage. If there are captive-bred birds in neighbouring cages their reactions are calm, rather like a budgie or canary that is used to people. Even to a person knowing little about finches, this comparison is a useful guide.

Birds legitimately kept or bred in captivity

Some birds can be legitimately kept in captivity. Generally these are kept as cage birds (finches and small song birds), birds of prey for falconry purposes, and birds bred for game shooting purposes. These birds are usually well cared-for, though since they are captive, any animal welfare-related offence is likely to come under s. 19 Animal Health and Welfare (Scotland) Act 2006. The most likely offence is the illegal trade in these birds (s. 6 WCA).

Contrary to popular belief, all birds kept in captivity do not need to be ringed, though a keeper must be able to prove that a bird is legally in his possession. Birds which may be sold alive, provided they are ringed and bred in captivity, are listed on Schedule 3, Part 1 of the WCA. Apart from birds bred for shooting purposes, birds bred in captivity must be ringed if they are being sold.

Private Breeders' rings are obtainable from several sources and are advertised in a number of specialist magazines. They come in a variety of colours and the breeder can choose what he wants stamped on the ring. In the main, breeders use numbers followed by their initials, the ring size and the year. Therefore, such a ring should read something like 053 PAC 10W.

British Bird Council closed rings are stamped with a four-digit number, followed by a B over a C, a code letter to indicate the size of the ring, and the year. International Ornithological Association rings are silver in colour and are stamped with a ring number, followed by a size code, the letters IOA, and the year.

Some rarer birds kept in captivity *must* be registered and ringed at all times. These birds are listed on Schedule 4 of the WCA.

Schedule 4 birds

Under Section 7 of the Wildlife and Countryside Act 1981, the keeper (who may not necessarily be the owner) of any captive bird of a species listed in Schedule 4 must have it registered with Animal Health and fitted with a unique closed leg ring, microchip, or have a licence for it to be kept unringed. Hybrids are not required to be registered.

Registration of Peregrines and Merlins is slightly different to other Schedule 4 listed birds. Peregrines and Merlins are considered to be registered if they have a valid Article 10 certificate, issued by the UK CITES

Management Authority (The Wildlife Licensing and Registration Service – WLRS).

Wild – disabled Schedule 4 birds

A person acquiring a wild Schedule 4 bird that has been injured or may be unfit for immediate release back to the wild, and who decides to care for the bird (s. 4(2)) WCA), must contact the Wildlife Licensing and Registration Service immediately to have it registered as wild-disabled. The rehabilitation of the bird will be monitored and a wildlife inspector may visit to ensure that rehabilitation is taking place and that the keeper has sufficient knowledge to successfully release the bird back to the wild. Wild or injured birds may only be taken into captivity for the purpose of rehabilitation and eventual release, and every care must be taken to avoid injuries becoming permanent. They must be examined by an avian vet and documentary proof of this must be completed and returned to WLRS.

Ringing of Schedule 4 birds

The Wildlife Licensing and Registration Service no longer issue any rings for Schedule 4 birds. Captive bred birds must be fitted with a uniquely marked closed leg-ring of a size which cannot be removed from the bird when its leg is fully grown. When this is not possible because of the physical or behavioral properties of the bird, it may be fitted with an unalterable microchip.

Breeders are responsible for obtaining and fitting their own breeder's rings, and ensuring their closed rings are uniquely numbered. There is no designated method of how this should be done, and rings might include the breeder's initials and telephone number or post code in the ring number. It is in the bird owner's interest to make sure that ring numbers are as unique to him or her as possible. Birds which lose their rings must be microchipped and registered under their microchip number.

Wild disabled birds which are temporarily in captivity while they are being rehabilitated for release back into the wild, do not need to be marked. Instead they must be registered under a 'UR licence' (a licence to keep a bird unringed), which will be valid for an appropriate period to be determined on a case by case basis. UR licences for Scotland are issued by Scottish Natural Heritage. If a bird is so disabled that a vet considers it is likely to remain in captivity permanently, it must be microchipped and registered under that number.

For any trade in those Schedule 4 birds or for their display to the public, an Article 10 certificate must be obtained from Animal Health, Defra (see COTES p136).

It was formerly quite common for young birds of prey to be taken from the wild and then laundered into the legitimate falconry, with a claim they had been bred from legitimately held captive stock. Since the development of DNA profiling for certain birds of prey, it has now become a relatively straightforward matter to prove conclusively the heredity and provenance of individual birds. In Scotland this DNA profiling may be able to be carried out for officers, free of charge, at Science and Advice for Scottish Agriculture, Edinburgh (see Specialist Examinations: Science and Advice for Scottish Agriculture (SASA) p208 and Veterinary Pathology p210).

Sibling relationships and maternity/paternity can be proven by the taking of a blood sample from the claimed parents and young, and analysing the DNA profiles produced. It is possible to obtain evidence as to whether an individual adult is related to an individual chick, whether two adults, or any of a combination of adults are related to a chick, and also whether two chicks are related and were produced by the same parents.

Adult to young relationships are easy to prove, especially in combination with declarations of ringing and parentage for Schedule 4 species, but sibling relationships are also valuable as these can still be used where the adults are claimed to have escaped or died. Chicks or eggs may have been taken from more than one nest or site, and if these are claimed to be a single clutch it is possible to negate this claim.

Breeding of birds of prey in captivity was long considered very difficult but as the understanding of bird biology and breeding requirements increased, so did the success with which they have been bred. All the commonly-kept species of birds of prey, such as peregrine falcons and most of the hawks, have now been bred in captivity and it is usually easy to see if a keeper is trying to breed from his birds. A few breeders have now also managed to breed golden eagles successfully in captivity.

A bird that is being kept for breeding will usually be kept isolated in an aviary, normally with solid sides, and with just the roof open to the sky (a skylight seclusion aviary). This ensures that the bird is as undisturbed as possible and is settled for the breeding cycle. Keepers with birds in seclusion aviaries will often be very unhappy about allowing people to see into them and risk upsetting the birds. If planning to visit a keeper who breeds birds it would be best to avoid the birds breeding season if at all possible.

It is fairly common practice to remove eggs from the aviary and to incubate these in an incubator, particularly with young inexperienced females. Removing eggs is also sometimes used to increase productivity and is a practice called 'pulling' eggs from a clutch. In these cases the first couple of eggs are removed, which stimulates the female bird to lay replacement eggs thus increasing overall clutch size.

During an investigation, if a constable suspects with reasonable cause that a specimen (in this case a bird) found in exercise of the powers of search is one in which an offence under Part 1 of the WCA is being or has been committed, he may take a sample of blood or tissue from it to determine its origin, identity or ancestry (s. 19ZD WCA). This is a procedure that formerly either required the consent of the owner of the specimen or a warrant.

Further, the constable may require the person to make available for blood or tissue sampling any other specimen in his possession or control which the constable suspects with reasonable cause to be a specimen that may assist in establishing the origin, identity or ancestry of the relevant specimen. In other words if the constable recovers young birds of prey that are suspected of being taken from the wild and they are alleged by the person possessing or controlling them to have been bred by him from his adult stock, samples may be taken from the young and the alleged breeding stock for DNA comparison.

Samples require to be taken by a vet and the constable is entitled under Section 19(ZD)(8) to have a vet present if it is likely that his or her services will be required. It is worth selecting a veterinary surgeon who has experience of birds of prey to examine and comment on the condition of each bird.

With the exception of very tame pet birds, all birds dislike being handled, and the stress of handling can cause fits or collapse, especially in the smaller species such as sparrowhawk or highly strung species such as goshawk. All injury to birds, including to their feathers and beaks which may become damaged if they fly into the aviary fence, must be avoided at all costs. In most situations keepers will be content to catch their own birds, as they will view this as the best way to reduce the risk of injury during the procedure. Situations will arise when the owner is either not present or does not wish to cooperate. In view of this, the police officers should be accompanied by someone suitably experienced to ensure that any birds can be safely caught and handled.

If blood samples are taken from a bird which is not identified in a permanent manner (for example a closed metal ring on the leg), it may be advisable for the vet, with the keeper's consent, to implant the bird with a microchip at the scene of the investigation. Most vets have or have access to suitable equipment; they should be requested to bring such equipment with them, and know how and where to safely implant birds of various sizes. If micro-chipping is not appropriate then cable-ties can be used (depending on the species).

Where it is likely that birds may need to be seized, arrangements should be made in advance to find suitable sites where they may be looked after by experienced and reliable bird keepers. Suitable carry-boxes and transport must be arranged in advance. Seized birds should always be transported individually in boxes, unless an experienced falconer considers the birds suitable to be kept together.

From the point of view of the birds' welfare, the best time to execute a warrant is early morning, avoiding the late afternoon or evening after the birds have settled. If the case involves taking samples from chicks or young birds, then it is important to wait until the chicks are large enough for a sample to be safely taken: in the case of species like goshawk or peregrine this is when the bird is about 18 days old. If at all possible, avoid periods when birds are likely to be incubating eggs.

If it is anticipated that birds may be seized, then prior arrangements should have been made for their long-term care and maintenance, bearing in mind that a case can take many months to be resolved through the courts

Officers should bear in mind the use of Animal Health Wildlife Inspectors. They are a free resource and can provide considerable expertise and evidential statements regarding captive birds of prey, particularly those on Schedule 4. They will also be able to take buccal swabs from birds for DNA purposes, if required, with the consent of the owner.

'Game' birds

Formerly covered by the ancient Game Laws, 'game' birds now come under the Wildlife and Countryside Act 1981. Though they are wild birds when they are *not* in captivity, when captive they are not covered by the Wildlife and Countryside Act, but their welfare comes under the Animal Health and Welfare (Scotland) Act 2006 (see definition of 'wild bird' on p62).

Since pheasants, partridges, grouse and ptarmigan, formerly referred to as 'game birds' under the now repealed game laws, can be killed or taken at certain times, their legal position is now little different to the position of ducks, geese and waders that can be shot. An exception under s. 2 WCA in relation to these birds is that they may be killed (or taken, in which case they would become captive) by a person with legal right to do so (for instance the owner of the land), or a person with the permission of the person with the legal right (for instance a gamekeeper, shooting tenant or a guest of a shooting tenant).

Pheasant, grey partridge, red-legged partridge, red grouse and mallard may be caught-up at any time *outwith* the close season. Authorised persons (landowner, gamekeeper etc) may only catch up *pheasant and partridge* (for breeding purposes) during the close season, though only in the 28 days immediately after the beginning of the close season (s. 2(3A) and 2(3B) WCA). The caught-up birds are generally penned and the eggs collected for hatching in incubators. Once the birds are caught up and penned they cease to be 'wild birds'. They are therefore not subject to the Wildlife and Countryside Act, and the birds and their eggs may be bought and sold without any restriction that might be imposed by section 6 of the Act.

Red grouse may be caught-up at any time for the purpose of preventing disease, though their captivity must not exceed 12 hours. (s. 2(3C) WCA). It is rare that they are not released immediately after being caught-up and dosed with relevant medicine. It seems that despite the intention of the Scottish Parliament to permit this, the means by which it is done (use of artificial light source and a net) may be illegal. It may well be resolved through the use of a new general licence.

Nest damage, disturbance or interference (including Schedule 1 birds).

It is an offence to intentionally or recklessly take, damage, destroy or interfere with any active bird nest, even when it is being built (s.1(1)(b) WCA), though intentional or reckless *disturbance* only applies to nesting birds on Schedule 1 (s.1(5) WCA). The disturbance also encompasses nests being built and dependent young. Disturbance is likely to arise where operations or activities cause these specially protected birds to change their behaviour with potentially adverse effects on their breeding success. In the worst case, they could desert a nest or fail to rear young successfully. The offence can range from disturbing Schedule 1 birds without a licence from SNH to do so (for example for photography), or carrying out game management or forestry operations activities near a known Schedule 1 bird's active nest. Forestry Commission Scotland has a range of excellent on-line guidance which can be found at http://www.forestry.gov.uk/website/forestry.nsf/byunique/infd-6vrjh2 For example this extends to, in the case of the capercaillie, an instruction to their foresters to mark an exclusion zone of 100 metres radius round the nest with tape.

Though disturbance of *non*-schedule 1 birds is not an offence, offences are committed by intentionally or recklessly blocking out (or blocking in) these nesting birds, or otherwise preventing them accessing their nest (s.1(1)(bb) WCA); removing or destroying active nests that from the point of view of the offender are in the wrong place or an inconvenience, or using machinery to remove sand from a sandy face in the knowledge there are sand martins nesting or trying to excavate a nest in that face.

It is not the intent of the legislation to prohibit otherwise lawful activities, such as forest operations, land development or even hedge trimming. There are many practicable reasons why these cannot be confined to the period outside the breeding season, but common sense should prevail. Most hedges can be checked for active nests beforehand, and some trees and bushes can be checked so far as is possible. With full-scale forest operations there may be areas rich in active nests that can be left till later, although some birds such as wood pigeons can nest for much of the year and it is difficult to avoid felling trees containing their nests or young. However it is necessary to consider these issues beforehand, and taking any reasonable mitigating measures and recording evidence of how decisions were reached may be helpful.

If a tree containing an active nest of a Schedule 1 species is felled, advice on what practical steps might be possible should be sought immediately by contacting the area office of Scottish Natural Heritage or RSPB Scotland, and in some cases Forestry Commission Scotland staff may be able to help. Correct identification is important to know what to do. In some cases, birds will return to nests if they are rebuilt on some kind of platform and left undisturbed, but this is a complex area, varying between species, and advice should be taken. A record of the incident and action taken should be kept.

Many ground-nesting birds' nests or chicks are flattened during agricultural operations such as harrowing, rolling or ploughing. Despite the fact that the operator may well know there are nesting birds in the field, this would not appear to be an offence as it is unlikely that he will know the *exact* location of the nest, nests or chicks, and it would be unreasonable to expect someone to painstakingly search a field before carrying out any operation. Unfortunately there is the potential to destroy many eggs or young of lapwing, curlew, oyster catcher or grey partridge in these operations. It provides the basis for an interesting counter-argument when someone complains of eggs or chicks being taken by predatory birds!

Cruelty

Cruelty against captive-bred birds or captive wild-taken birds is covered under the chapter relating to Cruelty to domestic and captive wild animals (p191). Wild birds must be captive for an offence under the Animal Health and Welfare (Scotland) Act 2006 to be committed against them. If they are not captive, the offence is within the Wildlife and Countryside Act 1981 at Section 1: intentionally or recklessly causing injury to a wild bird. Injury is normally caused to a bird in an attempt to kill it. If it can be proved that the intention was to deliberately injure rather than kill the bird, this could be an aggravation of the offence that the court is likely to take into consideration.

5. Wild Mammals

WILD MAMMALS of Scotland enjoy different levels of protection under the law. For example a wildcat is completely protected, but a rat has protection only against being cruelly treated. Some, like the rabbit and the hare, may be killed, but only by authorised persons or at certain times of the year. There are several different pieces of legislation, and some mammals may have protection under more than one of those. This chapter tries to explain which legislation protects which mammals and the levels of protection afforded.

Live trapping offences – see page p43
Tunnel trapping offences – see page p45
Snaring offences – see page p52
Shooting offences – see the section relevant to the species concerned

Schedule 5 of the WCA (includes pine marten, but see Schedule – for full list see p264

Section 9 of the Wildlife and Countryside Act 1981 gives certain protection to animals listed in Schedule 5 to the Act. The schedule lists the degree of protection given, for instance it may seem odd that the killing of a water vole may not be unlawful, but its place of shelter is protected, and it is an offence to disturb it while using its place of shelter. Similarly it is not an offence to kill *some* of the the butterflies on schedule 5, but it is an offence to sell or offer them for sale. Offences against each animal are listed on the schedule. Many of the mammals formerly on this schedule have been transferred to Schedule 2 of the Habitats Regulations for increased protection, with the pine marten, red squirrel and water vole being the only mammals remaining. Unless otherwise stated on the schedule, the relevant offences are to:

Intentionally or recklessly kill, injure or take an animal on Schedule 5 (s. 9(1)), or to possess or control a live or dead Schedule 1 animal, or any part of it or anything derived from it. (s. 9(2)) Exceptions to these offences are *if the person shows* that it had not been killed or taken, or had been killed or taken at or from a place (or sold at a place) in Scotland otherwise than in contravention of the relevant provisions, or that the killing or taking would not, had it been committed in Scotland, have been in contravention of the relevant provisions, or it had been brought from the place where it was killed in accordance with relevant regulations. (s. 9.3))

It is also an offence to intentionally or recklessly damage or destroy, or obstruct the access to, any structure or place which the Schedule 5 animal uses for shelter or protection, or to disturb it while it is occupying that structure or place (s. 9(4)).

This creates an interesting situation in relation to the red squirrel – is its place of protection or shelter its drey or the piece of woodland it inhabits? It is probably the former but as has happened during a housing development a coniferous wood of a few acres, home to some red squirrels, was cleared apart from a tree containing a drey and a handful of other trees to be dotted for aesthetic purposes among the new houses, and with the nearest alternative habitat some distance away.

Generally, the effort to protect a species should be proportionate to:
- the legal protection status of the species;
- the sensitivity of the species to disturbance or damage from various operations or activities;
- the potential effect of any damage/disturbance on the conservation status of the protected species, locally or nationally; and
- what is reasonable in terms of the practicality and cost of protective measures for lawful activities such as woodland management.

The law aims to balance the needs of lawful land management activities like forestry with wildlife protection. The intention is to strike a balance which seeks to avoid reckless or deliberate damage or disturbance, but does not place unreasonably onerous and impractical restrictions on legitimate land management practices. This dichotomy makes the role of the wildlife crime officer extremely difficult when faced with a barrage of complaints about the displacing of the red squirrels, some from people who may well have been against the development for other reasons.

There are fewer problems with forest management since, even in the case of a clear fell, there are usually areas of suitable woodland nearby or that could form safe corridors for displaced red squirrels to reach a new habitat.

During thinning operations the accessibility of nearby feeding and shelter areas to which red squirrels can escape should always be taken into account. If felling or thinning during the breeding season is unavoidable, trees containing red squirrel breeding dreys should be marked and where practical left unfelled, together with immediately adjacent trees. Ideally connection should be retained to breeding dreys by means of remaining tree crowns linking to adjacent woodland areas. However it will often not be possible to avoid loss or damage to dreys in clear felling operations.

Woodland managers should read the on-line guidance by Forestry

Commission Scotland, much of which is based on sensitive forest management, including appropriate timing of work to avoid the breeding season and based on timeous surveys to identify the species at risk.

The sale, offering for sale or transporting for sale of a live or dead Schedule 5 animal, or part thereof or anything derived it from is also an offence (s. 9(5)(a)), as is to publish an advert likely to be understood that the person buys, sells, or intends to buy or sell any of those things (s. 9(5)(b)).

Lastly it is an offence to knowingly cause or permit any of the foregoing except for s. 9(5)(b). In practical terms if an employer instructs an employee to kill or take a pine marten, then he commits an offence. The term 'knowingly' is important, and proof of this is crucial to a conviction.

Schedule 6 of the WCA (includes badger and hedgehog but see Schedule on p268 for full list)

Schedule 6 of the Wildlife and Countryside Act 1981 lists animals that may not be killed or taken by certain methods. Changes under the Wildlife and Natural Environment (Scotland) Act 2011 removed some species from this schedule, leaving only badger, hedgehog, red squirrel and all species of shrew.

Section 11 of the 1981 Act lists the relevant offences, which are:

To set in position any of the following articles, being an article which is of such a nature and so placed as to be likely to cause bodily injury to any wild animal included in Schedule 6 which comes into contact with it, that is to say any trap or snare, any electrical device for killing or stunning or any poisonous, poisoned or stupefying substance; or uses for the purpose of killing or taking any Schedule 6 animal any article as aforesaid, whether or not of such a nature and so placed as aforesaid, or any net.

The setting out of substances as described is easily understood. Less straightforward is the use of any trap or snare, since it must be of a type that is *likely* to cause injury. Some live-catch traps, for instance a mammal cage trap, would not be of that type, though a tunnel trap with a wide entrance that would allow access to larger non-target species, or a deadfall trap might. It would of course be essential for the prosecution to prove the presence of Schedule 6 animals in the area of the trap. Electrical devices are extremely rare, and a net is unlikely to cause bodily injury. With snares, it may depend on the type of snare set and the species caught as to whether injury is caused, or likely to be caused.

At first glance there may seem little difference between the terms 'set in position' and 'uses', though a device *'set in position'* need only be *'likely'* to cause injury. If any of these devices which may not necessarily cause injury are *'used'*, proof is required that they are *'for the purpose'* of killing or taking a Schedule 6 animal. The difference might be seen as a reckless act as opposed to an intentional act. This might mean that if there was evidence a live-catch trap or a snare had been set with the intention of catching a hedgehog then that is an offence.

It is also an offence under s.11 to use for the purpose of taking or killing a Schedule 6 animal-

- Any automatic or semi-automatic weapon
- Any device for illuminating a target or sighting device for night shooting
- Any form of artificial light or any mirror or other dazzling device
- Any gas or smoke not already covered by the term 'poisoned, poisonous or stupefying substance'
- To knowingly cause or permit any of the methods discussed.

Though a badger is included in Schedule 6, some of the offences listed may also be covered under the Protection of Badgers Act 1992.

Schedule 2 of the Conservation (Natural Habitats etc) Regulations 1994 (includes bats, cetaceans, otter, wildcat but see Schedule for full list – p275)

Schedule 2 of the Habitats Regulations lists European Protected Species of animals (EPS), with offences committed against them being covered by regulation 39. (see Conservation (Natural Habitats etc) Regulations 1994 – p133)

Schedule 3 of the Conservation (Natural Habitats etc) Regulations 1994 (includes pine marten, mountain hare, polecat and seals, but see Schedule for full list – p276)

Schedule 3 of the Habitats Regulations lists animals which may not be killed or taken by certain methods, with offences committed against them being covered by regulation 41. (see Conservation (Natural Habitats etc) Regulations 1994 – p133)

Hunting mammals with dogs

It is an offence under the Protection of Wild Mammals (Scotland) Act 2002 to hunt a wild mammal with a dog. Exceptions are rabbits or rodents, provided permission has been obtained from the owner or tenant of the land. The legislation is complex and since the provisions of the Wildlife and Natural Environment (Scotland) Act 2011 have improved the policing of poaching offences under the Wildlife and Countryside Act 1981 (see Poaching p178), it will be rare now for the 2002 Act to be used for anything other than illegal fox hunting.

It should always be borne in mind that, in Scotland, 'foot packs' of hounds are regularly used to control foxes. This is the use of a pack of hounds, controlled by men (or women) on foot, to flush foxes forward towards waiting guns. This has always been done purely for fox control rather than sport. Definitions are important, and under the 2002 Act, the term 'to hunt' means 'to search for or course'. This term is not further defined therefore it would be reasonable to give *hunt* its ordinary dictionary meaning of *diligent pursuit*. Other terms are used in the exceptions such as *stalking, searching* and *flushing*. None of these are defined under the Act either. It may therefore also be reasonable to apply their respective dictionary definitions of *pursuing game or a quarry by stealth, going about in order to find or ascertain the presence of a thing,* and *to drive out into the open*. None of the exceptions include the word *hunt*, however the exception at section 2(1) uses the word *search*, which as already stated is part of the definition of *hunt* in the Act. In the first sheriff court judgement relating to fox hunting with hounds the presiding sheriff considered that the activity struck at by the Act is the diligent pursuit of a wild mammal with dogs, and in terms of Section 10(1) (definitions) that included *searching*. (*Sheriff's judgement – PF, Jedburgh against Trevor Adams, 2004*)

The term '*mammals*' does not include rabbits or rodents, and references to *hunting with a dog* can include the use of two or more dogs. The crucial word is *deliberately*; this prevents a person being charged with an incident which has been unintentional or which has resulted from carelessness or even recklessness.

The main offences are to:

- deliberately hunt a wild mammal with a dog; (s. 1(1))
- being the owner or occupier of land, to knowingly permit a person to hunt; (s. 1(2))
- being a person having responsibility for dog, knowingly to allow it to be used to hunt. (s. 1(3))

This sounds straightforward, but there are many exceptions. Summarising what *can* be done, it allows the flushing of mammals from cover above ground by a dog under control provided it is done by the owner/occupier of the land or with that person's permission.

It also allows the flushing of a mammal above ground to be shot (as with 'foot packs,' or to be taken by a falconer. Those participating must 'act to ensure that the fox is shot' but an offence is not created if the fox is shot at and missed, or if it changes direction away from the waiting guns. If, in the process of chasing the fox towards the guns, the dogs (normally hounds) catch and kill the fox, no offence is committed as this is yet another exception (s. 2(2)).

It allows the use of a dog, under control, to be used to flush a fox or mink – no other mammal – from *below ground*, or a fox from an enclosed space within rocks or other secure cover above ground. The mammal must then be shot as soon as possible after flushing by a person holding a firearm or shotgun certificate, who is either the owner or occupier of the land or has that person's permission. Both methods are in common use to control foxes at dens, normally in April and May.

A fox that has gone to ground while being hunted may be dug out, but must not be released again for the hounds to continue to chase. From time to time people who are sometimes involved in badger digging dig out foxes, usually with the help of a dog to locate the fox. This is seldom carried out with the permission of the owner or occupier of the land and in these cases do not fall within any exception.

The term 'under control' is interesting. In terms of Section 10(4) of the Act (definitions) a dog is under control if the person responsible for the dog is able to direct the dog's activity by physical contact or verbal or audible command, or if the dog is carrying out a series of actions appropriate to the activity undertaken, having been trained to do so.

The Act makes no difference to the use of a dog to retrieve shot mammals, or to hunt for a wounded mammal. This remains perfectly legal.

Lastly, it allows an occupier of land or a person acting with that person's permission to use a dog under control below ground in order to locate a fox cub which is reasonably believed to be orphaned, but only if that person takes reasonable steps to ensure that the fox, once located, is despatched *by a single dog* or otherwise killed humanely (s.5(3)). This allows the despatch of fox cubs in a den after the vixen has been killed and it is suspected the cubs are too young to survive on their own. In practical terms this will invariably be after the vixen has been bolted and shot or has been snared or killed by other means.

There are pressure groups on both sides of the fox hunting debate. Police officers have to uphold the law as it stands, not as some might like it to be. The police must be completely impartial, separating legal issues from moral concerns. These investigations can be further complicated by the amount of potential suspects involved, the fact that where the alleged offence is occurring may not be easily accessible, the speed at which the activity may be moving forward, and the obvious drawback with this legislation in that it is largely untested in the court.

Because of the difficulties, police officers may consider a risk assessment of the implications of attending an incident. Those best placed to deal with this are wildlife crime officers because of their knowledge, training and the fact they already have suitable outdoor clothing and footwear.

It appears that the most likely grounds for complaint against a hunt is that there are either no people with guns in attendance to shoot a fox being hunted by hounds, or that the guns are in completely the wrong place and that the fox and hounds are headed in an entirely different direction. Having no guns in place is a straightforward breach of the Act. The wrong placing of the guns is an entirely different matter and likely to be difficult to prove since to a large extent the fox can choose its route.

The question may be asked, 'should the huntsman call off the hounds if they are heading away from the guns?' If he tries to do so and they do not respond could it be construed that they are no long *under control* and therefore the manner of the hunt does not fall within any of the exceptions? These are questions yet to be tested in court but worthy of consideration. If the hunting is to be legal, there is a requirement under section 2(3)(b) of the Act for steps to be taken to ensure the fox is located and shot 'as soon as possible after it is flushed'. The investigating officer may well try to establish whether the arrangements have satisfied this requirement.

The stopping of a hunt should not be carried out lightly and police should be sure that an illegal activity has been or is about to be carried out before doing so. Similarly with the power of arrest or detention, officers should consider if arrest or detention is really necessary and the practical difficulties of doing so, particularly if more than one arrest or detention is required. Would the same objectives be achieved, and perhaps better served, by noting all the details required, obtaining photographic or video evidence where possible, and considering the evidence at leisure and in collaboration with the specialist wildlife prosecutor? Against this, if key individuals are not detained could evidence be spirited away before it can be collected?

The question of who to charge has also to be established and there is much to be gained by identifying this person at an early stage. The huntsman in charge and/or the master of foxhounds are the most obvious choice. The owner or occupier of the land or owner of the hounds may also be considered as suspects in relation to the use of the land or the dogs (S. 1(2) and 1(3) of the Act). Other persons – or even everyone involved – may be committing an offence but again this may be a matter for reflection, consideration of available evidence and consultation with the fiscal. With that in mind, police officers should consider the value of interviewing certain witnesses under caution. It may also be helpful to get hold of any documentation that may show who were present and any 'orders' that may have been drawn up in advance.

It may also be of value to canvass the witnesses as to the particular reason for this hunt, i.e. to hunt a fox because of recent loss of lambs or loss of poultry. It is a requirement of the exemption under s. 2(3)(a) of the Act that the hunting is for one or more of the purposes listed in the Act, as authorised under paragraphs (a) to (f) of s. 2(1), namely:

- protecting livestock, ground-nesting birds, timber, fowl (including wildfowl), game birds or crops from attack by wild animals;
- providing food for consumption by a living creature, including a person;
- protecting human health;
- preventing the spread of disease;
- controlling the numbers of a pest species; or
- controlling the number of a particular species to safeguard the welfare of that species.

Officers may well consider the authority – or lack of authority – given for the hunt to take place on the land in question. Would the landowner be a suspect? Has the landowner given permission but permission been refused or not sought from the tenant? The reverse may also be the case: that a tenant has given permission, though the owner of the land may either have no knowledge or had he or she been aware, may have refused permission. These issues relate to who may be charged – or otherwise – with an offence under Section 1(2) of the Act.

Lastly, officers may consider who is the owner of the hounds being used. Was that person involved directly in the hunt? If so it is likely that consent for the use of the hounds would have been given, either implicitly or explicitly, possibly making the owner liable to be charged with an offence under Section 1(3) of the Act if the activity is found to be illegal.

Police powers – Section 7 of the Act

The Act gives power for police officers to stop and search, and to arrest a suspect. Detention is an option under section 14 of the Criminal Procedure (Scotland) Act as the offences are punishable by imprisonment of up to 6 months. Police may also search or examine a vehicle, animal or article which appears to belong to or be in the possession or control of a suspect, and may seize animals or articles which may be evidence in connection with the offence. A constable may enter land without warrant, but not a dwelling, in order to exercise these powers.

No chief constable will want to kennel 20 or 30 hounds or stable a couple of dozen horses for what might turn out to be many months. Photographic or video evidence would almost always serve the purpose just as well. Wild animals killed or injured as a result of the hunt are an entirely different matter and of course would be seized. A post mortem examination is likely to be of value to confirm that the fox was killed by hounds rather than the hounds encountering an already-dead fox. It should be borne in mind when seizing dead animals that the defence would also have a right to have them examined (Anderson v Laverock 1976). They should not be disposed of unless with the authority of the specialist wildlife prosecutor. There may be justification in seizing dogs injured as a result of a suspected illegal hunt and where a charge under the Animal Health and Welfare (Scotland) Act 2006, is under consideration.

If weapons are being seized, ensure that they are confirmed as unloaded and safe by an officer experienced in firearms before putting them in a police vehicle.

To raise awareness of the law with those involved with fox hunting, police officers should make a point of getting to know the main hunt organisers and getting advance details of their activities and of their strategies for ensuring that they work within the provisions of the Protection of Wild Mammals (Scotland) Act 2002. Where there appears a shortfall of knowledge, advice can be given to prevent a breach of the law. Preventing a crime is better than having to investigate one that has taken place.

Cruelty

Cruelty against captive wild animals is covered under the chapter relating to Cruelty to Domestic and Captive Wild Animals (p191). Certain cruel act committed against an animal that is *living wild* may be an offence under section 1 of the Wild Mammals (Protection) Act 1996. The offences are to mutilate, kick, beat, nail or otherwise impale, stab, burn, stone, crush, drown, drag or asphyxiate *with intent to inflict unnecessary suffering*. Examples might be to kick a hedgehog or to beat a seal pup to death. It is worth noting that in order to carry out some of these cruel actions against any of the fleeter wild mammals it would most likely have to be caught first, making it captive. In this case the offence may be better dealt with under the Animal Health and Welfare (Scotland) Act 2006.

It must be borne in mind that some mammals are regarded as pests and may *legally* be killed. Someone hitting a wild rabbit over the head with a stick and killing it, or stamping on a mouse to kill it does not *necessarily* commit an offence under the Act. If the person had deliberately injured but had not killed the rabbit or mouse, this is an act of cruelty and an offence under the Act would have been committed.

The term *with intent to inflict unnecessary suffering* is interesting. In Grampian in 2011 a golfer on a golf course whacked a semi-tame fox with a golf club. The liver and other internal organs of the fox were severely injured by the blow on its side, though not to the extent that immediate death followed. The golfer then left the injured fox, which died shortly after. By hitting the fox other than on the head it was reasonable to assume that the golfer had intended to inflict unnecessary suffering to the animal, and having done so, did not follow his first actions up by ending the suffering of the fox by then hitting it on the head. A post mortem examination was carried out on the fox to confirm the cause of death and that it had indeed suffered severe pain before dying. The golfer was prosecuted under the Wild Mammals (Protection) Act and found guilty. A charge under the Animal Health and Welfare (Scotland) Act 2006 would not have been valid as the fox was not under the control of man.

Cruelly killing or injuring a mammal such as a bat, dormouse, pine marten, otter, red squirrel or wildcat would be offences under this Act but may be more likely to be investigated under the Wildlife and Countryside Act or the Habitats Regulations since these mammals are included in one or more of Schedule 5 of the former Act or Schedules 2 or 3 of the latter Act. Powers and penalties are the same under both pieces of legislation.

An offence under the Wild Mammals (Protection) Act may occur if a trap such as a Fenn Mk IV or Springer No.4 were to be set in a tunnel with an entrance far larger than would be necessary to allow access to the mammals for which the trap is approved, and as a result caught, for instance, a hedgehog. A hedgehog is unlikely to be killed outright and would receive crushing injuries from the trap; something that any experience user of these traps would be expected to know. Though unnecessary suffering would undoubtedly be the outcome, difficulty may be encountered in trying to prove that the trap was set 'with intent' to do so, though this is certainly worthy of consideration. Such an incident would also constitute an offence under Section 50(1)(b) of the Agriculture (Scotland) Act, 1948, (knowingly use an approved trap in circumstances in which it is not approved).

If an animal is still alive, the opinion of a vet may be required to assess whether or not the animal has sustained injuries that are treatable or if it should be euthanased. An animal obviously very badly injured may need to be destroyed on the spot. Photographic or video evidence will be extremely helpful for court purposes. Graphic portrayal of injuries to an animal is often reflected in the severity of the sentence.

It must be proved that the injuries sustained by the animal were caused by the suspect. If this is not done then the defence argument might be that the animal was injured before the alleged act of cruelty took place. Along the same lines, if the animal is dead the defence might argue that the animal was dead when found by the suspect and any injuries were sustained before that time. An example may be a hedgehog being kicked about like a football. There would be no offence to kick an already-dead hedgehog so it must be proved that the animal was alive when the cruelty was inflicted. To establish this, an examination must be made by a veterinary pathologist.

As in other types of offences where there are dead animals, the carcass must be retained until the procurator fiscal authorises its disposal, since the defence may wish to have the animal examined to confirm or to contest injuries inflicted.

Police powers – Section 4

Where a constable has reasonable grounds for suspecting that a person has committed an offence under the Wild Mammals (Protection) Act and that evidence may be found on that person or in or on any vehicle he may have with him, the constable may without warrant, stop and search that person and any vehicle or article he may have with him; and seize anything which may be evidence of the commission of the offence. The penalty options include up to 6 months imprisonment, therefore a detention under section 14 of the Criminal Procedure (Scotland) Act is available.

Badgers

Badgers have an Act all to themselves: the Protection of Badgers Act 1992. The offences under the Act relate to any activity that causes, or is likely to cause, harm to a badger. This harm is likely to be as a result of badger digging or badger baiting for sport, or by someone damaging the sett or trying to get rid of the badgers as their presence is inconvenient. This latter category can include badgers being killed for the purposes of game management, farming or development.

The principle offences are those of deliberately taking, killing or injuring a badger (s. 1(1)); possessing a dead or a live badger (s. 1(3)), though there are common sense exceptions for possessing a dead badger killed accidentally or a live badger that is injured and being taken for treatment; being cruel to a badger (S. 2(1)(a)); digging for a badger (s. 2(1)(c) or interference with a badger sett (s. 3).

Interference can include damaging a badger sett or any part of it; destroying it; obstructing the access; causing a dog to enter a badger sett; or disturbing a badger when it is occupying a badger sett. The action must have been carried out with intent, or being reckless as to whether the actions would have any of these consequences.

For investigative purposes the definition of a badger sett is the legislative definition: *any structure or place which displays signs indicating current use by a badger.* (s. 14) It is therefore the statutory requirement that for the structure or place to be a badger sett there must be *more than one sign or indicator* visibly present that point to the fact that the structure or place is being used by a badger (*Sheriff's judgement, PF Jedburgh v Harris 2010*). These could be:

- The presence of bedding
- Latrines or dung pits connected to the sett by recently-used paths
- Pad marks identifiable as those of a badger at the sett entrance
- Well-used paths with pad marks evidencing use by a badger
- Remnants of fresh bedding present in freshly excavated soil
- Hairs snagged in entrances or in freshly excavated soil
- Foraging marks
- The shape of the entrance
- A freshly-dug latrine pit even though there is no dung in it

Whether or not some of these signs are indicative of no more than badger presence in the locality may well be a question of fact and circumstance for each case to be determined on its own merits, and in the particular combination or accumulation of them which might be in evidence. The presence of any *one* of the following signs, namely bedding, the presence of dung in latrines which can be linked by paths to the structure in question or the presence of paw prints at entrance holes must be considered to be evidence strongly pointing towards current use *though not enough in itself*.

Police powers:
(See also Police Powers under Other Legislation (p20) where the powers are identical to those under the Wildlife and Countryside Act 1981.)
It is worth a word of warning on the temperament of those involved in badger digging or badger baiting. Invariably these are men of violent disposition and should not be tackled. The police should be contacted immediately badger digging or baiting is suspected.

If caught 'in the act', badger diggers with terriers may well state that they are digging for foxes. This is where previous history of the sett is invaluable, so that there is proof that it is a sett. Even if this is not immediately available, the persons may well be committing an offence under the Protection of Wild Mammals (Scotland) Act 2002, since only landowners, land occupiers or those with their permission can use terriers underground for foxes.

The men may also state that they are trying to recover their terrier, with a claim that it ran into the sett, and that they thought they could dig it out.

This is easily disproved as few people go for a walk with their dog and take a spade with them.

A more likely situation is the discovery, after the culprits have gone, of a sett which has been dug. It is in these situations that a thorough scene of crime examination is crucial. With badger setts in particular, important considerations are sole impressions, soil samples, badger hair samples, dog hair samples if found, human hair samples if found or any item from which DNA can be obtained, or photographs to scale (or a plaster cast) of a spademark or other toolmark. As an aide to investigating officers, badger guard hair is noticeably oval in cross-section when rubbed between the thumb and forefinger. Examination of a sett that has been interfered with is likely to be a joint investigation between police and a badger expert.

If suspects are traced, then examination of the interior of a vehicle, tools, clothing and dogs may give a chance to match samples taken from the locus. If dogs can be traced within a day or two, it is not the most pleasant job but an examination of their faeces for the presence of badger guard hair may prove worthwhile.

In any search of suspects' houses, police officers should be aware of notes, diary entries or photographs or videos of badger digging or baiting. Video footage may also be recovered from a computer. Also note any contact details for a vet as this is a further possible source of evidence in the event that a dog required veterinary attention subsequent to baiting a badger.

Photographing or videoing old scars on dogs should be considered. This would be permissible during a search using police powers under the Protection of Badgers Act. Any dogs found with untreated bite injuries should be immediately taken to a vet for treatment. Where a person is charged, such dogs should be kept for evidence and for possible re-homing (under Section 13) on conviction. The investigating officer should discuss this with the wildlife specialist fiscal at the earliest opportunity. Under the Protection of Badgers Act it is likely to be permissible to take a dog as a production. A warrant may be necessary to keep the dog after treatment if the Animal Health and Welfare (Scotland) Act is being used since the police powers primarily facilitate animal welfare considerations; not the investigation of crime.

Licensing:

In some cases a licence can be obtained from Scottish Natural Heritage to carry out what would otherwise be an unlawful act. These licences are mainly used where a badger sett is in the way of development. It is worth noting that for the purpose of determining whether or not a licence will be granted, SNH use a different definition of a badger sett 'in use' to that in the Act. For development purposes the definition used by SNH is any sett in a known occupied territory.

It is important to note that licences can only permit someone to 'interfere with a badger sett' for the purpose of development, which sometimes means excluding them from the sett. It is not possible to license removal, translocation or killing of badgers for the purpose of development. As a general rule of thumb any development within 30 metres of a badger sett entrance could result in interference to the sett (primarily by causing disturbance to any badger in that sett or by damaging or blocking the tunnels that radiate from the sett entrances). In some cases, where more disruptive works are planned, such as blasting, this distance may be greater.

Badger setts are often found in woodland. This does not preclude any woodland management taking place, but it does mean that some work in the vicinity of badger setts may have to be covered by a licence. Most operations do not interfere with setts and can be carried out without a licence if they are carefully planned and supervised. As well as careful timing to try to avoid setts with cubs in early spring, the best protection from damage or disturbance will normally be to restrict or avoid forest operations close to the setts. Tunnels vary in length; most are under 15 metres, but exceptionally they reach about 20 metres. They are often quite close to the surface (about 60 cm deep) and so heavy machinery or large falling trees could readily cause collapse. A protection zone of a minimum of 20 metres is therefore required around the sett entrances. Operations causing prolonged high levels of noise or vibration may sometimes need a larger protective zone. The sett should normally be marked with brightly coloured nylon rope or similar, so that the boundary of the marked area is at least 20 metres away from any entrance to the sett which is believed to be in current use. Where there are concerns that this form of marking may attract malicious attention to the sett, alternative marking arrangements should be made. Within this marked zone forest operations should either be avoided or carried out with a high degree of sensitivity. There may also be opportunities to make the protection zone part of a larger indefinite retention. In clear felling operations, leaving a few trees around a sett is likely to lead to its identification and put it at risk from badger digging and other interference and they may be as well to be carefully removed.

Where a sett exists within an area which is due for thinning, trees in the immediate vicinity of holes should not be felled where there is a risk of felled trees damaging or blocking the mouth of the hole, and should be felled away from the hole or main badger runs. Any blockages which do occur should be removed immediately by safe means. The retention of un-thinned clumps of trees around setts should only be considered where they are not liable to act as a form of marker which may attract adverse attention to the sett. Again the 20 metre rule should apply to forest machinery.

Advice on licensing should be sought for:
- any mechanical cultivation or drainage within the 20 metre protection zone
- any timber extraction tractor movement within the 20 metre protection zone
- dragging heavy timber along the ground within the 20 metre protection zone
- any tree-felling within the 20 metre protection zone where damage or disturbance is expected and cannot be avoided, for instance between December and June at breeding setts; when large trees are likely to create a heavy impact or which cannot be felled away from sett entrances; or windthrow clearance where control of felling direction is difficult
- construction of roads or buildings entailing any mechanical construction or maintenance of earthworks within the 20 metre zone; any machine movement within the 20 metre zone, other than on metalled or tarred roads; any drilling, pile-driving or blasting within 100m of a sett; or any other construction or maintenance operation which is likely to cause damage or obstruct a badger sett or disturb a badger within a sett.

Badgers are generally very shy and secretive creatures and in the vast majority of cases badgers and humans co-exist very peacefully. However, on rare occasions badgers can cause damage to gardens, crops or property. In most cases this can be resolved by ensuring that badgers are not able to get access to the area in question. However, if this is not possible, and if serious damage might occur to that property it may be possible to get a licence to prevent such damage. Scottish Natural Heritage can issue licences to prevent serious damage to land, crops, poultry or any other property.

Seals

Atlantic grey seals and common seals (sometimes known as harbour seals) are found all round Scotland's coastline; often many miles up some of the larger rivers. Seals sometimes come into conflict with salmon farming, with fishermen operating nets, or with anglers. Because they can inflict damage on salmon stocks they may legitimately be controlled by shooting provided this is done under a licence granted by Marine Scotland.

The main reasons that people may be licensed to shoot seals are:
- to protect the health and welfare of farmed fish

* to prevent serious damage to fisheries or fish farms

The legislation giving protection to seals is the Marine (Scotland) Act 2010, with the main offence being intentionally or recklessly killing, injuring or taking a live seal (s. 107). It is not an offence to kill a seal humanely to alleviate suffering (s. 108(1)), nor is it an offence to take a disabled seal in order to tend and subsequently release it (s. 108(2)). In both cases this action must be reported to the Scottish Ministers as soon as reasonably practicable after doing so. (s. 108(3)) Failure to do so is an offence. (s. 108(4))

Though most offences will be investigated by the police, Marine Scotland, as a reporting agency, has the powers to investigate and report offences against this legislation. With offences committed against seals, if the initial complaint is made to Marine Scotland, it is highly likely that they will involve police officers in the investigation.

It is not an offence under Section 107 to kill or take a seal in accordance with a seal licence (s. 109). These licences are granted by the Scottish Ministers and authorise the killing or taking of seals:

(a) for scientific, research or educational purposes

(b) to conserve natural habitats

(c) to conserve seals or other wild animals (including wild birds) or wild plants

(d) in connection with the introduction of seals, or other wild animals (including wild birds) or wild plants to particular areas

(e) to protect a zoological or botanical collection

(f) to protect the health and welfare of farmed fish

(g) to prevent *serious* damage to fisheries or fish farms

(h) to prevent the spread of disease among seals or other animals (including birds) or plants

(i) to preserve public health or public safety, or

(j) for other imperative reasons of overriding public interest, including those of a social or economic nature and beneficial consequences of primary importance for the environment.

Copies of seal licences are sent to the relevant police wildlife crime officer for the area to which the licence relates.

The seal licence must specify the method which the licensee must use to kill or take seals, and they are not granted unless the Scottish Ministers are satisfied that the person has adequate skills and experience in using firearms.

The licence must not authorise a person to do anything which would contravene regulation 41 of the Conservation (Natural Habitats etc) Regulations. (Reg 41 of the Habitats Regulations covers prohibited methods of taking or killing animals, such as the use of devices for illuminating targets or crossbows, and any other means which is indiscriminate and capable of causing the local disappearance of, or serious disturbance to, a population of any species of animal listed on Schedule 3, which includes the common and grey seal.)

The licence must impose conditions specifying the maximum number of seals which may be killed or taken, and specifying steps which must be taken in relation to any seal injured when attempting to kill or take it in accordance with the seal licence in order to reduce the risk of it suffering unnecessarily. (s. 112(1))

It must also impose conditions specifying the type of firearm which must be used; the weather conditions in which a person may attempt to shoot a seal; how close a person must be to a seal before attempting to shoot it; prohibiting a person from attempting to shoot a seal from an unstable platform, and about the recovery of carcasses (s. 112(2)). Other conditions may be imposed by the Scottish Ministers if they consider them necessary.

> Note: There is no mention of minimum calibre of rifle for seals in this legislation. It was hoped to resolve differences of opinion about the suitability of some types of rifle for use in seal management under the new licensing system. It was not possible to complete the necessary ballistic tests in the short time available (before enforcement of the Act) and still provide sufficient notice of any possible changes. It has therefore been decided that the definition of firearm that will feature on seal licences meantime will remain as in the Conservation of Seals Act 1970. This definition is as follows: *'a rifle using ammunition with a muzzle energy not less than 600 foot pounds and a bullet weighing not less than 45 grains'*.

This effectively excludes any .22 rimfire rifles. Only centrefire rifles can be used, with the .22 Hornet using 45 grain bullets representing the lowest acceptable combination of bullet weight and energy. Expanding bullets designed to deform in a predictable manner must be used. During 2011, Marine Scotland carried out the planned ballistic testing on a range of rifles which *may* lead to changes in the firearms defined to be used for seal management under licence in future years. A Code of Practice which provides the wider context for any shooting under licence is available via the following link – http://www.scotland.gov.uk/Topics/marine/Licensing/SealLicensing/codeofpractice

Note that there are no longer any designated close seasons, though times when the shooting of seals should not be undertaken should be taken into account in the licence conditions. There is no mention of close seasons as such because under the Marine (Scotland) Act the whole year is now effectively a close season.

The intention is to limit the overall shooting of seals to levels that should not impact on seal populations (less than 1% of greys and slightly over 1.5% of commons) and therefore on that portion of the population that may be pregnant or lactating females. This will particularly limit the impact on vulnerable common seal populations. Marine Scotland has also, however, imposed conditions on certain licences, which further limit the level of shooting during breeding periods usually in relation to local seal Special Areas of Conservation (SACs).

It would be difficult to set a specific condition of not shooting 'pregnant or lactating seals' because of the difficulties involved in the identification of such animals amongst the wider population and the length of seal pregnancy.

The operation of licences is being monitored by Marine Scotland, and if the current measures prove inadequate the Scottish Ministers have the power under section 112(4)(d) to impose what might be considered the equivalent of the old 'close seasons'.

Failure to comply with a condition imposed is an offence (s. 112(5)). In any proceedings for such an offence, it is a defence for the person charged to prove that the person took all reasonable precautions and exercised all due diligence to avoid the commission of an offence.

Seals are now given protection at designated haul-out sites, and it is an offence to intentionally or recklessly *harass* a seal at these sites. A 'haul-out site' means any place which the Scottish Ministers, after consulting the Natural Environment Research Council, by order designate as such for the purposes of this section.

This is an offence not formerly covered by the now-repealed Conservation of Seals Act 1970. It would be worthwhile wildlife crime officers establishing the location of any designated haul-out sites in their force area. Note that the term of the offence is *harassment* and not disturbance

The offence of harassment will come into effect only when Marine Scotland designate specific haul-out sites through an order in the Scottish Parliament. This is likely to take place early in 2013. This process will include publication of guidance on the offence of harassment of seals. Designated haul-out sites are likely to include the 14 existing SACs for seals. These are:

SACs for grey seals:
- Berwickshire and North Northumberland Coast
- Faray and Holm of Faray
- Isle of May

- Monach Islands
- North Rona
- Treshnish Isles

SACs for common seals:
- Ascrib, Isay and Dunvegan
- Dornoch Firth and Morrich More
- Eileanan agus Sgeiran Lios mÛr (Lismore)
- Firth of Tay & Eden Estuary
- Mousa
- Sanday
- South-East Islay Skerries
- Yell Sound Coast

The Conservation (Natural Habitats) Regulations 1994 Regulation 41 prohibits the killing of seals using '*artificial light sources, devices for illuminating targets and sighting devices for night shooting comprising an electronic image magnifier or image converter*'. This effectively eliminates night shooting of seals. Night is accepted as being '*the period between the expiry of one hour after sunset and the beginning of the last hour before sunrise*'.

Police powers:
Section 126 – Police powers: search and seize
A constable may stop any person who the constable suspects with reasonable cause of committing an offence under this part and may-
> *(a) without warrant, search any vehicle or vessel which the constable reasonably believes to have been used in connection with the commission of the offence*
> *(b) seize any seal, seal skin or other thing liable to be forfeited under section 127*

The statutory power given under subsection (b) is without prejudice to the common law power to seize items that would be necessary as productions in a case

Section 127 – Forfeiture
The court by which a person is convicted of an offence under this Part may order the forfeiture of-
> *(a) any seal or seal skin in respect of which the offence was committed, or*
> *(b) any thing which the person possessed or controlled at the time of the offence which was capable of being used in connection with the offence*

Section 128 – Penalties and power for police officers to detain suspects

Section 128(1)

A person guilty of an offence under section 107 or 117 is liable, on summary conviction, to imprisonment for a term not exceeding 6 months or to a fine not exceeding level 5 on the standard scale, or to both

These are the main offences of intentionally or recklessly killing, injuring or taking a seal, or intentionally or recklessly harassing a seal at a haul-out site

Section 128(2)

A person guilty of an offence under section 108(4) is liable, on summary conviction, to a fine not exceeding level 4 on the standard scale

This is the offence of failing to comply with the requirement to report the killing of a seal to alleviate suffering

Section 128(3)

A person guilty of an offence under section 112(5) or 113(4) is liable, on summary conviction, to imprisonment for a term not exceeding 3 months or to a fine not exceeding level 5 on the standard scale, or to both

These offences relate to failure to comply with licensing conditions and failure to send a seal licence report within 10 days of the end of a reporting period

Section 128(4)

A person guilty of an offence under section 124 is liable, on summary conviction, to a fine not exceeding level 4 on the standard scale.

This is the offence of obstructing an authorised person

In summary, for the main offences under Part 6 of the Act of intentionally or recklessly killing, injuring or taking a seal, or intentionally or recklessly harassing a seal at a haul-out site, the power for a police officer to detain a suspect under Section 14 of the Criminal Procedure (Scotland) Act 1975 would be available.

If wildlife offences are difficult offences in which to secure a conviction, offences against seals may be some of the most difficult by reason of where the offence is likely to take place and the recovery of the evidence. The Act is now in line with other wildlife legislation, in that the offence is that of *intentionally or recklessly killing, injuring or taking a live seal.*

Police wildlife crime officers should make a point of obtaining a copy of licences relating to their area of responsibility and be aware of the various conditions imposed on the licence-holder. In particular the licence *must* give details of the number of seals allowed to be shot, steps to be taken to deal with any seal that is wounded, the minimum calibre of firearm to be used (which will normally be .222), weather conditions in which shooting can take place, how close the shooter must be, prohibiting the shooting to take place from an unstable platform (such as a small boat), and steps to be taken to recover the carcass.

Though the licence does not need to specify the area in which seals can be shot, the circumstances under which they can be shot and any period during which certain seals may not be shot, these are invariably included and become licence conditions. There are no longer statutory close seasons for seals, but the licence should take account of times when the shooting of seals should not be undertaken if they are likely to be heavily pregnant or nursing pups.

Seals often travel surprising distances up some of our larger rivers, and 30 miles inland is not exceptional. The seals can do considerable damage to salmon stocks and it is in these circumstances that persons are more likely to take a shot at one with an unsuitable calibre of rifle or even a shotgun.

Evidentially, the following facts are extremely difficult to establish, even if someone is seen shooting a seal, be it in the river or the sea:

- What species of seal had been shot or had been shot at? Consider how many people, as witnesses, can tell the head of a grey seal from that of a common seal, or even know what species of seals live in Scottish waters.

- Can the body of the seal be recovered for identification purposes? If a seal is shot after it has filled its lungs with air then it is likely to float, otherwise it is likely to sink. A floating carcass can be recovered with some difficulty; a carcass which sinks cannot, though it may wash ashore eventually. Can it then be proved that a seal carcass recovered was the one that was shot?

Even if the carcass can be recovered is there a possibility of a recovery of the bullet for a ballistics match, since the bullets often fragment on impact? Who can be contacted to look for and recover a bullet, especially since an x-ray is difficult with such a large carcass? (May be possible at the Royal (Dick) Vet School, Edinburgh, where large animals are x-rayed. Investigating officers should liaise in the first instance with their local Scotland's Rural College vet lab (SRUC – formerly SAC)). Some enquiries will begin with the recovery of a seal that has been shot and the investigating officer then has to work back from that point, making the task even more difficult.

Seals typically return to haul-out sites to rest between foraging trips at sea. The haul out site is not necessarily near the seals' foraging sites, which may be several miles distant. According to experts, adult common seals rarely feed beside their haul-out site, with the shallow water round the site more usually a site for social interaction. Note that the offence at haul-out sites is *harassment* and not disturbance.

> The dictionary definition of *Disturb*:
> To interrupt or cause to move from the normal position or engagement, or destroy the quiet or composure of

> The dictionary definition of *Harass:*
> To irritate; to annoy; to trouble by constant raids and attacks

In addition to any harassment of seals at a *designated* haul-out site, this must of course be as a result of an intentional or reckless act. It seems then that the reason seals leave their haul-out site will be well scrutinised by the court. It is unlikely that a boat innocently passing too close to a haul-out site and making the seals enter the water would constitute an offence. A boat deliberately driving straight at seals hauled-out, or creating considerable noise, may come in to the realms of an offence, though the intended outcome of the activity would need to be establish as an act to cause the seals to enter the water. If the same person is seen to carry out this type of conduct on a regular basis the case will be strengthened.

Any specific queries about seal licensing or individual seal licences should be addressed to:
Seal Licensing
Marine Scotland
Marine Laboratory
PO Box 101
375 Victoria Road
Aberdeen
AB11 9DB
Tel No: 01224 295579

Any queries about general seal policy should be addressed to:

Seal Policy Team
Marine Scotland
Area 1A-South
Victoria Quay
Edinburgh
EH6 6QQ
Tel No: 08457 741741
Email: marinescotland@scotland.gsi.co.uk

Scotland's Rural College at Inverness is funded by Marine Scotland to undertake post-mortems of seals shot under licence. They would be happy to assist with any work in this field that might be necessary to assist the police with the collection of evidence.

http://www.scotland.gov.uk/Topics/marine/science/Publications/TopicSheets/strandings

Bats

All UK species of bat are European Protected Species (EPS) and included in Schedule 2 to the Conservation (Natural Habitats etc) Regulations 1994. The main threats to bats come from development or demolition of, or alterations to, buildings. Timber treatment in lofts is now less of a problem as the products used are less dangerous to bats, and operators using the products are more bat-aware.

Nevertheless a number of alleged offences against bats are investigated by the police every year. Similar to the Protection of Badgers Act 1992, offences relate to any action that causes a threat to bats. Most common are instances where bats have either been blocked into or out of a building. Under the Habitats Regulations (reg. 39(1)) it is an offence to deliberately or recklessly: capture, injure or kill a bat; disturb it while it is occupying a roost; disturb it while it is rearing or caring for its young; obstruct or otherwise deny it access to a roost; disturb it in a way likely to significantly affect its local distribution or abundance, or likely to impair its ability to survive, breed or reproduce, or rear or otherwise care for its young.

Note that all of these actions have to be carried out intentionally or recklessly for an offence to be committed. However if a person were to damage or destroy a bat roost (its place of shelter) (reg. 39(1)(d)), whether or not the bats are present at the time, this is what is termed a 'strict liability' offence. In this case there is no need for proof that the action causing the damage or destruction was carried out deliberately or recklessly. It is also an offence to be in possession of a live bat (reg. 39(3)), though, as under the badger legislation, there are common sense exceptions.

Prior to an amendment to the Regulations in 2007, it was lawful to take dead specimens of bats where it could be shown that the animal had died from natural causes or by accident. This is now no longer the case. It is an offence to be in control of any bat *taken since 10 June 1994* (reg. 39(3)). The exception is where a licence for possession has been granted by SNH (or the Scottish Government, though in mid-2011 their licensing responsibilities were passed to SNH). Licences may be granted by SNH for a number of reasons, including the exclusion of bats from a dwelling, but they must not grant a licence unless they are satisfied that there is no satisfactory alternative, and that the action authorised will not be detrimental to the maintenance of the population of the species concerned at a favourable conservation status in their natural range.

Most bat incidents are likely to fall into the following categories:
- Roof repairs
- Structural alterations to buildings
- Demolition of buildings
- Domestic incidents, which are likely to be roost blocking, roost destruction or bat disturbance by householders, normally arising from fear, ignorance or hostility
- Chemical treatment to roof timbers
- Felling of mature trees

During investigations an expert from the Bat Conservation Trust, Scottish Natural Heritage or a local bat group should be asked to attend to assist the enquiry officer. The expert will be invaluable is assisting the collection of best evidence for a police report to the procurator fiscal. Any blocking of a roost must be reversed immediately otherwise bats trapped in the roost will die.

In general terms bats are not dangerous, do not carry disease and cause no structural damage to buildings, nevertheless a fatal case of rabies in Tayside in 2002, where the bat worker is believed to have contacted the disease from Daubenton's bats, must be borne in mind and health and safety issues must be uppermost in the enquiry officer's mind. Any handling of bats should be carried out wearing a stout pair of gloves, and if possible left to an experienced and licensed bat worker.

Advice – Bats in domestic properties

Bats are quite commonly found in people's houses. In most cases people don't even know that they are there. Bats don't chew cables or any other materials and are not destructive by nature. Anyone concerned about bats in their house should contact Scottish Natural Heritage, who will arrange for a bat worker to visit and advise about bats.

Sometimes householders may need to carry out repairs or renovations that might affect bats in their property. In rare circumstances householders can experience problems with bat roosts in their houses, for instance if there is a particularly large roost present. Most problems can be solved and a bat worker will be able to provide advice. In some circumstances owners or occupiers might need a licence to carry out works, or, may wish to have the bats excluded from the house.

Advice – Bats in non-domestic properties

If bats are likely to be found in a site proposed for development, or in a building to be repaired, modified or demolished, then a bat survey should be undertaken by a suitably qualified and experienced person. If bats, their roosts or even signs of bats are found then the expert should identify what impact the development might have on the bats, and if this can be avoided or minimised. If avoidance is not possible and the development might otherwise result in an offence being committed, then a licence from SNH would be necessary to be able to proceed. Surveys should be up-to-date and carried out according to best practice to ensure that there are no unnecessary delays in addressing licensing and planning applications.

Advice – Bats in trees

All of the bat species found in Scotland are known to use trees as roosts, and often the presence of a roost is difficult to see. Because bat roosts are protected *at all times*, but may only be used by bats at certain times of the year, care needs to be taken to make sure, if tree felling or surgery is carried out, that a bat roost isn't present. Forest operations, particularly tree felling can cause disturbance to foraging bats by altering their habitat, although this is unlikely to be an offence under the Regulations if good forest practice is followed. Damage to or destruction of bat roosts in trees or disturbing bats at roost sites is the most frequent risk for woodland managers to consider, especially as damage or destruction does not need to be deliberate or reckless to be a potential offence.

Key points to consider are limiting the scale of felling operations in relation to bat foraging distances, and trying to restrict or avoid felling in prime foraging habitat typically used by bats for feeding or roosting, such as old broadleaved woodland, riparian woods, pondsides and lochsides. Bats typically use linear features (e.g. woodland edges and forestry rides) to navigate from their roosting sites to their foraging areas. Woodland managers should be aware that felling operations can interrupt these linear features causing fragmentation and potentially disrupting the bats' movements to and from foraging areas and reducing foraging time. Certain species, notably brown long-eared bats, are particularly vulnerable to this as they will not generally cross open areas but tend to follow woodland edge. Woodland management that does not involve large scale clear felling operations is unlikely to create problems in this respect, but where larger scale management is planned, it is recommended that the effects on the above features are taken into account and sufficient connectivity of woodland retained.

The greatest risk of an offence under the Regulations is that of felling, and some other operations like forest road construction. Both could destroy or damage roost sites, which, as already stated, is an offence whether or not it is deliberate or reckless. Remember the roost sites are protected at all times, even when no bats are present. To reduce the risk of inadvertent roost disturbance and destruction, forestry operations should preferably be planned well in advance to allow time for survey work by a bat expert.

Areas particularly used for roosts include holes, cracks and loose bark. Older trees with any of these are particularly favoured, in particular oak, ash, beech, sycamore and Scots pine, but bats will use any tree with suitable cavities or crevices. Evidence in winter – more easily seen when deciduous trees are leafless – may be dark staining and streaks on the tree below the hole (although this is often due to water seepage); visible staining around the hole from oils in the bats' fur; or a maze of tiny scratch marks from the bat's claws around the hole, often around the top edge. These are often only visible close up. In spring and summer it may be possible to notice droppings below the hole – these have the appearance of mouse droppings but crumble to a powder of insect fragments and are often stuck to vertical surfaces as well as being scattered on the ground; noise of squeaking/chittering coming from hole, especially on a hot day in high summer or just before dusk as bats are getting ready to emerge; or a strong smell of ammonia or flies close to a hole. Bats can be seen emerging from their roost sites at dusk or returning before dawn, though of course better results can be obtained by an experienced person using a bat detector.

If a roost site is suspected the simplest answer is to leave the trees in question out of any felling operations, ideally leaving a buffer of adjacent trees around the roost tree to reduce disturbance to roosting bats. If a suspected roost trees must be felled, a specialist survey should be conducted to establish where roosts are and the felling may require to be licensed by SNH. Under the requirements of the Habitats Regulations, licences are unlikely to be issued except where there are reasons of public safety or other imperative reasons of overriding public interest including those of a social or economic nature.

Occupied bat boxes are roosts and therefore protected. Maintenance work, monitoring bat use or moving bat boxes to another site should be carried out by licensed bat workers.

The Bat Conservation Trust, Scottish Natural Heritage or Forestry Commission Scotland can all provide advice.

Cetaceans

Like bats, all cetaceans (whales, porpoises and dolphins) in the UK are European Protected Species (EPS) under the Habitats Regulations. The main threat to these mammals, particularly dolphins, is their being disturbed or harassed by people on boats or jet-skis (reg.39(1) and (2)). As EPS species, it is also an offence to be in possession of a part or parts of UK cetaceans without a licence, if taken after 10 June 1994. (reg. 39(3))

The vast majority of investigations are likely to be in relation to disturbance or harassment of dolphins. This poses the questions: when is a cetacean disturbed, when is it harassed and when is such conduct intentional or reckless?

It is first of all necessary to consider the meaning of the terms 'disturb' and 'harass', and to understand the difference between the two. The dictionary meanings are:

Disturb:
To interrupt or cause to move from the normal position or engagement, or destroy the quiet or composure of

Harass:
To irritate; to annoy; to trouble by constant raids and attacks

It is clear that to harass a dolphin is the more serious term.

Police officers are unlikely to be able to answer the question on whether or not a cetacean has been disturbed or harassed, and experts from one or more organisations will be required to establish this as a fact in any court case. Blatant cases are slightly more straightforward, such as continuously chasing after dolphins with a jet-ski or speedboat. This is much more likely to constitute harassment rather than disturbance. Complaints of boats with sight-seers going too close to cetaceans are much more difficult to prove.

There is no case-law to give guidance as to whether 50 metres or 250 metres is too close. A boat quietly drifting 50 metres from a whale cause may cause little or no disturbance, while the whale will certainly be aware of a boat 250 metres away with the engine running.

Assuming disturbance can be proved, it requires to be established whether the disturbance is intentional or reckless. This may depend on whether it can be established that the person had warning beforehand not to carry out the act. A reckless act, of course, is considerably easier to prove

Evidence of offences is most likely to come from people in boats who witness an incident either nearby or at a distance. Since one of the main criteria obviously involves distance between the offending boat and the particular cetacean, it is important to establish that the witness is correct about the distance. Distances over a mass of water with no landmarks are much more difficult to estimate than over an area of land, especially if the witness, the boat with the suspect and the cetacean are all in a straight line.

It is unlikely that the witnesses, unless experts in their own right, can prove to a court how the particular cetacean had been disturbed. This is likely to be the responsibility of an expert who was not at the scene but is speaking from scientific or practical experience of what would *normally* disturb or even harass such a cetacean.

Taking account of all the pitfalls, disturbance or harassment of cetaceans is an extremely difficult offence to prove, though this should not prevent police officers discussing with, and submitting cases to, specialist wildlife prosecutors.

Though occurring before the provision for *reckless* disturbance, a case of deliberate disturbance of dolphins under the Habitats Regulations was heard at Dingwall Sheriff Court on 17 March 2005. The sheriff's findings (*Sheriff's judgement – PF Dingwall v Davies 2005*) are particularly interesting. The sheriff emphasises the point that it is not enough for a person to act in a manner that is *likely* to cause disturbance. That the dolphins *were actually disturbed* must be proved.

It is good use of police time trying to reduce such offences; ensuring in areas where offences are most likely that those using boats and jet-skis, or even swimming with dolphins, are advised of what actions may constitute offences and how to avoid them. Such proactive preventive measures are also likely to aid a prosecution should someone ignore the advice given. Signage at key locations outlining the offence and the penalty is often successful.

6. Freshwater Pearl Mussels

FRESHWATER pearl mussels are listed on Schedule 5 of the Wildlife and Countryside Act 1981. As such it is an offence to intentionally or recklessly commit certain acts against them, in particular to kill, injure or take them. One of the main threats to these molluscs is gathering them in order to look for the rare pearls inside. (s. 9(1) WCA) To carry this out, wet suits are occasionally used, though the normal equipment will be a bucket with a glass bottom so that the mussels can more easily be seen on the river-bed, and a long cane or stick, often bamboo, with a split on one end, used for gripping the mussel and lifting it clear of the water. If these items are found in the possession of a person on a riverbank without a reasonable excuse – even without the witnessing of an attempt to take mussels – this may well be sufficient for the offence of, for the purpose of committing an offence, being in possession of items capable of being used. (s. 18(2) WCA) It is also an offence to sell or advertise for sale, a freshwater pearl mussel or any part of it. This would invariably be the pearl. (s. 9(5) WCA)

It is also an offence to intentionally or recklessly damage or destroy any place which the mussels use for shelter or protection. (s. 9(4) WCA) This, of course, is the river bed. The most likely example of this offence would be the disturbance of a part of the river bed used by mussels, possibly by the extraction of sand or gravel with a digger. The wording of this offence implies that the Schedule 5 animal need not be present at the time of the damage or disturbance. In the case of a freshwater pearl mussel, which does not move around the bed of the river in the manner of other creatures, it does not seem to be the case that *all* of the river bed is protected; just the places where the mussels are embedded in the sand and gravel. It is also an offence to intentionally or recklessly disturb a freshwater pearl mussel, which would include prodding it with a stick so that it was dislodged and washed downstream. (s. 9(4) WCA)

If suspects are still at the scene, an enquiry is relatively straightforward, and the investigating officer should seize any dead or injured mussels or any pearls. Live uninjured mussels should be photographed with a signed production label and returned to the river, preferably by experienced SNH staff. Someone with the necessary skills would be required to attend to find evidence in the river, again most likely SNH staff.

In cases where mussels have been killed and/or their place of shelter on the river-bed has been disturbed by work in the river with a tractor or JCB, it is essential to show that the act was intentional or reckless rather than careless or accidental. It must be demonstrated that the person involved was – or should have been – aware of the presence of mussels in the location being worked. It must also be demonstrated that the person should be aware that the work would kill, injure or at least dislodge the mussels, and was disregardful of the consequences. Further, it must be established that mussels were indeed present and that they suffered to some degree from the prohibited acts.

Work with a tractor or JCB is likely to completely destroy mussels that are run over, or mix mussels up with tons of excavated sand or gravel. The best that may be able to be done to establish if mussels have been destroyed is to have the river bed immediately upstream and immediately downstream surveyed by SNH staff for the presence of live mussels. A search immediately downstream is more difficult as any mussels there may well have been affected by silt and be buried.

Bear in mind that as well as identification of the suspect, the court will require identification of the mussel as being a freshwater pearl mussel, *Margaratifera margaratifera*, or of the pearl as having come from a freshwater pearl mussel. This is where the experts are essential and a case is likely to fail without their inclusion. So far as identification of the pearl is concerned, consulting a specialist jeweller is the best option.

Experts should be asked to examine any freshwater pearl mussel still containing part of the animal *as soon as possible*, and may well be able to give an accurate estimate of how long it has been dead, which could be of major importance in a court case. Officers should keep the mussels cool *and not freeze them until they have been examined.* Ensure mussels and pearls are retained in case the defence challenges the prosecution assertion that they are freshwater pearl mussels.

Very often the taking of mussels takes place repeatedly on the same part of a particular river, simply because they are known to be there and that they are accessible. Most often police will be alerted to people taking them by a landowner, water bailiff or someone having responsibility for the stretch of river. Normally these folks are excellent witnesses and will provide a detailed account of what had taken place. It is well worth police trying to liaise with these potential witnesses *before* an offence takes place and ensure that they have an action plan in hand, or at least the most appropriate telephone number to contact.

Be aware that all dead mussels or empty shells have not necessarily been the subject of crime; they may have been swept away and killed by a flood. In some cases, experts may be able to distinguish between those that have been subject of crime and those which have been killed through natural causes.

It is worthy of mention that shoddy or unauthorised river engineering works are beginning to have an adverse effect on mussels. It is not uncommon for fishing proprietors to make alterations to a river bed or bank which might result in large scale killing or injuring of mussels. Additionally, there is an increase in the number of mini hydro-electric schemes being set up. The preparation work for these schemes has the potential to cause silting of rivers during periods of heavy rain, with the consequent suffocation or injury to the mussels, and extreme damage to their habitat. Wildlife crime officers should make a point of liaising on a regular basis with SEPA and SNH, who may be the first organisations to be alerted to these threats to mussels.

7. Amphibians, Reptiles and Invertebrates

THE SAND lizard, great-crested newt, smooth snake and natterjack toad are listed as European Protected Species (EPS) on Schedule 2 of the Habitats Regulations. Of these species, only the great-crested newt is present in Scotland, and its distribution is sparse, mainly in the central lowlands, Scottish Borders, Dumfries and Galloway and within 30 miles of Inverness. The main threat against all amphibians and reptiles comes from development, where their habitat is sometimes destroyed. As EPS species, the offences are identical to those that are committed against bats (see Bats p108).

Great-crested newts live in and around ponds, even up to 250m from the pond. If it is suspected that great crested newts are present, forestry or development work should not be carried out within 50m of a pond during the breeding season. Avoid features likely to be used by great crested newts, such as dead wood piles, within 250m of the pond and try to limit the work to 25% of that 250m zone in any one year. If newts are encountered, no work should be carried out within the 250m zone.

If development or forest operations are essential and you know that great crested newts are present, and if the work is likely to kill newts or damage their breeding, resting or hibernating place (i.e. the work cannot be kept within the limits described above), then a licence from SNH should be sought prior to undertaking the work.

A licence application will require evidence:
- of the existence of a breeding site or resting place
- that there is no satisfactory alternative to damaging or destroying the breeding site or resting place, and
- that there will be no detriment to the maintenance of the species at 'favourable conservation status'. In order to fulfil this last criterion it is usually necessary to carry out some form of mitigation or compensation work to offset the effects of the proposed operations. Mitigation work can range from using amphibian-proof fencing to exclude newts from an area temporarily while operations are carried out, to moving the newts to a newly created and suitable site.

If great crested newts or their eggs or larvae are found during operations, stop work immediately and seek advice from Scottish Natural Heritage on how to proceed. Anyone who finds they have inadvertently damaged or destroyed a breeding site/resting place during operations should get in touch with SNH for advice on what to do next. Remember that breeding sites or resting places are protected at all times, even when no great crested newts are present.

The following species of amphibians and reptiles are listed under Schedule 5 of the Wildlife and Countryside Act 1981: adder, common frog, viviparous lizard (also referred to as the common lizard); palmate newt; smooth newt; slow worm; grass snake; common toad. None on this list has the *full* protection given to most species in that schedule (for more detail see Schedule 5 p264). It is, however, an offence to sell or offer for sale any of these species, and the adder, grass snake, slow worm and viviparous lizard have additional protection against anyone intentionally or recklessly taking, killing or injuring them. It would be an offence under the Animal Health and Welfare (Scotland) Act 2004 to cruelly ill-treat *any* captive amphibian or reptile.

A surprisingly high number of invertebrates, particularly butterflies and moths, are listed on Schedule 5 of the Wildlife and Countryside Act 1981. They are too many to mention, but in relation to those listed it is an offence to sell or offer them for sale. In some cases it is also an offence to kill or injure them, for example in the case of the marsh fritillary or the swallowtail.

8. Plants

PLANTS often seem the poor relations when considering the different aspects of wildlife crime. Nevertheless a small number of offences take place in Scotland either against plants or involving plants. Examples might be the removal of growing plants such as snowdrop bulbs to sell to garden centres, often as far away as the south of England, the sale of wild-taken native bluebell bulbs, or in some cases the large-scale removal from the wild of sphagnum moss, usually for the making of wreaths or the lining of flower baskets.

This section only deals with offences under the Wildlife and Countryside Act, 1981. For other offences relating to the trade in plants see chapter on COTES on p136. For offences in relation to European protected species of plant, see The Conservation (Natural Habitats, etc) Regulations 1994 on p133. For offences in relation to the release of invasive species of plant see Introduction of new species on p123.

The main offences under the WCA are to intentionally or recklessly *pick, uproot or destroy* any wild plant included in Schedule 8, or any seed or spore attached to any such wild plant (s. 13(1)(a)); or, not being an authorised person, to intentionally or recklessly *uproot* any wild plant not included in that Schedule. (s.13(1)(b))

Plants on Schedule 8 are the rarer, specially protected, plants and include many mosses. A glance at the plants listed on Schedule 8 is enough to show the extreme difficulty in enforcing this section. Few police officers – even wildlife crime officers – could identify more than a handful of these plants and would rely in most cases on a complaint being made by, and assistance from, an expert.

It is also an offence to sell, offer or expose for sale, or possess or transport for the purpose of sale, any live or dead wild plant included in Schedule 8, or any part of, or anything derived from, such a plant (s. 13(2)(a); or publish or cause to be published any advertisement likely to be understood as trading in any of those plants. (s. 13(2)(b))

It should be noted that the native bluebell (*Hyacinthoides non-scripta*), though listed in Schedule 8, is only subject to the provisions of Section 13(2), not Section 13(1). It is not an offence to pick or dig either the native bluebell or the Spanish bluebell (*Hyancinthoides hispanica*) with the permission of the landowner, but it is an offence to become involved in any commercial transaction in relation to the native bluebell.

It is worth noting the definition of 'sale' at section 27(1) of the Act. This includes 'hire, barter and exchange, and cognate expressions shall be construed accordingly'. In a case in North Wales a company involved in the selling of bulbs cleared a large tract of bracken in exchange for the native bluebell bulbs dug up during the work. The value of bluebell bulbs was substantial and both the company and the landowner were reported for prosecution.

A defence (s. 3), which covers damage to Schedule 8 plants during otherwise lawful activities, extends the responsibility of the person involved to minimising the damaging consequences to the plant once he has become aware of the result of his otherwise lawful operation or activity. An example may be the crushing of plants on Schedule 8 during timber or agricultural operations when the plants were initially either not seen or not recognised for what they were. The operator must have taken reasonable precautions to avoid causing damage and have been unable to foresee the outcome. Once the error has been realised, however, the work must cease if it is going to cause further damage.

There will be many cases, as already stated, where the only people who can report a case to the police are botanists or similar experts who realise the significance of the evidence they encounter. The evidence may be in the form of recent signs of digging in an area formerly holding rare plants, or may indeed be a sighting of someone actually digging plants.

Where a person is caught in possession of plants, obtaining identification of the plants is more straightforward. However trying to link plants back to their original habitat may be extremely difficult and is likely to mean a fairly specialised scene of crime examination being carried out. Soil samples may have to be taken and compared, as will any companion plants in the wild and companion plants adhering to recovered plants.

The investigating officer should look for evidence (or the lack of evidence) on the plants of horticultural-type soils, eg peat, sand, perlite or charcoal as these may indicate the plants have been in a nursery. Also look for evidence of root growth. If it conforms to the shape of a pot then it has been in a nursery for a while (though does not necessarily mean that it is not wild). Wild plants can be dug from the wild and then heeled in or housed in nursery conditions before they are sold on. This may mean they look like artificially propagated plants. The main points to look for are:

- Uniformity in shape and size – the cleaner and more uniform they are the more likely they are to be propagated

- Insect damage
- Root growth and health, although long periods out of soil whether from the wild or a nursery could mean the roots deteriorate. Look for the roots growing in the shape of a pot
- The presence of horticultural materials – is the sphagnum moss surrounding the plants native or a species used in horticulture, eg New Zealand sphagnum moss
- The time of year – is it the correct time of year to be selling the species in question?

To prove a case, the enquiry officer may need to seek out an expert who can almost act as a forensic botanist.

With recovered plants or bulbs, advice should be sought regarding returning the plants to the wild, though this must always be done in consultation with the specialist wildlife prosecutor, since a defence solicitor would be entitled to have the plants examined.

Some landowners allow people on to their land on payment to dig up plants that are not on Schedule 8. This arrangement mostly applies to digging snowdrop bulbs in springtime after the flower is dying back. Large quantities are often harvested and police officers should be aware of this legitimate practice. The same practice formerly took place with bluebell bulbs, though any commercial activity in native wild bluebells was banned in 1998. An advert in a horticulture column of a newspaper offering bluebell bulbs for sale from a private address or with a mobile telephone number as the only contact must be treated with suspicion.

Scottish Natural Heritage will be able to provide advice and identification of plant species. Plantlife (Scotland) will be able to provide the same advice and identification. The Royal Botanic Gardens, Kew, has specialists who can advise on the illegal trade in wild plants and specialise in Traditional Asian Medicines, tree species/timber, orchids and tropical plants. If good digital images can be forwarded, they can identify plants quickly. The Royal Botanic Garden in Edinburgh also has a range of botanists and bryologists.

9. Introduction of New Species

THE LEGISLATION relating to the introduction of new species is covered under section 14 of the Wildlife and Countryside Act 1981. This section was amended by the Wildlife and Natural Environment (Scotland) Act 2011, with the considerable changes coming into force on 2 July 2012 (through the provisions of the Wildlife and Natural Environment (Scotland) Act (Commencement No. 4 Savings and Transitional Provisions) Order 2012.) In broad terms section 14 governs the keeping, release, allowing to escape and sale of invasive, non-native, and invasive non-native species. It also allows for Codes of Practice and Control Orders to be created to reduce the risk of escapes. Since there are substantial changes to what the law was formerly, it is set out in more detail than some of the other sections.

It should be noted that the release, planting, keeping and sale are strict liability offences. This means that the prosecution does not need to prove any intention, knowledge, recklessness or negligence on the part of the accused, simply that the offence took place. However, a person accused of a release, planting or keeping offence may successfully establish a defence if they can show that they took all reasonable steps and exercised all due diligence to avoid committing the offence. This due diligence defence is designed to recognise efforts made by people to comply with the legislation. Ultimately it is always a matter for the Court to determine whether the defence of due diligence has been established. This will depend on the circumstances of each particular case but compliance or non-compliance with the Code of Practice on Non-native Species could be used as evidence in a criminal prosecution.

There have been many examples over the years of the accidental or deliberate release of invasive new species of animals, plants, fish, etc. to the wild in Scotland. Examples, to name but a few, are grey squirrel, mink, Himalyan balsam, Japanese knotweed, ruffe and signal crayfish. In some cases these species have gone on to colonise large areas, often to the irreversible detriment of our habitat or indigenous flora and fauna.

The seriousness with which both the UK Government and the Scottish Government view this is reflected in the prison sentence available to courts where persons are convicted of illegally introducing invasive new species: a sentence of up to 2 years imprisonment.

Prior to the Wildlife and Natural Environment (Scotland) Act 2011 the principal offence related to the release of non-native species *into the wild*. The legislation has changed significantly, with the main change being a move away from an extensive 'black list' approach – listing species that can't be released or planted – to a presumption against release. This precautionary approach is justified by the fact that it is extremely difficult to guess whether a species will become invasive. The point is not whether the species is native to Scotland, the UK or any other administrative boundaries; a species must not now be moved beyond its native range. If that native range is only a small part of Scotland, for example only one river catchment area, then the rest of the country is off-limits. It would now be an offence, as an example, to translocate hedgehogs to Orkney, an area outwith their native range. The term *'into the wild'* is removed so far as animals are concerned, but remains for plants; for example you can plant non-native plants in a garden but not in the wild.

The police are responsible for the enforcement only of Section 14(1) to 14B. Sections 14C to 14J relate to Control Orders, with the creation and enforcement of the Control Orders being carried out by a 'relevant body,' defined at subsection (P)(6) as Scottish Ministers, Scottish Natural Heritage, the Scottish Environment Protection Agency or the Forestry Commissioners. Search warrants can be obtained under subsection 14(N) by members of these relevant bodies, however a constable must be present during the execution of any warrant which authorises that force may be used. (s. 14N(5)) Other persons or equipment considered necessary for the search may be taken on to the land. (s. 14O(1))

Offences

The main offences with which police officers are likely to become involved are:

Section 14 (1) *Subject to the provisions of Part I of the Act, any person who –*
   (a) releases, or allows to escape from captivity, any animal—
      (i) to a place outwith its native range; or
      (ii) of a type the Scottish Ministers, by order, specify; or
   (b) otherwise causes any animal outwith the control of any person to be at a place outwith its native range,
   is guilty of an offence.

In other words it is an offence to release or allow to escape from captivity any animal to a place 'outwith its native range'. 'Native range' is defined as a locality to which the animal or plant is indigenous and excludes any locality to which a plant or animal has been introduced (intentionally or otherwise) by any person (s. 14P(2) and (3)). Bear in mind that there is no requirement for this to have been committed 'intentionally or recklessly' for an offence to be committed.

The native range of a *hybrid* animal or plant is defined as any locality within the native range of both parents of the hybrid animal or plant. Any hybrid which has at least one parent non-native to the hybrid's location is considered to be a non-native species in that location.

Being defined as a non-native plant or animal does not necessarily mean that the plant or animal will be subject to active control measures. However, where appropriate, control of invasive non-native species – beyond the general prohibition on release of non-native species under section 14 – can be required under a Species Control Order (This is dealt with section 14D of the 1981 Act, though *not* covered in this book since it does not relate to a criminal matter and is the remit of other organisations).

Some species are naturally expanding their range, for example the collared dove arrived in Great Britain in 1953. If a range is increased naturally (for example, in response to climate change) then this larger area will be considered to be the native range of the animal or plant.

However, if the range is only expanding as a result of direct human activity then this will not be considered to be the animal or plant's native range – this includes natural range expansion following direct human activity. For example, the harlequin ladybird (*Harmonia axyridis*) is native to eastern Asia but has been introduced into Europe from where it has spread to Britain (and Scotland). As it is only present in Europe due to human action importing it to that region, it is outwith its native range in Europe. Although it spread naturally within Europe to Britain, because of the manner by which it was introduced in Europe initially, it is still outwith its native range when it spreads to Britain.

Animals and plants that were once native in a location but have become extinct are considered to be 'former natives' (though if they re-establish themselves without the help of man they are considered to have extended their natural range and so be a native species once again). For the purposes of the 1981 Act former natives are considered to be outwith their native range and it is therefore an offence to release a former native without a licence. The environment may have changed considerably since a former native was present as a species in Scotland and the impact of the former native species on the environment and on land use would need to be assessed before it can be released into the wild.

Japanese knotweed is an example of a plant that is in Scotland and considered in the code of conduct to be non-native. It is a native of Japan, China and Korea but was deliberately introduced to the UK early in the 19th Century by plant collectors. In its native range it spreads both by seed and vegetatively (in the UK only by vegetative means) but without human assistance it would not otherwise have crossed oceans etc. to establish in Great Britain. It is therefore a non-native species in Great Britain.

The ruffe, listed in Schedule 1, Part 2 of the Wildlife and Countryside Act 1981 (Keeping and Release and Notification Requirements) (Scotland) Order 2012, is a freshwater fish that is native to southern Britain. It is thought to have been introduced to Loch Lomond as a bait fish by anglers. Without human assistance it would not have been able to move outside of the catchments in its native range. It is therefore a non-native species in Loch Lomond and anywhere else outwith southern Britain (unless it naturally extends its native range).

The European hedgehog has a native range spanning mainland Britain, most of Europe, Asia and North Africa. It was introduced to the Outer Hebrides in the 1970s to control slugs in gardens. Hedgehogs would not otherwise have been able to cross the sea to reach the Hebrides. It is therefore a non-native species in the Outer Hebrides and any other Scottish islands.

Under section 14(1)(a)(ii) it is also an offence to release or allow to escape from captivity any other animal specified in an order made by the Scottish Ministers. (in this case the Wildlife and Countryside Act 1981 (Keeping and Release and Notification Requirements) (Scotland) Order 2012)

An animal is considered to be in captivity if it is under human control and is constrained from free movement into a new area. An example of this would be an animal (say wild boar, beaver or prairie dogs) held within an enclosure from which it cannot escape. An offence is complete when a person allows an animal to escape from captivity to a place outwith its native range.

Allowing a non-native animal to escape from captivity will include situations where steps are not taken to ensure the animal is contained. For example, not repairing a hole in the fence of an enclosure, or releasing the animal to an enclosure which is not of a sufficient specification to keep that animal contained.

A person should take all reasonable steps and exercise all due diligence to avoid committing an offence when he or she is responsible for a non-native animal. For example, if the person introduces an animal into an enclosure outwith its native range, the enclosure is of a suitable specification to prevent escape and evidence can be provided that its security is inspected and maintained on a regular basis, it is reasonable to conclude that all due diligence has been exercised. This would include taking steps to prevent damage to the enclosure, for example, in the case of a storm blowing down nearby trees. If a tree had damaged the enclosure, despite the person taking all reasonable steps to avoid this happening, and no action had been taken within a reasonable timescale to repair it to a suitable standard, then it may be difficult to show that all reasonable steps had been taken and due diligence exercised.

Subsection (1) does not apply to the common pheasant and red-legged partridge where those animals are released or allowed to escape from captivity for the purpose of being subsequently killed by shooting. (s. 14(2A) WCA)

The offence at subsection (1)(b) applies where an animal that is *not* in captivity for the purposes of section 14(1) is enabled by some act or omission to move to a new place outwith its native range. An example might be a non-native sea squirt that becomes attached to the bottom of a person's boat before it arrives in Scotland. It is not 'in captivity', however, whilst the sea squirt may have been outwith the person's control, by moving the boat that action will have caused the sea squirt to be at a place outwith its native range. The boat owner should have followed good practice advice regarding antifouling and regular haul-out of the boat, thereby taking reasonable steps and exercising all due diligence to avoid committing the offence. If the person scrapes that sea squirt off the boat and washes it into the harbour in Scottish waters, that action will have caused it to be at a place outwith its native range. In addition, moving that boat from the harbour to another area while the sea squirt is still attached to it would move the sea squirt to other locations and may constitute a further offence.

When someone is moving equipment, or substances such as soil or water, which may contain animals or plant material, it is important that they assess whether species are likely to be present which would be outwith their native range at the intended destination. They must take all reasonable steps and exercise all due diligence to avoid committing the offence of causing the animals or plant material to be at a place outwith its native range. For example:

Moving Water

A company pumping water for the purpose of a hydroelectric scheme between catchments should take steps to establish if the source catchment is known to contain fish which would be outwith their native range in the new catchment. If so the company should take steps (such as screening agreed with appropriate experts) to prevent those fish being moved to the new catchment and therefore being caused to be at another place outwith their native range.

Moving Soil

A company moving materials such as soil that contains animals should follow good practice guidance such as that found in the Environment and Efficiency section of www.business.scotland.gov.uk In addition, they should follow the guidance outlined in the Code of Practice to Prevent the Spread of Non-Indigenous Flatworms to ensure that non-native flatworms (such as the New Zealand flatworm) and flatworm eggs are not transported to new areas.

The Wildlife and Countryside Act 1981 (Keeping and Release and Notification Requirements) (Scotland) Order 2012

This Order, commenced on 2 April 2012 to facilitate the operation and enforcement of section 14 of the 1981 Act, makes provision about the release of certain animals, the keeping of invasive animals and notification requirements in relation to the presence of invasive animals under the Wildlife and Countryside Act 1981 as amended by the Wildlife and Natural Environment (Scotland) Act 2011.

Part 1 of Schedule 1 of the Order lists the types of animals specified for the purposes of section 14(1)(a)(ii) of the 1981 Act (types of animal which it is an offence for a person to release or allow to escape from captivity). At present only deer of any species are listed on Part 1, the offence being to release them or allow them to escape to the Outer Hebrides and the islands of Arran (including Holy Island), Islay, Jura and Rum.

In relation to Part 2 of Schedule 1 the types of invasive animals are specified for the purposes of section 14ZC(1)(a) of the 1981 Act. (See Appendix E for complete list).

Section 14(2)

Subject to the provisions of Part I of the Act, any person who plants, or otherwise causes to grow, any plant in the wild at a place outwith its native range is guilty of an offence.

· To 'plant' is an easily recognised term and includes placing or setting seeds, seedlings or plants (or parts of plants) into a medium from which they can grow. This includes placing an aquatic plant (or propagating parts of that plant) into water.

To 'otherwise cause to grow' may include throwing cuttings of plants which would come in to the category of 'being out of their native range,' or complete plants of this type which have been weeded out of a garden or pond, over the fence into woodland or dumping them in the countryside where they take root. If a non-native plant is planted in a garden in such a way that it spreads into the wild that will also be an offence. The essence of the offence is that the non-native species, as a direct result of someone else's actions, finish up growing unwanted on someone else's land. Bear in mind that the approach is one of creating a presumption against any release.

'In the wild' is not defined in the Act, however the Code sets out that the term encompasses both natural and semi-natural habitats in both rural and urban environments. Examples of habitats *not* 'in the wild' are allotments and private gardens, burial grounds, amenity locations, agricultural and horticultural land, including reseeded grassland, and roadside verges and railway embankments in a built-up area (elsewhere, verges and embankments are wild). Although it is not an offence to plant or cause a non-native plant species to grow in these areas, it can be an offence to permit a non-native plant species to spread from such an area into the wild.

A company moving materials such as soil that contains or may contain plants should follow good practice guidance (in the Environment and Efficiency section of www.business.scotland.gov.uk); otherwise they could be responsible for a plant contained within the material spreading to a new location outwith its native range.

It is a defence to a charge of committing an offence under section 14(1) or (2) for an accused person to show that he or she took all reasonable steps and exercised all due diligence to avoid committing the offence (s. 14(3) WCA). However where this defence involves an allegation that the offence was due to the act or default of another person, the person charged shall not, without leave of the court, be entitled to rely on the defence unless, within a period ending seven clear days before the hearing, he has served on the prosecutor a notice giving such information identifying or assisting in the identification of that person.

Wildlife and Countryside Act 1981 (Exceptions to section 14) (Scotland) Order 2012

This Order, commenced on 2 April 2012, facilitates the operation and enforcement of section 14 of the 1981 Act. Part 1 and Part 2 of the schedule to this Order specifies the types of animal and the types of plant to which the offence provisions in section 14(1)(a)(i) and 14(2) of the Wildlife and Countryside Act 1981 do not apply, thereby taking them outwith the ambit of an offence. (See Appendix F for complete list)

Part 1 is extremely brief, and permits the release of fish caught by rod and line, though only if released at the same location as they were caught and on the same day. Part 2 comprises a substantial list of trees and plants that are exempt from the section 14.

Section 14 ZC – Prohibition on keeping etc. of invasive non-native animals or plants

Note that subsections 14ZC to 14B now deal with **invasive** animals or plants rather than **certain** animals or plants.

'Invasive' is defined as being an animal or plant which, if out of control of the person, would be likely to have an adverse affect on biodiversity, environmental interest or social or economic interests. However offences under this section are only created in respect of those species on lists made by Scottish Ministers.

Section 14ZC(1) *Subject to the provisions of this Part, any person who keeps, has in the person's possession, or has under the person's control –*

  (a) any invasive animal of a type which the Scottish Ministers, by order, specify;
  or

  (b) any invasive plant of a type so specified,

  is guilty of an offence.

Section 14ZC (1) (a) of the 1981 Act makes it an offence for any person to keep, have in the his possession, or under the his control any invasive animal of a type listed in Part 2 of Schedule 1 of the Wildlife and Countryside Act 1981 (Keeping and Release and Notification Requirements) (Scotland) Order 2012. Interestingly this list includes a grey squirrel. The wording of the defence below may just about permit a person to have one 'under his control' in a live catch trap until it can be killed, provided that is done as soon as possible.

It is a defence to a charge of committing an offence under subsection (1) to show that the accused took all reasonable steps and exercised all due diligence to avoid committing the offence (s. 14ZC(3) WCA). However where this defence involves an allegation that the offence was due to the act or default of another person, the person charged shall not, without leave of the court, be entitled to rely on the defence unless, within a period ending seven clear days before the hearing, he has served on the prosecutor a notice giving such information identifying or assisting in the identification of that person. (s. 14ZC(4) WCA)

Section 14A – Prohibition on sale etc. of invasive animals or plants

Section 14A (1) *This section applies to –*

  (a) any type of invasive animal; or

  (b) any type of invasive plant,

  the Scottish Ministers, by order, specify.

Section 14A (2)

Subject to the provisions of this Part, any person who –

> *(a) sells, offers or exposes for sale or has in the person's possession or transports for the purpose of sale any animal or plant to which this section applies; or*
>
> *(b) publishes or causes to be published any advertisement likely to be understood as conveying that the person buys or sells, or intends to buy or sell, any such animal or plant,*
>
> *is guilty of an offence.*

Section 14B – Notification of presence of certain invasive non-native animals or plants etc.

Section 14B enables the Scottish Ministers to make provision about the notification of the presence of invasive animals and plants at any specified place outwith their native range where persons are, or become, aware of the presence of such animals or plants.

Article 4 and Part 3 of Schedule 1 of the Wildlife and Countryside Act 1981 (Keeping and Release and Notification Requirements) (Scotland) Order 2012 lists the relevant invasive species (meantime only mammals – coypu, muskrat, muntjac, rabbit (other than European rabbit)). Where an occupier of land is, or becomes, aware of the presence of an invasive animal of a type listed in Part this Schedule, that person must notify Scottish Natural Heritage without delay. Failure to do is an offence. (s 14B(4))

Section 14P – Interpretations:

Section 14P (1) *This section applies to sections 14 to 14O only.*

Section 14P (2) *Any reference to the native range of an animal or plant, or a type of animal or plant, is a reference to the locality to which the animal or plant of that type is indigenous, and does not refer to any locality to which that type of animal or plant has been imported (whether intentionally or otherwise) by any person.*

Section 14P(3) *The native range of a hybrid animal or plant is any locality within the native range of both parents of the hybrid animal or plant.*

Section 14P(4) *Any reference to an invasive animal or invasive plant, or type of such an animal or plant, is a reference to an animal or plant of a type which if not under the control of any person, would be likely to have a significant adverse impact on –*

> *(a) biodiversity;*
>
> *(b) other environmental interests; or*
>
> *(c) social or economic interests.*

Section 14P (5) *Any reference to premises –*

(a) includes reference to land (including lockfast places and other buildings), movable structures, vehicles, vessels, aircraft and other means of transport; but

(b) does not include reference to dwellings.

Section 14P (6)*Any reference to a relevant body is a reference to –*

(a) the Scottish Ministers;

(b) Scottish Natural Heritage;

(c) the Scottish Environment Protection Agency; or

(d) the Forestry Commissioners.

Section 14P(7) *Any reference to an animal includes a reference to ova, semen and milt of the animal.*

Section 14P(8) *'Plant' includes fungi and any reference to a plant includes a reference to –*

(a) bulbs, corms and rhizomes of the plant; and

(b) notwithstanding section 27(3ZA), seeds and spores of the plant.

The re-vamped section 14 of the Act, though at first glance complex, should be much more straightforward for police officers to enforce. The clear difficulties in the past have been to prove that species have been released 'into the wild,' or that they are not 'ordinarily resident in Great Britain'.

Dealing with animals rather than plants, and taking as an example a current (2012) issue in certain parts of Scotland where escapee beavers exist outwith the official Knapdale trial area, section 14(1) would now appear to be suited to deal with any new releases or escapees. Looking at the elements of the offence, bearing in mind the principle of section 14 is now the presumption against release, and assuming there is evidence that a person *released or allowed beavers to escape from captivity* they would then be existing in *a place outwith their native range;* their native range (assuming they are European rather than North American) currently being continental Europe.

Proof of the species involved may come from dead specimens, photographs/video footage or evidence from an expert of distinct and unique traces of their presence. In relation to plants, consideration could be given to photographing/videoing them, then drying and retaining them.

There will be few investigations under this section where assistance or advice will not be required, at least in the initial stages, from Scottish Natural Heritage. Experts there will be able to advise on common species and of their native range. Other organisations that may be able to assist, depending on the species and circumstances involved, could be SASA, The Royal Zoological Society of Scotland (RZSS), the National Museum of Scotland, Royal Botanical Garden, Edinburgh, RBG, Kew or local council zoo and dangerous wild animal licensing officers.

The habitat leads (SNH, Marine Scotland, SEPA and Forestry Commission Scotland) all have information on their websites however queries should be directed to SEARS (Scottish Environment and Rural Services) in the first instance:

24/7 Customer service telephone number: 08452 30 20 50

Email: info@sears.scotland.gsi.uk

10. The Conservation (Natural Habitats etc) Regulations 1994

THESE REGULATIONS make provision for the purpose of implementing, for Great Britain, Council Directive 92/43/EEC (the 'Habitats Directive') on the conservation of natural habitats and wild fauna and flora. The regulations, colloquially referred to as the Habitats Regulations, are lengthy and complex and only the most likely breaches of the regulations are covered here.

Animal and plant species of Community interest (i.e. endangered, vulnerable, rare or endemic in the European Community) and in need of strict protection are listed on Annex IV of the Habitats Directive. They are protected from taking, killing or disturbance or the destruction of their habitat. Schedule 2 of the Habitats Regulations lists the UK animal species on Annex IV. They are referred to as European Protected Species (EPS). Some species formerly on Schedule 5 of the Wildlife and Countryside Act 1981, which also lists threatened animal species, were removed from that Schedule in 2007 and are now listed on Schedule 2 of the Habitats Regulations, which gives them additional protection. The list includes all species of bat (see Bats p108), all species of whale, dolphin and porpoise (see Cetaceans, p112), large blue butterfly, wildcat, dormouse, sand lizard, great-crested newt, otter, smooth snake, sturgeon, natterjack toad and marine turtles.

Summarising the complex regulations, it is an offence in Scotland, in relation to EPS, to:

Reg 39 (Schedule 2 species)
- Deliberately or recklessly capture, injure, kill or harass a wild animal of EPS.
- From 1 May 2007 possess or control, or transport, sell or exchange or offer to sell or exchange, any live or dead EPS (or part thereof or anything derived from) taken in the wild in the EU since the date of implementation of the Habitats Directive, 10 June 1994, except under licence.

Prior to the Conservation (Natural Habitats etc) Amendment (Scotland) Regulations 2007 coming into force, it was lawful to take dead specimens of EPS where it could be shown that the animal had died from natural causes or by accident and it is not an offence to possess these, though if they were obtained *after 1994* a licence should have been obtained from the Scottish

Government (though the licensing authority from mid 2011 changed to Scottish Natural Heritage). The most common breach of the law now is the picking up of a road-killed otter or wildcat for taxidermy purposes.

It is not an offence to have in your possession, *but not for the purpose of sale or exchange,* any EPS that was taken lawfully from a member state either prior to the implementation of the Habitats Directive in 1994 or from a non-EU country or territory without contravention of the laws of that country or territory.

- Deliberately or recklessly disturb a wild animal of EPS while it is occupying a structure or place which it uses for shelter or protection; to obstruct access to its breeding site or resting place, or otherwise to deny the animal the use of the breeding place or resting site, or to damage or destroy that breeding site or resting place
- Disturb a wild animal of EPS while it is rearing or caring for its young; or in a manner that is, or in circumstances which are, likely to significantly affect the local distribution or abundance of the species to which it belongs; or in a manner that is, or in circumstances which are, likely to impair its ability to survive, breed or reproduce, or rear or otherwise care for its young.

Reg 41 (Schedule 3 species)

The Habitats Regulations prohibit killing or taking species listed on Schedule 3 of the regulations by certain methods (reg 41(1)). Note that the words 'deliberately' or 'intentionally' are not used, nor required, in this regulation. Schedule 3 includes mountain hare, pine marten, polecat, common and grey seal. The prohibited methods include the use of tape recorders, artificial light sources or other devices for illuminating targets, explosives, nets or traps which are non-selective according to their principle or conditions of use, poisons, crossbows and semi-automatic or automatic weapons capable of holding more than 2 rounds of ammunition.

It should be noted that under the provisions of the Wildlife and Natural Environment (Scotland) Act 2011, the pine marten and polecat were removed from Schedule 6 of the Wildlife and Countryside Act since it was considered that they had sufficient protection under Schedule 3 of the Habitats Regulations.

Schedule 7 to the Wildlife and Countryside Act now allows 'hares' to be shot at night. Hares are not defined, and under Regulation 41(d) to (g) of these Regulations it is an offence to take or kill mammals in Schedule 3 by any sort of artificial light source. This would mean that night shooting of mountain hares, Schedule 3 mammals, remains unlawful unless using natural light. (see section 12YA and Schedule 7 of the Wildlife and Countryside Act 1981 – p268)

Reg 43 (Schedule 4 plants)

Schedule 4 of the Habitats Regulations lists the European Protected Species of plants. Those found in Scotland are Killarney fern, slender naiad, floating leaved water plantain, and yellow marsh saxifrage. It is an offence in relation Schedule 4 plants to intentionally or recklessly pick, collect, cut, uproot or destroy such a plant or anything derived from it; possess specimens of these plants or derivatives of them, or to sell, exchange or offer for sale or exchange these plants or derivatives of them.

Police powers

See Police Powers under Other Legislation where the powers are identical to those under the Wildlife and Countryside Act 1981 – p20

Specific offences against bats (see Wild mammals – Bats p108)

Specific offences against cetaceans (see Wild mammals – Cetaceans p112)

11. Illegal Trade in Endangered Species (COTES)

OFFENCES in relation to the illegal trade in endangered species are covered by the Control of Trade in Endangered Species (Enforcement) Regulations 1997, as amended by the Control of Trade in Endangered Species (Enforcement) (Amendment) Regulations 2005 and 2009. Given this title, it is not surprising that the regulations are normally referred to as COTES.

In recent times, the public has become increasingly aware of the importance of preventing further loss of endangered wildlife and preserving our remaining biodiversity. After habitat destruction, illegal trade and conservation offences are among the most significant risks faced by endangered species. Wildlife trade offenders have been shown to be involved in other types of crime, working independently or as part of organised networks.

The Convention on the International Trade in Endangered Species of Wild Fauna and Flora (CITES), regulates *legal* international trade in endangered species and is implemented through European and domestic legislation.

European Council Regulation 338/97 (as amended) and Commission Regulation 865/2006 on the protection of species of wild fauna and flora incorporate all of the provisions of CITES as well as additional stricter measures concerning European species and stricter import, housing, and transport conditions for live specimens. The specific implementing offences for violations of the EU Regulations are contained in provisions in the Customs and Excise Management Act 1979 (CEMA) and in the Control of Trade in Endangered Species (Enforcement) Regulations 1997 (COTES). The general CEMA provisions are used to cover the illegal import and export of CITES species, an 'assigned matter' for the UK Border Agency. COTES is the national legislation which covers trade offences once the species has entered the UK. The statutory enforcers are the police.

The CITES Regulations list species of conservation concern in one of four annexes, depending on the extent to which they are endangered by trade. Species of greatest concern are listed in Annex A and are critically endangered by trade. No *wild-caught* animal or plant taken from the wild that is listed in Annex A is allowed in commercial trade. Annex A specimens are also prohibited from being sold or purchased in EU countries unless an exemption certificate (Article 10) has been issued. *Legal trade in Annex A specimens can only be carried out if the specimens are either captive-bred or artificially propagated.* In addition, captive-bred animals must be accompanied by an Article 10 certificate issued by Animal Health, Defra.

So what is the overall impact of the crime? Consideration needs to be given to both the environmental and economic impact. Some species, though on the same Annex, are much rarer than others. The tiger in Asia, for example, is more at risk of extinction than the elephant. On a more local scale the golden eagle and the common buzzard are both Annex A, yet there is no question that the golden eagle is by far the rarer of the two. When cases are reported for prosecution the investigating officer would probably consider the following two factors and, where relevant, obtain an impact assessment for the procurator fiscal:

- Environmental impact: Loss of threatened or endangered species or their habitat; the habitat loss may be irreplaceable.
- Economic impact: Costs of protecting endangered wildlife; effect on income-generating schemes for local communities; loss of revenue for eco-tourism; loss of revenue because of threatened species protection.

Offences

The main offences are:

- Knowingly or recklessly making a false statement for the purpose of obtaining a permit (Reg 3(1)).
- Knowingly or recklessly making a false import notification (Reg 3(2)).
- Knowingly falsifying or altering any permit or certificate (Reg 4(1)).
- Knowingly using a permit, certificate or import notification for any specimen other than that for which it was issued (Reg 4(2)).
- Knowingly using a specimen of a species listed in Annex A of the Principal Regulation otherwise than in accordance with the authorisation given at the time of issue of the import permit or subsequently (Reg 4(3)).
- Knowingly contravening any condition or requirement of a permit or certificate (Reg 6).
- Where an import permit or any certificate in respect of a live specimen of a species listed in Annex A specifies an address at which the specimen must be kept, it is an offence without reasonable excuse, to cause or permit that specimen to be transferred from that address without prior written authorisation from the Secretary of State; or to

keep that specimen at premises other than the specified address or location without prior written authorisation from the Secretary of State (Reg 7).

* To purchase, offer to purchase, acquire for commercial purposes, display to the public for commercial purposes, use for commercial gain, sell, keep for sale, offer for sale or transport for sale, any Annex A specimen without having an Article 10 certificate (Reg 8(1)).

* To offer to purchase, acquire for commercial purposes, sell, keep for sale, offer for sale or transport for sale, any Annex B specimen which has been imported or acquired unlawfully (Reg 8(2)).

(There are safeguards in relation to offences under Regulation 8 if the person proves that at the time the alleged offence was committed he had no reason to believe that the specimen was a specimen of a species listed in Annex A, or as the case may be Annex B, and in relation to Regulation 8(2) if at the time when the specimen first came into his possession he made such enquiries as in the circumstances were reasonable in order to ascertain whether it was imported or acquired unlawfully; and that at the time the alleged offence was committed, he had no reason to believe that the specimen was imported or acquired unlawfully.)

Split listed specimen (Reg 8A) – presumption in favour of Annex A
In 2007 a court case was brought against a trader of traditional Asian medicines on ten counts of offering for sale specimens of controlled species contrary to regulation 8 of the COTES Regulations. The indictment related to traditional Asian medicines claiming to contain ingredients derived from endangered species, namely musk deer, bear and orchids. The major defect with the case concerned species that, in different countries, are not always listed in the same Annex, in other words one country may list the species on Annex A, while in another country it is on Annex B, making it a 'split-listed' species. Unless its origin is known, it is therefore not always possible to determine whether a particular split-listed specimen derives from a species (or subspecies or geographical population) listed in Annex A or one listed in Annex B. In the 2007 case this resulted in the failure of the prosecution, because in order to prove the relevant offences in the COTES Regulations it was necessary to prove the Annex from which the specimen derived. This new regulation made under the Control of Trade in Endangered Species (Enforcement) Regulations 2009 introduces a presumption that, where it is not reasonably practicable to identify whether a specimen of a 'split-listed' species belongs to Annex A or B to the Principal Regulation, it shall belong to Annex A. This will enable

the prosecution to proceed with a charge under the offence in regulation 8(1).

Police powers
Regulation 9 – *Powers of entry*

(1) If, on an application made by a constable, a justice of the peace or sheriff is satisfied that there are reasonable grounds for believing—

(a) that there is any unlawfully imported or acquired specimen on premises specified in the application; or

(b) that an offence under these Regulations has been or is being committed and that evidence of the offence may be found on any premises, and that any of the conditions specified in paragraph (2) applies, he may issue a warrant authorising any constable to enter upon and search those premises; and such a warrant may authorise persons to accompany any constable who is executing it.

(2) The conditions referred to in paragraph (1) are –

(a) that admission to the premises has been refused; or

(b) that refusal is apprehended; or

(c) that the case is one of urgency; or

(d) that an application for admission to the premises would defeat the object of the entry.

In some investigations where a police officer is of the view that entry and search would be permitted without a warrant, he or she may dispense with the need for one. The conditions at (2) above are not normally a statutory requirement, though in a search warrant request under COTES one or more of these conditions must be shown to apply. Conditions (b), (c) or (d) are the most likely to be put forward in a search warrant request; if condition (a) is the position, and admission has been attempted but refused, by the time a warrant is granted it may be too late to recover the items sought.

Like a search warrant under some other wildlife legislation, a police officer may take individuals who are not police officers to give advice during the search.

(3) A constable who is, by virtue of paragraph (1), lawfully on any premises may, in order to determine the identity or ancestry of any specimen, require the taking from any specimen of a sample of blood or tissue provided that—

(a) the sample is taken by a registered veterinary surgeon; and

(b) the taking of such a sample will not cause lasting harm to the specimen.

In any search where it is anticipated that a blood sample may be required, the investigating officer should arrange the services of a suitable vet in advance, who should be aware of what is required and take the necessary equipment for the job. Ideally the vet should be experienced in working with the species at issue, should be able to satisfy the requirement at (b) above and should be aware that he or she may in due course have to attend court to give evidence.

(4) An authorised person may, at any reasonable time and (if required to do so) upon producing evidence that he is so authorised, enter and inspect any premises where he has reasonable cause to believe a specimen is being kept, for the purpose of –

(a) ascertaining whether the premises are being used for any of the following activities: purchase, offer to purchase, acquisition for commercial purposes, display to the public for commercial purposes, use for commercial gain, sale, keep for sale, offer for sale or transport for sale contrary to Article 8 of the Principal Regulation; or

(b) verifying information supplied by a person for the purpose of obtaining a permit or certificate; or

(c) ascertaining whether any live specimen is being kept on premises at the address specified in the import permit issued for that specimen as that at which the specimen is to be kept; or

(d) ascertaining whether any condition of a permit or certificate has been or is being observed.

An 'authorised person' is a person duly authorised in writing by the Secretary of State for the purposes of these Regulations, and will almost always be a wildlife inspector. The inspection may be by arrangement or unannounced. In cases where police officers are present the inspection will invariably be unannounced. Unless under warrant, there is no power for the police officer to enter, and entry should be by invitation of the owner or occupier of the premises. If the police officer requires to seize any item, and is not there under the terms of a search warrant, a search warrant may need to be sought (See Regulation 10)

(5) An authorised person who is, by virtue of paragraph (4), lawfully on any premises may, in order to determine the identity or ancestry of any specimen for the purposes specified in that paragraph, require the taking from any specimen of a sample of blood or tissue provided that –

(a) the sample is taken by a registered veterinary surgeon; and

(b) the taking of such a sample will not cause lasting harm to the specimen.

(6) Any person who intentionally obstructs an authorised person acting in accordance with the powers conferred by this regulation shall be guilty of an offence and shall for every such obstruction be liable on summary conviction to a fine not exceeding level 3 on the standard scale.

(7) If a person, with intent to deceive, pretends to be an authorised person, he shall be guilty of an offence and liable –

> *(a) on summary conviction, to a fine not exceeding level 5 on the standard scale, or to a term of imprisonment not exceeding three months, or to both; or*
>
> *(b) on conviction on indictment, to imprisonment for a term not exceeding two years or to a fine, or to both.*

Regulation 10 – Powers of seizure

A constable who is, by virtue of regulation 9(1) above, lawfully on any premises may seize any thing where he has reasonable grounds for believing that such seizure is –

> *(a) necessary for the protection of the constable or any person accompanying him; or*
>
> *(b) otherwise essential to effect seizure of the specimen referred to in that paragraph; or*
>
> *(c) necessary for the conservation of evidence; or*
>
> *(d) in the interests of the welfare of the specimen.*

Regulation 11 – Forfeiture

> *(1) The court by which any person is convicted of an offence under these Regulations –*
>
> *(a) shall order the forfeiture of any specimen or other thing in respect of which the offence was committed; and*
>
> *(b) may order the forfeiture of any vehicle, equipment or other thing which was used to commit the offence.*
>
> *(2) In paragraph (1)(b) 'vehicle' includes aircraft, hovercraft and boat.*

Power of arrest

There are **no** powers of arrest or detention directly within the COTES Regulations. However since 21 July 2005 a power of arrest exists which is fairly complex to trace back to its origin. The origin of the arrest power is as follows:

Section 307 of the Criminal Justice Act 2003 deals with enforcement regulations implementing European Community legislation on endangered species and at sub-section (1) defines 'the 1972 Act' as the European Communities Act 1972.

It also defines 'relevant Community instrument' as

> (a) Council Regulation 338/97/EC on the protection of species of wild fauna and flora by regulating trade therein, and
>
> (b) Commission Regulation 1808/01/EC on the implementation of the Council Regulation mentioned at (a)

Section 2(2) of the 1972 Act states, *inter alia*, 'subject to Schedule 2 to the Act, makes provision for the purpose of implementing any EU obligation to the United Kingdom, or enabling any such obligation to be implemented.'

Section 3(1) of the Criminal Justice Act 2003 (Commencement No.10 and the Saving Provisions) Order 2005 brought these arrest powers into force in Scotland on 21 July 2005.

Section 307(4) of the Criminal Justice Act 2003 states:
> In Scotland, a constable may arrest a person –
> (a) who has committed or attempted to commit an offence under regulations made under Section 2(2) of the 1972 Act for the purpose of implementing any relevant Community instrument, or
> (b) who he has reasonable grounds for suspecting to have committed or to have attempted to commit such an offence

As a custodial sentence is available for all of the offence listed above under COTES, detention by a police officer under Section 14 of the Criminal Procedure (Scotland) Act, 1995 is an option.

Wildlife and the Law: Frequently asked questions

THE FOLLOWING provides quick answers to some of the most regularly posed questions about Scottish wildlife law.

If I find an illegal trap or snare should I leave it set?
If an illegal trap or snare has been set, leaving it in that state could well result in a bird or mammal being caught. Birds will invariably be caught during daylight while mammals will mostly be caught at night. This should be taken into consideration if the witness has to leave the scene before the police arrive. If the trap is a live-catch trap, the bird can be released by the police when they attend. Bear in mind that if the trap is removed or sprung by a lone witness, then there is no corroboration that it was ever set, though this should not over-ride the welfare of wildlife.

What should I do if I find a buzzard in a crow cage trap?
Firstly, if a decoy bird (usually a carrion crow) is used in a crow cage, which is the case around 90% of the time, then it must have food, water, shelter and a suitable perch. This will also accommodate the welfare requirements of any bird caught. If a cage is set without a call bird, food is used to attract crows in to it, so there will be a food supply for any birds caught but no legal requirement for anything else. The cage must be checked at intervals of no more than 24 hours, so unless weather is extreme with heavy rain and wind, the birds caught will come to no harm (though it must be said that if a bird caught is kept away overlong from eggs or chicks they could chill). If a buzzard (or other non-target bird) has entered the trap the only way that you can get it out without the crows being released would be to catch it, (and of course risk getting injured by sharp talons) take it out of the trap and release it – all providing the trap isn't padlocked. It is important to bear in mind that unless there is evidence that the bird has been inside longer than 24 hours the trap operator is not committing an offence. To release the buzzard in this case

could be seen as interference, though probably not an offence since there would be no *mens rea* (criminal intent) involved. It is much better to either make contact with the trap operator, if he is known, or ask the police to do so, quoting the police code on the sign or tag on the trap. This would allow the WECO to easily trace who is using the trap and either (a) make telephone contact to have the buzzard released in advance of the normal checking time; or (b) meet the trap operator and visit the trap with him. If there are grounds to believe that an offence is being committed – no sign on trap; no food/water/shelter/perch; birds suspected of being in cage more than 24 hours; trap baited with domestic livestock such as hen or lamb carcass – then the police should be called. If this is the case the trap should be left as it is. If there is a welfare issue and the police cannot attend within a reasonable time, they should agree some alternative solution.

What should I do if I find a dead animal or bird in the countryside and I think it has been poisoned?
Most pesticides used to kill wildlife are extremely toxic to humans as well as to animals or birds, and anything suspected to be bait or the victim of poisoned bait should not be touched. A WECO should be contacted as soon as possible. If the bait or victim has to be left, covering it with branches or some other material may prevent any further birds – though not animals, which could find it through their sense of smell – being put in danger until the police can retrieve it. Though pesticide abuse still occurs, it must be borne in mind that many animals or birds die of natural causes or as the result of accidents.

Is it legal to chase hares with dogs?
It is completely illegal not only to deliberately chase hares with a dog or dogs but to attempt to do so, search for them for this purpose or even to be in possession of anything capable of being used to commit the offence, which could be a lurcher-type dog. It is important to report this type of incident to the police as soon as possible since anyone involved is normally away from the area within a short time. If a vehicle registration number can also be obtained, and also the type and colour of the dogs that is a good start to an investigation. One witness to this offence is sufficient to convict.

Is it an offence to open freshwater pearl mussels to see if there is a pearl inside?

Freshwater pearl mussels are completely protected and it is an offence even to lift live mussels off the river bed.

Is it an offence to keep a collection of wild birds' eggs?

If the eggs were taken before 1954 – and it is up to the person having the eggs to show that this is the case – no offence is committed in keeping the collection. It is, of course, an offence to take the eggs of any wild bird, or to sell any wild bird's egg, no matter when the egg was collected.

Is it an offence to keep a dead bird or animal killed on the road and have it stuffed?

In general it is an offence to possess a dead bird or a dead protected animal (for example a badger or pine marten as opposed to a rabbit or hare, which can legitimately be controlled in any case). However there is an exception if the person in possession of the protected animal or bird can show that it died or was killed other than as a result of a crime being committed against it (see next question for more detail). Road traffic victims would fall in to this category and could legally be kept and used in taxidermy. To be on the safe side it may be worth having the animal or bird examined by a vet, (though they may not always be able to tell how it died without opening it up) or reporting the find to a police wildlife crime officer. From 15 February 2007 dead otters and wildcats, since they are European Protected Species (EPS), may not be taken for taxidermy without a licence from Scottish Natural Heritage. Those already in someone's possession that were taken after 10 June 1994 must be registered with SNH.

I have found a dead barn owl by the roadside and would like to have it stuffed for my own use. Can I legally do this? I may wish to sell it later. Is this OK?

If you want to have this specimen mounted by a taxidermist you can simply commission a taxidermist to do this for you. Providing that you only use the specimen for your own personal use, no paperwork is required for this transaction. If you later wish to sell the stuffed bird or use it in any way commercially, you will need an Article 10 Certificate from Animal Health, Defra. In order to obtain this you will need to prove details of legal acquisition

145

from the wild and cause of death. This would include where and when the bird was found, who found it, the cause of death of the bird and which taxidermist mounted the bird. If you were not the finder of the bird you would require a signed letter from the finder stating that he or she gave it to you free of charge.

Is it legal to dig up wild plants?

All plants on Schedule 8 of the Wildlife and Countryside Act 1981 are protected. These are the rarest wild plants and it is an offence even to pick such a plant. The more common plants, such as bluebells, snowdrops and primroses may be dug up provided the landowner has given permission, though it is a specific offence to engage in any commercial trade in native wild bluebells (*Hyancinthoides non-scripta*).

Can I cut down a tree or a bush or demolish a building containing a bird's nest?

Spring and summer are the main nesting times for birds. It is an offence to damage or destroy a nest while it is being built or is in use if this is done intentionally or recklessly. To avoid any risk of committing an offence, checks should be made for active nests so far as this can reasonably be done. No-one expects trees to be climbed to ensure there are no nests in them. Once the bird has finished using the nest – remember some birds can have more than one clutch of eggs during the season – the nest can be removed and any work undertaken.

If I have bats in my loft what should I do?

In most cases bats and their human hosts live in harmony. It would do no harm to report their presence to the Bat Conservation Trust, Scottish Natural Heritage or to a member of a bat group for their records, as the bats may be one of the rarer species. Some bats come into lofts of houses to breed during the spring and leave again in autumn. If they pose problems during this time action must not be taken against them that would disturb them or obstruct, damage or destroy their roost. The person proposing any action can obtain advice from Scottish Natural Heritage and must first have a licence from SNH to carry out any action that otherwise would be an offence. Like the otter and the wild cat, all UK species of bats are European Protected Species (EPS) and have full protection under the Conservation (Natural Habitats etc) Regulations 1994. A licence must be obtained from SNH to keep a live bat, or any dead bats taken after 10 June 1994.

I have found a wild peregrine which is injured. What should I do with it?
Provided it was not you who caused deliberate injury to the bird you can take it solely for the purpose of it being tended and released it when it is no longer disabled. The bird should be placed with someone who has experience in tending injured wild birds and ensuring their successful release. Many disabled and injured birds will require treatment by an avian vet. Your WECO should be able to help direct you to a suitable falconer or rehabilitator. The person tending the bird must then register the bird with the Bird Registration team at Animal Health, Defra, and its progress may be monitored by an Animal Health wildlife inspector.

Do I need any kind of licence to hunt birds and rabbits with my bird of prey?
You don't require any form of licence to hunt rabbits with your bird of prey, though you must have the landowner's permission. Certain species of wild birds may also be hunted for the purposes of falconry but for this you will require a Quarry Licence obtainable from Scottish Natural Heritage. If a falconer with an English address wants to fly his raptor at quarry birds in Scotland he should also apply to Scottish Natural Heritage for a Quarry Licence.

There is a parrot advertised on the internet which I wish to purchase. The seller stated he is local and gave a mobile telephone number. What do I need to know to ensure I stay within the law and that I am not ripped off?
First you need to ascertain the species and whether it is listed under CITES. If the bird is on Annex A you need to check whether the seller has the correct paperwork to allow the sale. If the bird originated outside the EU can the seller prove legal import? If it was bred in captivity within the EU can this be proved? Lastly, you should go to the seller's house to see the parrot, and not agree to meet in a car park or other such venue. Because his/her address is then identifiable this is less likely to lead to an illegal sale.

I have a young Hermann's tortoise that I no longer want and my friend would like to buy it. Can I sell it?

The Hermann's tortoise is on Annex A. If the plastron (the bony plate on the underside) exceeds 100 mm in length then the tortoise requires to be microchipped before sale. In any case you will need to apply to Animal Health, Defra, for an Article 10 certificate before sale. This is likely to be a transaction-specific certificate if the tortoise is under 100 mm, which you must show to the buyer or pass on a photocopy. With a microchipped tortoise you are likely to receive a specimen-specific certificate which you must pass on to the buyer, as this is the tortoise's 'passport'.

I want to display my Bengal eagle owl at a local fair and have been told I need to apply for an Article 10 certificate as the bird is Annex A. Is this correct?

The Bengal eagle owl (*Bubo bubo bengalensis*) is on Annex B and you do not require an A10.

A friend of mine has a stuffed leopard that until it died recently was a zoo animal. Is this legal?

Despite the leopard being on Annex A, it is legal to possess a taxidermied specimen provided it had been obtained legally and there is documentary evidence to this effect (an A10 or proof the specimen was gifted). To display it to the public or to sell it on requires an Article 10 certificate.

When cleaning out the attic I found a stuffed tiger head which I would like to sell. What paperwork would I need?

If it is pre 1947 (and this is up to you to establish) you would not need a licence to sell it. If it is not, then you wouldn't be allowed to sell it without first having obtained an Article 10 certificate.

I recently bought a stuffed golden eagle at a local auction. The auctioneer said the bird had been obtained before 1947 and I wouldn't need what he called an Article 10 certificate. Is this right?

If that is the case that is correct. If it turns out not to have been the case then the person selling the specimen has broken the law.

A friend gave me a buzzard that he recently shot by accident. Can I have it stuffed?
The fact it was shot, whether accidentally or otherwise, makes its possession illegal. You should either contact the police or get rid of the bird.

I saw a rhino horn on a base at a recent auction sale. Can this legally be sold?
Since 18 February 2011 the sale of rhino horn mounted on a base or a plaque has been illegal

Since these regulations are complex, to try to clarify the provisions in relation to keeping specimens of Annex IV animals, here are some questions which might be asked by owners or potential owners of specimens:

In 1997 I found a dead otter by the roadside and had it stuffed. It now sits in my living room. Is it an offence for me to keep this otter?
Yes. You took it after the 10 June 1994, so it does not qualify as a lawfully taken specimen. However, you may be able to get a licence from Scottish Natural Heritage to keep this specimen if you can provide details of how it was found and the purpose for which you require it.

Our school has a collection of 5 stuffed bats, 2 natterjack toads preserved in alcohol, and the skin of a Scottish wildcat. These were all found dead in Scotland, between 1990 and 2005. Do we need a licence?
For the specimens taken prior to 10 June 1994, you don't need a licence, provided they were not taken in contravention of the laws of Scotland at the time. You will need a licence for specimens taken after this date. As the licences are for educational purposes they are likely to be granted.

I have inherited a stuffed otter. Can I sell it?
No. It is an offence to sell any European Protected Species without an Article 10 certificate. Furthermore, if it was taken after 10 June 1994, you will require a licence to keep the specimen.

I run a small museum which includes 2 stuffed specimens of lynx. Both were taken from the wild. One of these was purchased from the Spanish wildlife authorities in 2002. It had been run over by car. The other was a Eurasian lynx taken from Estonia in the same year. It had also died an accidental death and was given as a gift to the museum by a wildlife charity. Do I need licences for these specimens?

You will certainly need to apply for a licence to keep the lynx taken from Spain, as it was taken after 10 June 1994. However, the Estonian Lynx is from an excluded population, and therefore may not require to be licensed. However, you should be satisfied that the lynx was taken in accordance of the laws of Estonia at the time. Otherwise you may be committing an offence.

Occasionally I find dead otters by the roadside near my house. I move them into the bushes so that they don't prove an environmental hazard. Is this OK?

Moving dead European Protected Species for such purposes is not an offence. But it would be an offence if you decided to keep the specimens or parts of the specimens.

12. Taxidermy, and Trade in, or Commercial Use of CITES Specimens

TAXIDERMY is a trade practised professionally in the UK by up to 200 full time taxidermists, including a small number working for national or larger private museums, and many more on an amateur basis.

Legal trade in animals or their derivatives is a huge business, with specimens for the taxidermy market playing its part. Whether an exotic species or one that is indigenous to the British Isles, controls are firmly in place to monitor the trade or movement in any creature (or plant) deemed to be endangered in any way. This is done by way of licensing systems run internationally by the management authorities of the majority of countries in the world. To operate legally any person trading in a protected species must do so within the regulations set out to control such trade.

Whatever law or regulation is used, the criteria are the same UK-wide. A taxidermist or dealer *must* follow four golden rules:

1) Any specimen must be legally obtained.
2) All protected specimens (species) must be logged with full details of acquisition, and tagged.
3) Licences must be obtained where applicable to sell, hire, barter, exchange or make commercial gain.
4) Proof of legality must be given to the buyer at the point of sale – usually by way of a label giving details.

CITES

CITES (The Convention on International Trade in Endangered Species of fauna & flora), is the international system for monitoring trade or movement in certain higher profile or endangered species of wildlife. Species are listed in one of three Appendices, depending on the degree of protection or monitoring which is deemed necessary.

- Appendix I includes obvious species such as tiger and the majority of big cats; rhino; elephant; rare macaws and parrots
- Appendix II includes many birds of prey (including those found in the UK, and the African lion – the only big cat currently not on App I).

* Appendix III includes some species of duck, eg. teal

Permits for international movement are granted when it can be proved that the specimen has been legally obtained. There is generally no distinction between a wild specimen and one that is captive bred in a zoo: permits are required for either. A full classified list can be found on the CITES database on www.cites.org

International movement of these specimens will require export documents from the country of origin and import documents for the country receiving the specimen. It is therefore always worth checking when a taxidermist is in possession of such a specimen, that he or she has either the relevant import/export documents if from abroad, or that the log book shows it has been received from a zoo within the UK or Europe. If received from a zoo, details of the seller's Article 10 certificate should be noted unless it was a gift.

EC Regulations

EC Regulation 338/97 and EC Commission Regulation EC865/2006

For movement and trade within the European Union, CITES is administered by Council Regulation EC338/97 and Commission Regulation EC865/2006. Basically the EU has re-written CITES and in some cases added stricter control for use within its own borders. A UK-based taxidermist/dealer therefore should abide by EC Regulations and will only get involved with CITES proper when trading with a country outside of the EU.

EC Reg 338/97 has taken the Appendices of CITES and re-listed them in one of four 'Annexes'. All CITES App I and some of App II are listed under Annex A and so on down the line to Annex D. Unless dealing outside of Europe the only Annex that affects UK taxidermists/dealers is Annex A.

EC Reg 865/2006 dictates how 338/97 is administered and confirms among other things the licensing requirements for species listed under Annex A. The enforcement tool in the UK, as it is with CITES itself, is the Control of Trade in Endangered Species Regulations 1997 (COTES).

Article 10 certificates

The certificates, often referred to as Article 10 licences or A10s, are issued by Animal Health, Defra (or another EU state Management Authority). The certificate is only required if specimens are to be used for commercial purposes. An A10 is not required simply to possess an Annex A CITES specimen or to give it away.

Trade or any commercial gain in a species listed on Annex A requires an individual (one for each specimen) Article 10 certificate that has been issued to the seller. It is illegal to make a commercial gain on such a specimen without a licence *and although the seller's licence covers the purchaser, it is also illegal to purchase a specimen without the seller having an Article 10 certificate (COTES Reg 8).*

There are three exemptions to this ruling and they are:
1) Any specimen mounted prior to 1 June 1947, which is considered an 'antique' and requires no licence (even a tiger).
2) Any specimen that is being prepared by the taxidermist for the owner of that specimen (a commission) does not require a licence.
3) Any specimen given or received as a gift (without commercial gain) requires no licence.

A taxidermist/dealer should, *upon receipt of a listed species or soon after,* apply for an Article 10 certificate for each specimen. This licence allows the named person to sell, offer for sale, transport for sale, display, hire, exchange, barter and keep for commercial gain.

There are two types of Article 10 certificates:
* The transaction certificate. This is a licence that will state what it may be used for. If for a sale, it will cover one trade only by the person named on it and from the address shown. In some cases the licence may only allow educational display and/or breeding, but not sale. This is the usual type of licence taxidermists go for as it covers them for keeping for sale as well as for the sale itself. Legally the taxidermist is not required to pass the licence on to the buyer. It may even confuse the buyer into thinking it will allow him or her to sell on using the same document. If the buyer wishes to sell on, he or she must apply for another transaction licence. Of course the buyer must be sure that the taxidermist has a licence in the first place so it is a legal requirement for the seller to either show the licence, give a photocopy or list the number on the 'proof of legality' label

* The specimen-specific certificate. This is the passport-type licence that stays with the specimen for its tradable life. *It is a legal requirement for the taxidermist or the seller to pass this type of licence on to the buyer.*

Specimen-specific certificates will only be issued if one or more of the following conditions are met:

- The specimens must have been introduced into the European Union when the conditions relating to species listed in Annex A or in Appendix I to the Convention or in Annex C1 to Regulation EC 362/82 did not apply to them.
- The specimens must have been born and bred in captivity. Captive breeding can be more complex than just breeding in a cage, aviary or enclosure. Animal Health will confirm whether a specimen would be considered to be captive bred.
- The specimens are 'worked' taxidermy specimens which were taken from the wild in the UK in line with domestic legislation.
- The specimens must be uniquely and permanently marked. A live specimen may be marked with a microchip. Taxidermy specimens can also be permanently marked with a microchip transponder encased in resin (or any other similar material) in the skull cavity.

'Worked' and 'Unworked' specimens

An Article 10 certificate is not required to sell Annex A worked specimens acquired before 1947. Specimens are defined as 'worked' for CITES purposes if the specimen was made before 1 June 1947 and no further work has been carried out in it since that date. Specimens obtained before this date but which are not substantially altered from their natural state do not qualify for this exemption.

Rhino horn and elephant ivory

Rhino or elephant ivory products are sometimes offered for sale at auction. For rhino horn, worked would include a taxidermied rhino head including horn(s), mounted or un-mounted, or rhino horn carved or fashioned into a complete and identifiable artistic or utility object. Unworked would include a rhino horn mounted on a plaque, shield or other type of base for wall hanging; rhino horn removed from a plaque, shield or other type of base, or rhino horn with minimal or rudimentary carving.

For elephant ivory *antique* worked specimens of ivory acquired in their finished worked state before 1 June 1947 are covered by the antiques derogation (Article 62(3) of EC Regulation 865/2006) and may be used commercially without a certificate. Examples of ivory which may be considered to be 'worked' are ivory items made for jewellery, adornment, art, utility or musical instruments, including whole tusks where the surface has been carved. Unworked would include a whole uncarved elephant tusk or a whole polished elephant tusk.

The commercial use of any raw elephant ivory tusks or raw rhino horns is banned within the UK. All applications to Animal Health for Article 10 Certificates will be refused.

Domestic Legislation

Though the criteria governing the taxidermy trade under the Wildlife and Countryside Act 1981 is the same throughout the UK, since devolution, taxidermy issues under the Wildlife and Countryside Act by Scottish-based taxidermists/dealers are administered by the Scottish Government.

Birds

The Wildlife and Countryside Act was the first Act in the UK to require taxidermists and dealers in derivatives of protected species to register as such (s. 6(2)).

Since 1995 General Licences have permitted the trade. (see General Licence No 14 under Annual General Licences p251). Most bird species listed under the Wildlife and Countryside Act are therefore tradable under the general licence by anyone. A general licence does not actually need to be applied for or held. The criteria for this and any other licence is the same- specimens must be legally obtained; they must have full details of acquisition held in a log; they must be tagged; and proof of legality must be given at the point of sale.

A taxidermist in Scotland must also send in an annual return to the Scottish Government prior to 31st December each year advising what has been sold.

Mammals/reptiles/amphibians/insects/plants

The Wildlife and Countryside Act also protects some mammal/reptile/ amphibians/insects (and plant) species indigenous to the UK. For a taxidermist/dealer to trade in those species listed a Schedule 5 licence (for Scotland) is required at the point of sale. This is an individual licence granted by Scottish Natural Heritage which is usually issued on request and is required whatever the age of the specimen. This is unlike EC Regulations/CITES, which have a cut-off date for antiques.

In addition, from 1 May 2007 under the Conservation (Natural Habitats etc) Regulations 1994 it is an offence in Scotland to possess or control, or to transport, sell or exchange or offer to sell or exchange, any European Protected Species taken in the EU since the date of implementation of the Habitats Directive – 10 June 1994, except under licence from Scottish Natural Heritage. (see Offences under the Conservation (Natural Habitats etc) Regulations 1994 – p133)

The legal requirements of a taxidermist/dealer

As explained earlier, the various licences all list similar criteria resulting in the necessity to follow the four golden rules. These legal requirements need to be explained more fully to be of use to police officers when checking if a person is operating within the regulations.

1) Any specimen must be legally obtained

This is relatively self-explanatory. The specimen must not have been obtained as a result of committing an offence. Legal specimens are road-kills, birds that have flown into windows, specimens that have died naturally, etc.

2) All protected specimens (species) must be logged with full details of acquisition and tagged.

It is a legal requirement for anybody in possession of *protected* specimens to list certain details in either a log book or log sheet. Although many of the details may be necessary to obtain a licence, only (a), (b), (c) and (d) below are legal requirements. Most taxidermists will also get the donor to sign the sheet as a form of proof, although this is not a legal requirement.

a) Species (common name & scientific name)
b) Source of acquisition – name and address of donor/finder.
c) Date of acquisition;
d) Cause of death;
e) Date of death;
f) Place of death (if known) – nearest town, road number etc
g) If captive bred, parental details & hatch date.
h) Licence numbers (if known).
i) Was specimen given free of charge or was there a commercial transaction (to be included in log from 1 March, 2004)

Once the specimen is logged a reference number (Log No.) must be given to each specimen, written on the log sheet and a *tag with the same number attached to the specimen at all times.*

The Guild of Taxidermists recommends to its members that an individual log sheet be used for each specimen. This can then be stored in a ring binder and the appropriate licence (where necessary) can be stored with the log sheet. When applying for a licence the applicant can simply photo-copy the sheet and include it with the application. This is preferable to photo-copying a ledger book page with numerous specimens listed.

3) Licences must be obtained where applicable to sell, hire, exchange or barter, display for commercial gain etc.

It is a legal requirement (under EC Reg 338/97 & Community Reg 865/2006) for anybody wishing to: sell; hire; advertise for sale or hire; display for sale, hire or commercial gain; keep for sale, hire or commercial gain; transport for sale, hire or commercial gain; or in any way make a commercial gain; to *first* acquire an Article 10 licence to do so, *though this is only necessary for species listed on Annex 'A' of EC Regulation 338/97*

For species listed on any other Annex of EC Regulation 338/97 no licence is required for the commercial gain on such a specimen within Europe, although proof of legality will be necessary.

When operating under the Wildlife and Countryside Act the General Licences are already there (licences 13 and 14) and for species listed on Schedule 5, it is only necessary to have the appropriate SNH Schedule 5 licence at the point of sale, hire etc.

Some confusion can arise over what is keeping for sale and what is not. If a person is a known taxidermist/dealer, it may be argued that any specimen possessed and on the person's commercial property is being kept for commercial gain, and therefore requires a licence. Many taxidermists are also collectors, and may wish to keep particular specimens, which could negate that argument. If that specimen is being displayed in a commercial way (advertising the exponents work) it could be thought of as a commercial gain and would therefore require a licence. On the other hand it may not be displayed or advertised in any way, and might even have a label stating 'not for sale.' A common sense approach is required if this situation is encountered.

If the trader has separate commercial premises, then anything held there could certainly be interpreted as being held for commercial gain. Any legally-acquired item held at home, however, could be his or her own property and not for commercial gain. A difficulty arises in that many taxidermists work from home. To eliminate these problematic issues it is the recommendation of the Guild of Taxidermists that all specimens are covered by a sales licence whatever the situation.

4) Proof of legality must be given at the point of sale/commercial gain.

This is a legal requirement, although sometimes forgotten or ignored. A few taxidermists will not put their name to all of their work, however proof of legality must give: name/address of original seller (trade label); the species (common name & scientific name); the log number; the cause of death; the date of acquisition; a statement saying something like 'I/we confirm that to the best of our knowledge this specimen was legally obtained'; and preferably the transaction licence number if applicable. Whether EC Regulations or the Wildlife and Countryside Act, this is the criteria of the licences and technically should enable a trace to the origin of the specimen. In reality there are thousands of specimens on the market, be they months old or years old that display nothing.

Police powers

Police powers under COTES are discussed in that chapter – p136.
Also see chapter Police powers under the Wildlife and Countryside Act – p16.

As in other aspects of wildlife crime investigation, police officers may need advice from Animal Health or a taxidermist before embarking on a taxidermy-related investigation. These offences may in fact be relatively common, but the Guild of Taxidermists estimate that only about 30% of the taxidermy trade is seen. Each day throughout the UK, auction houses ply their trade and sometimes sell (in ignorance or otherwise) protected specimens without the necessary licences being in force. On e-Bay there are thousands of private sales where no questions may be asked. The only trade that is really known about is where taxidermists/dealers apply for licences.

Specimens listed on EC Regulation 338/97 that require an Article 10 licence can be sold 'on behalf of the licence holder' by auction houses or High Street shops on a sale or return basis. There is no requirement for the auction house to have a licence in their name, though it would be sensible for them to check that a licence is in force in the vendor's name.

There are, unfortunately, opportunities to 'legalise' an illegal specimen. Taking the transaction certificate as an example, to apply for such a certificate a taxidermist must fill in the appropriate form with the necessary details and include a copy of his or her log sheet/book. A fairly common species like tawny owl, kestrel etc will attract little attention providing plausible details are given. The taxidermist, now in possession of an Article 10 for a tawny owl, can legally sell the bird. The taxidermist will show the Article 10 to the buyer and technically he should put the log number on his label. There is no legal requirement for the taxidermist/seller to pass on the licence to the buyer.

After the sale the taxidermist retains the Article 10 certificate (there is no legal requirement for the seller to return the 'used' licence to Animal Health). There is therefore nothing to stop him selling another tawny owl – or another 20 tawny owls – using the same Article 10. There may well be many mounted tawny owls or other specimens around with the same log number.

It is worth noting from an enforcement point of view that should a police wildlife crime officer suspect an individual of committing taxidermy-related offences, and be aware of a particular sale under a transaction licence, a check could be made with Animal Health after a short period of time to see if that licence has been returned. Likewise under the terms of the general licence, a check could be made in January the following year with the Scottish Government to ensure that the particular individual has sent in his return (by 31st of December) of the previous years trading. The returns are stated as a condition of the licence.

An example of illegal practice may be as follows. A shot peregrine is received by a taxidermist. He gets an A10 on a legal one that for whatever reason is no good for taxidermy purposes and swaps it for the shot one. Shot birds upon receipt are often skinned out immediately and the carcass discarded, potentially hiding the evidence. To the casual observer a skinned shot bird is sometimes difficult to spot, though an expert can often identify the signs.

A dishonest taxidermist (it must be emphasised that most are honest) may not even bother with Article 10s but dress a new specimen to look old (prior to 1/6/1947), put it in an old case, perhaps from a broken collection, and it looks like it doesn't need a licence. Only an expert can tell.

Within the Guild there are experienced taxidermists who will help police officers with any case where an expert opinion is required. In an agreement with Animal Health, certain members of the Guild are there to assist when provenance is required for a licence application. Each of those nominated members, geographically placed around the UK and with at least 20 years experience, can bring the expertise that the police may require. Many are used to acting as an expert witness in court and often a case is brought to a successful conclusion with the help of a Guild member.

The Guild members can on most occasions age a specimen, identify species and write training manuals. They can also advise an investigating officer if a specimen is worth x-raying for shot (when a bird has been shot, a pattern of 'chips' will be seen in the main flight feathers). These little nicks in the feathers are clear and sharp, almost like someone has cut them. If the 'chips' appear on quite a few flight feathers, it is consistent with having been shot from close to medium range. It is then worth moving forward to an x-ray, which may prove the point by revealing shot, which is sometimes embedded in wing bones and just under the skin. Although the 'chips' referred to can also be caused by thorns or mantling in heather, consistent sharpness in the chips indicated they have been caused by high velocity, indicating shot from a cartridge.

With mammal pelts, the hole or holes in the pelt caused by shot will result in a bruise on the inside of the skin, again caused by high velocity. A rifle bullet that goes right through the body is likely to leave a small entry wound and a larger exit wound.

This decoy bird, with no perch, undrinkable green water and with no tag on the Larsen trap, died

A multi-catch cage trap being used for rooks and jackdaws, with an explanatory sign also bearing the police code and telephone number

Round version of Larsen trap legally set and displaying tag on top

Larsen trap legally set with decoy and displaying tag (top right)

Live and dead kestrel in funnel design cage trap

Letterbox-design trap. To be set legally this trap would need to display a sign or tag, and if used with a decoy, would require shelter for the bird

Home-made 'Clam' trap which the user admitted setting for a buzzard

Buzzard caught in a spring-over trap

A mink live-catch trap. Most live-catch traps are varying sizes on this design

Rabbit box trap. Padlocks minimise interference

Mk IV Fenn trap set illegally – entrance not restricted

Mk IV Fenn trap set legally as bridge or rail trap – entrance restricted

A particularly bad example, with a mountain hare caught because the tunnel entrance was unrestricted

Fenn Mk IV trap set in the open on perimeter of a pheasant pen. The trap was covered with grass

Fox snare with stop and anchored to tree – legally set

Snare legally set at 'midden' or 'stink pit'. It may be gory, but is legal

Snare set illegally on fence, where the captured animal could jump over and be suspended

Snare illegally set attached to a very light drag (the thin light-coloured piece of wood)

Snare set on log over burn, where any animal caught would be suspended over the water

Old design of self-locking snare

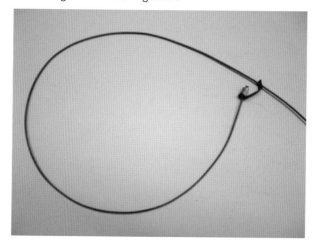

Hen harrier chicks in long heather

Recently poisoned buzzard beside woodpigeon bait

Granules of pesticide visible on woodpigeon bait

This sand martin colony was flattened while the birds were still nesting

Workman removing an active house martin nest

Oyster catcher shot with air gun. The pellet is still in the bird

The result of one day's egg collecting by egg thief

Juvenile freshwater pearl mussels

Badger sett. Note how the entrance is worn smooth by the badgers

A sett that has been dug. The depth was 3 metres
and would be many hour's work

Typical injury caused by badger to Patterdale terrier entered into a sett

Deer illegally shot with .22 rifle

Dead hare left in field after coursing incident. (Note that external injuries are minimal)

Typical dog used in hare coursing

The remains of 8 roe and a fallow deer gralloched in a forest car park by a poacher

A home made cage for poaching salmon. The fish, swimming upstream, enter and, like a lobster pot principle, cannot find their way out

Instrument for foul-hooking salmon

13. Poaching

WHILE MOST forms of poaching pose little conservation risk to the species taken, poaching offences form around half of the wildlife complaints made to the police. In some cases there are considerable animal welfare issues, such as shooting and injuring deer, killing female animals with dependent young or panicking domestic livestock by running dogs through a field of cattle, sheep or horses. Where there may be some conservation risk is through salmon poaching, where large numbers of fish are taken against the principle of the legitimate anglers' catch and release policy in an effort to conserve vulnerable stocks.

Deer Poaching

All four species of deer in Scotland – red, sika, fallow and roe – are subject to poaching, regularly being shot from the roadside. It is also common for the smaller roe deer to be taken by poachers using dogs. This latter offence takes place mainly in periurban areas, and is very often for 'sport' rather than for profit. Though less common, deer, again mainly roe, are sometimes deliberately snared. While legally-taken deer are invariably sold to a venison dealer, the outlets for poached deer are less obvious. There is no doubt that some are bought by unscrupulous hotels and restaurants, though many will be sold to friends and neighbours of the poacher.

Main offences:

The main offences relating to deer poaching, which are under the Deer (Scotland) Act 1996, are:
- Taking or killing deer without lawful authority or written permission (s.17(1)).
- Taking or killing deer by means other than using a proper calibre of rifle and ammunition. This is quite complex, with the use of slightly less powerful rifles and ammunition being permitted against roe deer compared with the larger deer species. Generally speaking the use of a shotgun is not allowed against deer, though there are exceptions. The use of dogs, snares or crossbows are illegal (s. 17(3)).

- Taking or killing deer at night, though there is an exception to this if authorised by Scottish Natural Heritage (s. 18(1)).
- Using a vehicle to drive deer (s. 19(1)).
- Shooting deer from a moving vehicle (s. 20(1)).
- Two or more people acting together to commit any of the offences already mentioned. This may include one person shooting, while the second is the driver of a vehicle being used (s. 22).
- Illegal possession of deer or of firearms or ammunition in circumstances which make it reasonable to infer that the person obtained the deer by committing a relevant offence, or had used the firearm or ammunition for the purpose of committing the offence, or knew that a relevant offence had been committed in relation to the deer, or knew that the firearm or ammunition had been used for the purpose of committing that offence. (s.23)). For policing purposes this is usually the easiest offence with which to start an investigation
- Take or kill deer outside the designated close season for that particular species. There is an exception to this if authorised by Scottish Natural Heritage (s. 5)
- An attempt to commit any of these offences is an offence in its own right (s. 24).

Authorisations

Scottish Natural Heritage issues authorisations under the Deer (Scotland) Act 1996. Authorisations allow individuals to cull deer in circumstances when they would not normally have the legal right to shoot them, for example to prevent deer damaging the natural heritage (natural habitats). Authorisations are required when shooting deer in the following circumstances:

- during the close season
- at night – the shooting of deer is not permitted between one hour after sunset and one hour before sunrise
- driving deer with vehicles- in order to take or kill for the purposes of deer management.

The new general authorisation

The Wildlife & Natural Environment (Scotland) Act 2011 made a number of changes to the Deer (Scotland) Act 1996. These changes, which cover the close seasons and owner and occupier rights, mean that to shoot any deer in the close season will require authorisation from Scottish Natural Heritage.

A new general authorisation came into force on 1st April 2012. (see

Appendix B on p254 for a copy). This allows occupiers suffering damage to improved agricultural land or enclosed woodland to control deer in the close season. This can be obtained from SNH by telephoning 01463 725362 or from their website.

Changes to Section 5 and 26 of the Deer (Scotland) Act, which cover the close seasons and owner occupier rights, mean that from the 1st April 2012 the previous exemption for the rights of owners and occupiers to cull deer *outwith the shooting season* to prevent damage on improved agricultural ground and in enclosed woodland has been removed; the right for the occupier to cull deer to prevent damage *within the shooting season* in enclosed woodland and on improved agricultural land remains. Any deer culled *out of season* must now be culled under authorisation from SNH.

SNH now issue authorisations which can be general or specific in their nature. A general authorisation is in place for owners and occupiers suffering damage to improved agricultural land or enclosed woodland to cull deer for the purpose of preventing damage. This general authorisation covers the period from 1 April to 31 March. It does not allow the culling of female deer, over 1 year old, of any species between the period of the 1st April to the 31st August.

The owner, owner's employees, the occupier's employees or any other person normally resident on the land can carry out control under any general authorisation or specific authorisation on enclosed woodland and improved agricultural land without the need to be on the SNH fit and competent register.

Those operating under a general authorisation, must have read and understood the general authorisation and carry out any control in accordance with the conditions listed on the authorisation.

Night shooting for public safety may now be authorised by SNH. This relates to the culling of deer to reduce or prevent impacts by deer on public roads. This is not a measure to allow shooting of deer at night where it is deemed unsafe to do so during daylight hours. Any application for such an authorisation must detail why daylight/in season/out of season control have not been sufficient to address the problem.

Occupiers are defined in the Deer (Scotland) Act 1996 as any tenant or sub-tenant, whether in actual occupation of the land or not. In order to operate under the general authorisation, occupiers would need to be able to satisfy a Court that they were preventing damage to their legitimate objectives and this should be reflected in any lease and/or agreement that occupiers are operating under.

Owners and Managers of Woodland need to be particularly aware of how these changes may affect their operations. In any woodland, female deer cannot be culled from 1st April to 31st August without a specific authorisation.

The definition of enclosed land is also of central importance. It is defined by the Deer (Scotland) Act 1996 as meaning enclosed by a stock-proof fence or other barrier and unenclosed shall be construed accordingly. It is for those operating under the general authorisation to be satisfied that the land is enclosed. Fencing that contains – or excludes – cattle and sheep may not necessarily keep out deer, which can jump normal stock fencing.

Collaboration and consultation between the various interests on any given piece of land is highly desirable and all possible steps should be taken to ensure that there is an effective dialogue between as many as applicable of the owner, the occupier(s), sporting tenants, controllers, neighbours and the deer management group. It remains the case that anyone operating under an authorisation, general or specific, should be able to demonstrate that no other reasonable means of control would be adequate. Longer term problems may be more effectively addressed through dialogue with other deer managers in the area, including through local Deer Management Groups than by recourse to authorisations.

Fit and competent persons

The Wildlife and Natural Environment (Scotland) Act 2001 (at s. 17A of the Deer (Scotland) Act 1996) makes provision for Ministers to ensure that a person who shoots deer (with some exceptions) may require to be registered with Scottish Natural Heritage as being a fit and competent person to do so, or to be supervised by a registered person. In support first of all of a voluntary principle of regulation the 'deer industry' has been given some time to agree a standard and achieve a good uptake of that standard. SNH will review this in 2014 (as per s. 17B of the 1996 Act). Whether or not an Order is made by Scottish Ministers to commence registration depends on the outcome.

Section 33 – Licences

All venison lawfully marketed must pass through the hands of, and be properly recorded by, a licensed venison dealer. Licences to deal in venison are issued by the local Council and are valid for 3 years. There are 'hunter' exemptions to enable a hunter to trade in small quantities of deer that he shot, or had been involved in the hunting, provided that they have not been processed more than evisceration and lower legs and head removed. When in this condition there should be a 'hunter's declaration' as to the normality, including a health declaration, by the hunter of the animal before and throughout inspection. If they are processed more than this then the hunter's tag may legally be absent but he must have undertaken the work in registered premises and have a local authority licence. Wild game meat laws are derived from EC852/2004, EC853/2004 and EC 854/2004.

Venison dealers have a legal obligation to keep records of purchases of venison (s. 34). Any constable and any person authorised in writing by the Secretary of State or Scottish Natural Heritage may inspect these records. The prescribed form of the records to be kept is made under and reproduced in *The Licensing of Venison Dealers (Prescribed Forms etc) (Scotland) Order, 1984*. For policing purposes, the main entries on this form are:

* Date of purchase
* Species
* Place where deer killed (e.g. name of estate, etc)
* Name and address of seller
* Registration number of vehicle delivering the deer

These records, *especially the vehicle registration number*, are vital when following up a report of deer poaching. Under a Scotland-wide operation, Operation Moon, police wildlife crime officers visit venison dealers regularly to ensure that they are keeping their records accurately.

Police powers

A constable may seize any deer liable to be forfeited on conviction of an offence under the Act (s. 27(1)). Deer seized must be kept until the defence either has an opportunity to examine them, or declines to do so (*Anderson v Laverock 1976*). The investigating officer should liaise with the specialist wildlife prosecutor in this regard.

Where a sheriff or justice of the peace is satisfied on oath that there are reasonable grounds to suspect that a relevant offence (Section 5, or Sections 17 to 22) to have been committed *and* evidence of the commission of the offence is to be found on any premises or in any vehicle, he may grant a warrant authorising a police officer, at any time or times within one week of the date on the warrant, to enter, if necessary by force, the said premises or vehicle for the purpose of detecting the offence. (s. 27(2)). This allows the officer to search every person who is found in, has recently left or be about to enter the premises or vehicle to which the warrant relates, and seize relevant items. A police officer may also stop and search a vehicle without warrant in cases of urgency or other good cause (s. 27(4).

If a person is found committing an offence under Part III of the Act, a police officer may arrest him. Part III would cover all of the offences listed except the offence of taking deer out of season. All of these offences, including taking or killing deer out of season, are punishable by imprisonment, therefore a detention under Section 14 of the Criminal Procedure (Scotland) Act, 1995, would be applicable.

Deer (Close Seasons) (Scotland) Order, 2011:

This order specifies the close seasons for various species of deer. These are:

Red deer	Males	21 October to 30 June
	Females	16 February to 20 October
Sika deer	Males	21 October to 30 June
	Females	16 February to 20 October
Red/Sika hybrid	Males	21 October to 30 June
	Females	16 February to 20 October
Fallow deer	Males	1 May to 31 July
	Females	16 February to 20 October
Roe Deer	Males	21 October to 31 March
	Females	1 April to 20 October

There would be no offence in an authorised person shooting a muntjac deer, were one to escape, at any time of the year. None should be in the wild in Scotland.

Some deer poaching investigations will emanate from a call with information from a game dealer, who will be well placed to give assistance and advise on how the particular deer was killed. In these types of incidents, the deer may well be available as a production and the police officer's job will be to link the deer with the person who sold it to the game dealer, though this may not necessarily be the person who killed the deer. In cases such as these, there should be little difficulty obtaining a search warrant if evidence is required to prove how the deer was killed. The evidence might take the form of snares, dogs, firearms or another weapon such as a crossbow.

In cases where dogs have been used to take deer, the police would be unlikely to seize the dogs, but may consider whether a warrant is required in order to find the dogs and take photographic or video evidence of them, or even DNA or other samples. If the incident took place within the previous 24 hours or so the investigating officer may consider taking samples of the dog's faeces for examination for deer hair. (Deer stalkers increasingly take trained dogs with them to track and hold wounded deer, which is not an offence).

In some cases, deer will be found in the back of a vehicle during a vehicle stop-check. If the occupants cannot give a reasonable account of why they have possession of the deer, then the easiest offence to prove, and the best starting point, is unlawful possession of the deer. The occupants can be detained by the officers and if necessary the more technical aspects of the investigation undertaken in due course. Firearms and live and spent ammunition may also be in the vehicle and likely to be relevant to the offence.

Even if deer are not found in a vehicle, but there is fresh blood and deer hair without a reasonable explanation of why they are there, may be enough for a detention on suspicion that the occupants have taken deer without lawful authority. DNA procedures have advanced to the stage that blood samples can be identified as coming from a particular species of deer. SASA provide this service to the police free of charge. The recovering of human DNA from animals, such as from deer legs that have been cut off, may soon be a possibility. At the University of Strathclyde, scientists at the Centre for Forensic Science are advancing this process.

Evidence of deer poaching may come from someone who finds deer gralloch (head, feet, intestines, etc) in a wood or some other place, giving a reasonable indication that the deer was not taken by someone with permission to do so. Often these grallochs are from deer shot at the roadside at close range, and in many cases there is evidence that the deer has been shot in the head. These cases can be extremely difficult to solve, though if there is a suspect it may be worth having the heads x-rayed to see if there is a bullet which could be recovered for forensic comparison with the suspect's rifle. The chances of a comparison are slim, however, as most bullets hitting bone fragment on impact. If bullets are removed from a carcass they must be handled extremely carefully and in a manner which does not risk scratching them otherwise evidentially they are likely to be worthless.

Snares set for deer pose another problem. There is seldom time available for police officers to maintain a watch on the snares to catch the suspect returning – even if the appropriate surveillance authority can be obtained. The snares may simply have to be removed, but may well be worth examination for DNA as if DNA is found and matched, the suspect may have difficulty explaining how his DNA was found on the snare.

There is another option if there is a suspect. There are various substances, visible only under ultra-violet light, which can be used as a contaminant to coat the snare and transfer to the suspect when he next touches the snare. Before coating the snare with the contaminant, the snare must be pulled or knocked so that it is no longer in a 'set' position and cannot catch an animal. Regular checks must be made on the snare after coating to see if it has been set up again. If this is the case, the sooner the suspect can be traced and examined for contaminant the better. The longer the delay, the more justification he can use in court that he was contaminated by contact with some other person rather than from the snare. Contaminants available include ultra-violet paste, Cyphermark and Smartwater.

Particular care should be taken when dealing with a deer poacher holding a rifle, shotgun or crossbow. Officers taking possession of firearms must ensure immediately that they are unloaded. If unfamiliar with weapons, an authorised firearms officer, or gamekeeper or farmer who is experienced with firearms should be sought to unload it or to demonstrate that it is unloaded. Never put a firearm that may be loaded into a vehicle or building.

Fish Poaching

The legislation covering fish poaching is the Salmon and Freshwater Fisheries (Consolidation) (Scotland) Act 2003. For the purposes of this section, the term 'salmon' should be taken to include sea trout. The offences relate to salmon and sea trout unless other fish are specifically mentioned.

Apart from in public waters, freshwater fishing rights are private. It is not the fish but the right to fish for them that is owned. The rights to freshwater fishing belong to the owner of the land that is adjacent to the water (riparian ownership). Salmon fishing rights are heritable titles, which may be held with or separate from the land, and carry with them the subsidiary right to fish for trout and other freshwater fish. This right must not be exercised in a way that will interfere with the rights of the riparian owner. Where the right is held separate from the land, the proprietor of the fishing right has an implied right of access for the purpose of exercising the right to fish for salmon.

It is a criminal offence to fish for salmon without the legal right or without written permission from the owner of that right. In the case of fishing for trout and other freshwater fish, fishing without permission is usually a civil rather than a criminal offence. However, where a Protection Order is in force it is a criminal offence, without legal right or written permission, to fish for or take freshwater fish in the inland waters in the prescribed area (s.12). Protection Orders are made by the Scottish Government under Section 48 of the Act. There are currently 14 Protection Orders in force in various parts of Scotland. It is also a criminal offence to fish for or take fish from a stank – any pond or reservoir which has been stocked and has neither inlet nor outlet – without authority. (s. 11)

The powers of police officers and water bailiffs are broadly similar. Bailiffs have certain powers on rivers that police don't have, but, unlike police officers, cannot stop a suspect's vehicle. Very often police officers and water bailiffs work together, and police, water bailiffs and Marine Scotland regularly share intelligence on poachers and poaching activity.

Main offences

Many of the offences that relate to fish poaching mirror those that relate to deer poaching. The offences are too numerous to give details of all of them, but the main offences are:

- Fishing by means other than a rod and line or a net and cobble, a cobble being any form of boat. (s.1(a) and (b)) To be legal, a rod and line must be used in the recognised sporting method of enticing the fish to bite the lure. The rod and line must not be used with a large hook and lead weight – or indeed with any legal tackle – in a manner designed to foul hook fish by ripping the hook or bait through the water. Any use of a net, with or without a cobble, must be legitimate. There will be few occasions, apart from coastal or estuarine nets used by fishing companies, when netting is legal. Exceptions may be in freshwater lochs to remove unwanted species, such as perch or pike, or in a pond or loch, where all owners of the pond or loch are in agreement.
- Fishing for salmon or sea trout without lawful authority or written permission. (s. 6) There may also be circumstances when other freshwater fish may not be taken or fished for without such authority.
- Two or more people acting together to commit any of the offences already mentioned. (s. 7) This may include one person fishing illegally, while the second is waiting with a gaff or landing net, or simply keeping watch. *The penalty for s. 7 includes imprisonment.*
- The use of explosives, noxious substances or electrical currents to take fish. (s. 5) The most likely noxious substance is Cymag, a grey/white power that gives of deadly hydrogen cyanide sodium when exposed to moisture. This effectively suffocates fish. Cymag, formerly used to gas rats and rabbits, was banned in 2004, though stockpiles may remain. *The penalty for s. 5 includes imprisonment.*
- Illegal possession of salmon or trout, or of instruments or substances in circumstances which afford reasonable ground for suspecting that the person has obtained possession of the fish, or instrument or substance as the result of, or for the purpose of, committing any of the earlier mentioned offences. (s. 9) For policing purposes this is

invariably the easiest offence with which to start an investigation. There is no penalty built in to this section: the penalty would be that relating to the method of taking the fish of fishing for them. In other words if the fish have been taken by explosives, the instruments possessed relate to that method or if there are two or more persons involved then the penalty for s. 9 will include imprisonment. *One witness to this offence is sufficient.*

- Taking dead salmon or trout. (s. 8)
- Fishing in a stank or loch, the fishing right of which are owned by one person, without the legal right to do so. (s. 11) A 'stank' means a reservoir or pond with neither inlet nor outlet sufficient to allow access or egress by fish.
- Fishing for or taking freshwater fish in contravention of a prohibition contained in a protection order. (s. 12)
- Fishing by net for salmon or sea trout during the weekly close time. (s. 13(3)) This extends from 1800 hours on a Friday until 0600 hours on a Monday. One witness to this offence is sufficient.
- Fishing by rod and line for salmon or sea trout on a Sunday. (s. 13(2)) *The annual close time varies from river to river. One witness to this offence is sufficient.*
- Fishing for salmon during the annual close time. (s. 14) *One witness to this offence is sufficient.*
- Fishing for trout during the annual close time (s. 17), which is from 7 October to 14 March, both inclusive. *One witness to this offence is sufficient.*
- Fish for, buy, sell, expose for sale or possess any unclean or unseasonable salmon. (s.18)

  This relates not only to fish that have spawned (kelts), but to fish just about to spawn, the test of which is to gently squeeze the fish from behind the gills towards the vent. If eggs or milt run from the vent then the fish is about to spawn. Catching a kelt or unseasonable salmon is not an offence if it is caught accidentally and returned to the river. *One witness to this offence is sufficient.*
- A person in possession of salmon who believes; or in possession of salmon in circumstances in which it would be reasonable for that person to suspect, that a relevant offence has at any time been committed in relation to the salmon, commits an offence. (s. 20)

NOTE: It is a defence for an accused to show that the salmon had not been unlawfully taken even if the circumstances initially gave rise to suspicion that it had been so taken. This should not be read as a reverse burden of proof: the prosecution must prove both that the person was in possession of the salmon and that he should, in all the circumstances, have suspected or believed that the salmon had been illegally taken. A 'relevant offence' (any of the foregoing offences in this Act) in relation to the taking of the salmon may be committed in Scotland under this Act, or in England or Wales under the law applicable there. An exception exists in respect of anything done in good faith for purposes connected with the prevention or detection of crime or the investigation or treatment of disease. *Unlike in section 9, no proof is required under this section that the suspect was the person who actually took the fish.* Examples would be a person in possession of salmon with clear marks on the bodies of having been taken in a net; with clear marks on the body consistent with having been foul-hooked; by evidence of having paid a price well below market value for the salmon or where evidence is available that the person had been told that the fish had been poached. In some investigations this may be a preferred starting point. *This is an important section for policing purposes in that the penalty includes imprisonment. In addition, a person who commits an offence under this section may be convicted on the evidence of one witness.*

- An attempt to commit any of these offences is an offence in its own right

Newer legislation, including 'set lines'

It is worth a quick mention of some of the newer regulations. It is an offence to sell or offer for sale rod-caught salmon – (The Conservation of Salmon (Prohibition of Sale) (Scotland) Regulations 2002). It is also an offence to fish for eels, since the European eel is now a species of conservation concern – (The Freshwater Fish Conservation (Prohibition on Fishing for Eels) (Scotland) Regulations 2008). The Aquaculture and Fisheries (Scotland) Act 2007 has amended the 2003 Act in that a gaff or tailer for landing fish may no longer be used, and landing nets must now be made from mesh which is knotless and made of non-metallic material. (s. 3)) In bank fishing for fish of the family Salmonidae the angler may only use one rod and must hold the rod while he is using it. The family Salmonidae includes salmon, trout, grayling and char. In bank fishing for *other* freshwater fish a person may use up to 4 rods and does not require to have hold of them. In fishing for *any* species of fish from a boat, there may not be more than 4 rods in use. The legislation is silent on the number of anglers and it would appear that while in a boat an angler may use more than one rod to fish for salmonids. (all s. 3A)

Section 33A of the 2003 Act (which came into force on 1 August 2008) makes it an offence for any person to intentionally introduce any live fish or spawn of any fish into inland waters, or possess such with the intention of introduction without previous written agreement of the appropriate authority (either Scottish Ministers or District Salmon Fishery Boards). The provisions apply to all introductions of freshwater fish to any inland Scottish water system. They do not apply to fish farms (including introduction of brood-stock into hatcheries) or to appropriate ornamental fish-keeping facilities. There is a derogation under the Wildlife and Countryside Act 1981 (Exceptions to Section 14) (Scotland) Order 2012 that allows the return of rod-caught fish provided they are returned to the same location as where they were caught and on the same day.

Police and water bailiffs' powers
Section 52 (1) – Search under warrant
A sheriff or justice of the peace, upon information on oath that there is probable cause to suspect that:

    (a) a breach of any of the provisions of this Act has been committed; or

    (b) any salmon or trout illegally taken, or any illegal nets or other engines or instruments are concealed, on any premises or in any vehicle, may by warrant under the hand of such sheriff or justice authorise and empower any constable or water bailiff to enter such premises or vehicle, if necessary by force, for the purpose of detecting such offence, or such concealed fish or instruments, and to seize all illegal nets, engines or other instruments, or any salmon or trout illegally taken, that may be found on such premises or in such vehicle.

Section 52 (2) – Conditions of search warrant
A warrant granted under this section

    (a) may specify the time or times in the day or night at which it may be exercised; and

    (b) shall not continue in force for more than a week from the date on which it is granted.

Section 52 (3) – Extended powers of search warrant
A person authorised by any such warrant may search every person who is found in,

or whom the person so authorised has reasonable ground to believe to have recently left or to be about to enter those premises or that vehicle.

Search warrants under this section may not be obtained in relation to the enforcement of Protection Orders

Section 53 – Powers of constables
Section 53 (1) – Stop and search of vehicle without warrant

A constable who has reasonable grounds for suspecting that an offence against any of the provisions of this Act has been committed, and that evidence of the commission of the offence is to be found in any vehicle, but who considers that by reason of urgency or other good cause it is impracticable to apply for a warrant to search such vehicle, may stop and search that vehicle and any person who is found in, or whom there are reasonable grounds to believe to have recently left or to be about to enter the vehicle.

Section 53 (2) – Search of premises without warrant

A constable who has reasonable grounds for suspecting that an offence against any of the provisions of the Act is being committed and that evidence of the commission of the offence is to be found in any premises (other than a dwelling-house or any yard, garden, outhouses and pertinents belonging thereto or usually enjoyed therewith) but who considers that by reason of urgency or other good cause it is impracticable to apply for a warrant to search such premises, may search them without warrant.

These powers are broadly similar to police powers contained within section 19 of the Wildlife and Countryside Act 1981.

Section 53 (3) – Other police and water bailiff powers

Any constable may exercise any of the powers conferred on a water bailiff by section 55 of this Act.

Police powers in Section 55 are:
Section 55 (1)
    (a) examine any dam, fixed engine or obstruction, or any lade and for that purpose, enter on any land
    (b) stop and search any boat which is used in fishing or any boat which there is reasonable cause to suspect of containing salmon or trout
    (c) search and examine nets or other instruments used in fishing or any basket, pocket or other receptacle capable of carrying fish, which there is reasonable cause to suspect of containing salmon or trout illegally taken
    (d) seize any fish, instrument or article, boat or vehicle liable to be forfeited in pursuance of this Act

Section 55(6)

It shall be lawful for a water bailiff, without any warrant or other authority than this Act, to seize and detain any person found committing an offence against any of the provisions of this Act and deliver such person to a constable.

This is a rather unusual way of giving the police power of search, seizure and arrest in relation to offences committed against the provisions of this Act. Nevertheless the police and bailiffs' powers of search with and without warrant, entry on to land, seizure and arrest are extremely strong.

Power of arrest

While there is a power of arrest for offences under the Act, the only offences that are punishable by imprisonment are s. 5 – use of explosives, noxious substances or electrical devices; s. 7 – two or more persons acting together; s.20 – in possession of salmon which the suspect knows, or should have known, had been taken against the provisions of the 2003 Act; and s. 58 – obstruction of a constable or bailiff.

Powers under either section 53 or 55 may not be utilised in relation to the enforcement of Protection Orders

Section 54 – Power of constables and water bailiffs to enter land

Any constable or water bailiff may enter and remain upon any land in the vicinity of any river or of the sea coast during any hour of the day of night for the purpose of

    (a) preventing a breach of the provisions of this Act; or

    (b) detecting persons guilty of any breach of those provisions

This section would seem to dispense with the requirement to obtain RIP(S)A authority to carry out surveillance. Powers under this section may not be utilised in relation to the enforcement of Protection Orders

Section 58 – Offences in relation to obstruction

Any person who refuses to allow a constable or a water bailiff to exercise any power conferred on them in pursuance of this Act commits an offence. The penalty for s. 58 includes imprisonment.

Section 59 – Power of court in trial for offence to convict of another

If upon trial for an offence under Section 9, 16 or 20 of this Act, or any rule of law relating to reset, the court is satisfied that the accused is:

    (a) not guilty of the offence charged, but

    (b) guilty of another of those offences it may acquit on the offence charged but find the accused guilty of the other offence, for which the accused would be liable to punishment.

(S.9 is unlawful possession of salmon or trout; s. 16 is buying or selling salmon in the close season; s. 20 is the possession of salmon illegally killed, taken or landed.)

Many offences will be investigated by police acting along with water bailiffs. Water bailiffs are experts in their own field and their assistance to the police will make the investigation and the reporting of the offences much easier. Unless an investigating police officer is a seasoned angler, he or she should not consider speaking to technical issues in court, such as the breaking strain of fishing line, hook sizes and the purpose of illegal implements. This is far better carried out by water bailiffs or ghillies who deal with these instruments on a more regular basis.

Police officers shouldn't be overly concerned about attending an incident without the assistance and guidance of a water bailiff. If an offence seems to have been committed, even though the officer is not exactly sure what that offence is, he or she should be aware in particular of section 20 of the Act – possession of salmon in circumstances in which it would be reasonable for that person to suspect that a relevant offence has at any time been committed in relation to the fish. (This could include marks on the fish, poaching implements found along with the fish, or simply suspects coming away from a river with fish but no obvious means of having legally caught them). The power of detention under Section 14 of the Criminal Procedure (Scotland) Act, 1995, available for this offence should be sufficient to deal with the incident until an expert can be summoned to assist.

Some incidents are clear-cut offences, such as someone using nets on a river or having large lead weights and a large treble hook on the end of a line. Some other offences are more difficult to detect. The following is guidance on some of the more common types of salmon poaching.

Foul hooking

This method consists of deliberately trying to foul hook salmon by jerking the line and hook through the water, allowing them briefly to sink again, then repeating the jerking motion. The person fishing may be using a fishing rod or simply have the line, which is usually of a breaking strain considerably stronger than would be used for normal fishing, tied to a piece of wood. The 'business end' is likely to consist of a lump of lead and a large treble hook.

The poacher may in fact just use an ordinary lure with a large treble hook on it. It is not the equipment the poacher is using that necessarily creates the offence: it is the manner in which he is using it. The rod, reel, line and lure may be completely legitimate for ordinary fishing, but being used in an unlawful way. Foul hooking may be referred to by different names in different parts of Scotland, such as 'jigging', 'sniggering', 'ripping', 'pointing' etc, but the method used is always to use a violent jerking motion to retrieve the line.

Occasionally a salmon does get accidentally foul hooked by a person fishing legitimately. A fish caught in this way must be returned to the water.

With a salmon that has been foul-hooked, there is usually a mark somewhere on the body, normally in the form of two small (or sometimes not so small!) parallel slits or rips, where the hooks have gripped. Examination of the mouth normally shows that there is no hook mark that would have been consistent with being genuinely caught. It is this crucial type of evidence that a water bailiff or ghillie can describe to the court.

Illegal netting

A poacher may use a net on a river to sweep up fish in a pool, or to hang at slack water in a tidal area. With these types of poaching, the poacher is often in attendance while the net is being worked, and may well also have a dinghy or even a wet suit.

Fish caught will have marks consistent with netting, usually dark lines round the body just behind the gills where they have been trying to get through the net or where they have been stuck in the net.

Other types of net, especially off-shore or in an estuary, may be set then left for some time. These nets are more difficult to link to the person setting them unless time can be taken to wait until they are checked. The one advantage is that there may be time to set up an operation to catch the persons responsible. Such an operation should always include water bailiffs, since they have access to boats.

Bear in mind that those involved may well have salmon scales on their clothing. Clothing can be seized and the scales examined by the Freshwater Fisheries Laboratory, Faskally, Pitlochry. In due course (though in 2012 this facility is not yet available), the DNA lab at Science and Advice for Scottish Agriculture will be able to match scales with individual fish.

The use of a cage

Wire cages are occasionally used, often with considerable success, to take salmon at a part of a river where their passage is likely to be restricted to, or where they would favour, a particular route upstream. This may well be at a part of a dam or weir that is broken and allows more water through than the rest of the dam or weir.

The cages are constructed of wire netting or gridweld mesh and likely be about 4 feet long by 3 feet deep by 2 feet high. The end of the cage facing downstream has an entrance, sometimes a funnel, in the manner of a lobster pot, extending into the cage. This allows the fish to enter, but since they would need to find the narrow part of the funnel to escape, they seldom succeed. In addition their natural tendency is to keep facing upstream against the current otherwise they may drown.

A cage is most likely to have success when there is a run of salmon on, which is normally just after heavy rain raises the height of the river, encouraging salmon to move upstream to spawn. Like the use of Cymag, there are favourite parts of a river for the use of a cage.

Gassing

Though 'gassing' is the term used, the fish are not in fact gassed. The substance used is normally a white powder called 'Cymag' that, prior to Government approval being withdrawn on 31 December 2004, was used for the gassing or rats and rabbits. When exposed to moisture, the powder gives off poisonous hydrogen cyanide gas. In a salmon poaching situation the hydrogen cyanide bonds with the iron within the haemoglobin of the salmon's blood and prevents the admission of oxygen, suffocating the fish.

Normally this method is employed in a pool where there are a lot of salmon. This may well be just downstream from a waterfall that is temporarily impeding the progress of the fish up the river. The Cymag will be emptied in to the waterfall so that the hydrogen cyanide is dispersed during the tumbling action of the water. The salmon then begin to suffocate and often start leaping out of the water, sometimes even landing on the bank. It is likely that the poachers would operate a net across the river downstream to catch some of the dead or dying fish but invariably many that are killed by the Cymag are not collected. It is often the presence of many dead fish downstream which alerts bailiffs and police to the fact that the river has been 'gassed'.

Fish seized that have been killed by Cymag must be taken with some urgency to the Freshwater Fisheries Laboratory at Pitlochry as evidence of the use of this substance disappears rapidly. If a large number of fish are involved, a minimum of 6 fish, independently labelled with the string through the mouth and gills, should be forwarded.

Cymag tins may still be traceable through their codes and numbers, though stocks of the substance and becoming more scare with each passing year after the 2004 ban on its production and use.

> WARNING: If Cymag tins are recovered, the contents are
> extremely dangerous if exposed to moisture and extreme caution
> should be used in handling and transporting them. Assistance or

advice can be obtained from Science and Advice for Scottish Agriculture, Edinburgh, where staff can also carry out a presumptive test on the contents. It is worth discussing with the specialist prosecutor whether there is really a requirement to keep the tins for court purposes, or whether a photograph and a label would suffice.

Any operation or investigation beside or on water is hazardous. Officers should not take risks, carry a reliable torch, use proper footwear for the job, such as walking boots or wellingtons and ensure someone else knows where the investigation or operation will take place.

Lastly, if salmon taken contrary to the Act are seized as productions they must not be destroyed or disposed of without consultation with the procurator fiscal. Failure to allow the defence solicitor access to the fish to examine them is likely to be fatal to further court proceedings. (*Anderson v Laverock, 1976*)

Poaching and legally taking, killing or trading in 'game' and quarry species

Offences in relation to 'game' birds, formerly pheasant, grouse, black game, partridge and ptarmigan, are no longer covered by the various Game Acts, which have been repealed. As the species listed are now included in the definition of 'wild birds' within the Wildlife and Countryside Act 1981 these offences are now covered by that Act.

Main offences

The main offences are:

- To intentionally or recklessly take, kill or injure a wild bird, (s. 1(1)). There is an exception for an 'authorised person' to take or kill certain birds (former 'game' species, some wildfowl and some waders) outside the close season. An 'authorised person' is the owner of the land on which the taking or killing takes places, or someone authorised by the landowner. Taking or killing birds on a Sunday or Christmas Day (other than where permitted) is simply an offence under section 1(1). Shooting or taking birds listed in Schedule 2 Part1 ('game' birds), on a Sunday or Christmas Day, is an exception thought rarely takes place, but pest species may still be shot under one or more of general licences 1 to 4. *Single witness sufficient in relation to the unauthorised taking, killing or injuring of grouse, pheasant, partridge or ptarmigan.* (see

Single witness evidence p29 for more detail)

- Intentionally or recklessly kill, injure or take a wild hare during the close season (s. 10A). *Single witness sufficient.*
- Intentionally or recklessly kill or take a wild hare or rabbit without the permission of someone who has a right to give that permission (s. 11G). *Single witness sufficient.*
- Attempts to commit any of these offences is an offence in its own right (s. 18(1)). *Corroboration is required for an attempt to commit an offence.*
- Having possession of any thing capable of being used to commit an offence against the Act is an offence (s. 18(2)). *Corroboration is required for this subsection.*

It is worth noting that to deal with hare coursing offences, the Wildlife and Countryside Act 1981 is now a far better option that the Protection of Wild Mammals (Scotland) Act 2002. One of the advantages is that single witness evidence is sufficient. In addition, the use of the dogs for coursing might be considered an offence under s.18(2) as being 'anything capable of being used for committing the offence'.

It is generally an offence to kill, injure or take any wild bird. There is an exception in the Wildlife and Countryside Act 1981 (s.2 (1A)) which permits this, outside the close season, to facilitate sporting shooting provided the shooter has a legal right (by being the owner of the land) or appropriate permission. The species that can be shot are listed in Part 1 of Schedule 2 of the Act.

Legally taking or killing 'game' species

Pheasant, grey partridge, red-legged partridge, red grouse and mallard may be caught up outwith the close season. Only pheasant and partridge may be caught-up for breeding in the 28 days immediately after the beginning of the close season (s. 2(3A) and 2(3B)). The caught-up birds are generally penned and the eggs collected for hatching in incubators. Once the birds are caught up and penned they cease to be 'wild birds'. They are therefore not subject to the Wildlife and Countryside Act, though as captive birds would be subject to the Animal Health and Welfare (Scotland) Act 2006.

Red grouse may be caught-up at any time for the purpose of preventing disease (s. 2(3C)) provide they are released within 12 hours. Grouse are frequently caught in nets, using artificial light at night, so that they can be dosed for worms. Despite the fact that this has been done for years it was technically illegal. This subsection now is intended to allow the taking of grouse by authorised persons for this and other medicinal purposes, however section 5(5)(c) details the legal use of nets to take 'game birds,' including grouse, and states that this must be only for the purpose of breeding. Section 5(1)(c)(v) and (vi) also state that it is an offence to take birds using an artificial light source. This anomaly may well be resolved through the issue of a new general licence. Having said that, since the advent of medicated grit that can be set out in a tray or an upturned turf and is effective in prevention of large worm burdens, few grouse are now caught up and dosed.

In Scotland, on a Sunday or Christmas Day, birds which may be shot (in addition to 'pest' species, are: black grouse; red grouse; grey partridge; red-legged partridge, pheasant; ptarmigan (Schedule 2 Part1). In practice, shooting etiquette dictates that the shooting of these birds on these days is discouraged and very rarely takes place.

Police powers – see powers under the Wildlife and Countryside Act

With offences in relation to the poaching of 'game' species now being under the Wildlife and Countryside Act 1981 rather than the outdated game laws, all offences are punishable by imprisonment therefore a police officer may detain a suspect under section 14 of the Criminal Procedure (Scotland) Act 1995.

The time bar under the 1981 Act of 6 months from the date sufficient evidence of the commission of the offence goes before the procurator fiscal, but not more than 3 years after the date of the commission of the offence also applies. This is considerably better than the 3 months that applied under some of the now repealed game laws.

Since the poaching of game – apart from hare coursing – is less common than it used to be, not every police officers has had experience of dealing with these incidents. Gamekeepers, landowners and farmers encountering poaching offences have sometimes complained that a poaching incident they have reported to the police has not be dealt with satisfactorily and that the police are unsure of the law in relation to poaching. They state that this tends to make them reluctant to report poaching incidents to the police, which in turn results in police officers having less chance to become familiar with the legislation. The Wildlife and Countryside Act 1981 is more familiar to modern police officers than the outdated game laws were and should be easier to work with. In addition, the powers given to police under the Act apply equally throughout, and will make dealing with poachers much more effective.

Officers should consider what productions must be seized to help to prove the case. Any dead birds or animals which are alleged or suspected to be the subject of the crime must be seized. Pheasants, rabbits or whatever other animals have been seized should never be disposed of before discussing the case with a specialist wildlife prosecutor. The defence must be offered an opportunity to examine the dead animals to confirm (or otherwise) that they have been killed by the method alleged. Disposing of the carcasses and denying the defence this opportunity may be fatal to a conviction. (*Anderson v Laverock, 1976*)

Instruments used in poaching must be seized. These are normally nets or traps of some sort. *If firearms have been used and are to be seized it must be confirmed that they are unloaded before they are put in a vehicle.* If officers are not sure about how to do this, they should have a police officer, gamekeeper or farmer attend who is familiar with weapons and can ensure that they weapon is made safe.

Live animals, such as dogs and ferrets, should not be seized, though officers should consider with regular offenders whether it is worthwhile to take photographs or video footage of dogs involved with a view to (a) asking the court for forfeiture, and (b) helping to identify those involved if the dogs continue to be used in coursing. A vehicle used in the commission of the offences can be forfeit by the court, and officers should consider whether it is justified in seizing it for this purpose.

When dealing with poaching cases it may be prudent to have any mammals or birds that are recovered examined to confirm the cause of death. This could start with an x-ray (an airport or prison may allow their facilities to be used) to see whether there may be lead shot, a bullet or an air pellet in the carcass. If there is, and it is to be recovered, photographing x-rays at different angles to give a 3-dimensional perspective would allow easier recovery. Recovery should be carried out by a veterinary pathologist.

In cases where the mammal (or a bird) has been taken by another means, e.g a snare or dog, then an examination by a veterinary pathologist would be required to prove the cause of death. Photos of the progress of the examination are of value to the prosecutor and the court. As in most wildlife cases a series of photographs of the locus, and a map showing where particular items were recovered or where particular incidents took place are invaluable.

Where justified by repeated conduct by the accused, e.g. hare coursers, consideration should be given to requesting a bail condition that the accused are not allowed to go more than a mile from their home with their dog or anyone else's dog.

Close seasons in Scotland listed at s. 2(4) WCA are:

   Woodcock – 1 February to 31 August (this extends to 30 September in the rest of the UK)

   Snipe – 1 February to 11 August

   Pheasant – 2 February to 30 September

   Partridge – 2 February to 31 August

   Wild duck and geese – 1 February to 31 August (though above the high water mark of ordinary spring tides the close season does not take place until 21 February)

   Black grouse – 11 December to 19 August

   Ptarmigan and red grouse – 11 December to 11 August

   Any other bird which may be killed or taken (eg coot, golden plover – 1 February to 31 August)

Shooting seasons in Scotland

For those who shoot, this might be more easily understood if the *shooting seasons* are listed. These are:

   Woodcock – 1 September to 31 January (1 October to 31 January in the rest of the UK)

   Snipe – 12 August to 31 January

   Pheasant – 1 October to 1 February

   Partridge – 1 September to 1 February

   Wild duck and geese – 1 September to 31 January (though above the high water mark of ordinary spring tides this is extended until 21 February)

   Black grouse – 20 August to 10 December

   Ptarmigan and red grouse – 12 August to 10 December

   Any other bird which may be killed or taken (eg coot, golden plover – 1 September to 31 January)

In addition, the Scottish Government can declare a period of special protection for birds in Schedule 1, Part II or Schedule 2, Part 1. This would generally take place during periods of extreme weather.

Trade in 'game' and quarry species

The birds that can be shot, taken or sold are listed on schedules of the Wildlife and Countryside Ac t 1981. The relevant schedules are:

Schedule 2, Part I – Birds that can be taken or killed outside the close season. They include pheasant, partridge, coot, greylag goose, mallard, woodcock etc.

Schedule 2 Part IA – Birds that may not be killed or taken on Sundays or Christmas Day. They are the wildfowl species, woodcock and snipe.

Schedule 3 Part IA – Birds that may be sold alive if legally taken. They are mallard, red grouse, pheasant, grey partridge and red-legged partridge.

Sale of 'game birds' and wildfowl

Schedule 3 Part II – Birds that may be sold dead at all times, lists only the woodpigeon.

Schedule 3 Part IIA – Birds that may be sold dead if legally killed. These are the same as the birds listed in Schedule 2 Part I, with the exception of the species of geese, goldeneye, pintail and moorhen.

This change in the law brought about by the provisions of the Wildlife and Natural Environment (Scotland) Act 2011 means that the birds in Schedule 3 Part IIA can be sold throughout the year *provided they were taken legally.* (s. 6(2) WCA) Section 27 WCA defines a 'sale' as including hire, barter and exchange, and cognate expressions shall be construed accordingly. Any offer to exchange or trade for other birds or goods in kind would still be treated as a sale.

14. Restriction of Use of Lead Shot over Wetlands

IT HAS BEEN known for many years now that waterfowl die from lead poisoning after ingesting lead shot which has fallen into wetland habitats. Under the terms of the African-Eurasian Waterbird Agreement (AEWA), signatory Governments are obliged to endeavour to phase out the use of lead shot over wetlands. The Environmental Protection (Restriction on Use of Lead Shot) (Scotland) (No.2) Regulations 2004 (SSI No. 2004/358) represents Scotland's response to this.

In practice, the new legislation formalises the shooting community's voluntary *'Code of Good Shooting Practice'*, endorsed by key shooting and countryside organisations, which for several years has called on all those who shoot to avoid depositing lead shot in wetland areas used by feeding waterfowl.

The new Scottish legislation differs from that in place in England or Wales, but is similar to that imposed in Northern Ireland. It follows a habitat–based approach as opposed to a combined species/site restriction. For example, in England or Wales it is illegal to shoot any duck, goose, moorhen or coot with lead shot, or to use lead shot on a specific published list of SSSIs. In Scotland, shooters will continue to be able to use lead shot to shoot species such as duck, geese, game, pests or clays *as long as this does not occur on or over wetlands.* Duck flying over, or geese coming into a dry stubble field, can still be shot with lead. The big difference is that the use of lead shot over wetlands to shoot *any* species is now prohibited.

The difference of approach in Scotland should be carefully noted in cross-border areas where the restrictions will apply (e.g. the Solway Firth and River Tweed). The Regulations in Scotland were finalised following an extensive consultation process both on the early policy and the final draft Regulations which included consideration of the approach in England and Wales and the effects of any restrictions on shooting bodies and their members. The Regulations are proportionate and are not intended to unnecessarily restrict those shooting outwith wetland areas.

The offences appear simple, though correct interpretation of the terms is crucial.

- Any person who uses lead shot for the purpose of shooting with a shotgun on or over wetlands, or causes or permits another person to do so commits an offence (reg. 5)

- Regulation 6 creates an offence by bodies corporate

Interpretations:
These regulations have the following interpretations:

Lead shot means any shot made of
 (a) lead; or
 (b) any alloy or compound of lead where lead comprises more than 1% of that alloy or compound

Alternative non-lead cartridges currently available include steel (soft iron), bismuth, tungsten-based materials (including Hevi Shot), tin etc.

Shotgun means a smooth bore gun but does not include any shotgun chambered for 9 millimetre or smaller rim fire cartridges

Wetlands has the meaning given in Article 1(1) of the Ramsar Convention. Article 1(1) states:

> 'For the purposes of this Convention wetlands are areas of marsh, fen, peatland or water, whether natural or artificial, permanent or temporary, with water that is static or flowing, fresh, brackish or salt, including areas of marine water the depth of which at low tide does not exceed six metres.'

For the purposes of the legislation, the reference in that Article to
 (a) temporary in relation wetlands means wetlands which are covered with water on a seasonal, intermittent or regular basis; and
 (b) peatlands means only peatlands with visible water

The Ramsar Convention means the Convention on Wetlands of International Importance, especially as Waterfowl Habitat signed at Ramsar on 2 February 1971, as amended by:
 (a) the protocol known as the Paris Protocol done at Paris on 3 December 1982; and
 (b) the amendments known as the Regina Amendments adopted at the extraordinary of the Contracting Parties held at Regina, Saskatchewan, Canada, between 28 May and 3 June 1987

It should be stressed that the Regulations do not implement the Ramsar Convention but rather use the recognised definition of what constitutes a wetland for the purpose of the Regulations.

Advice to a shooter should be 'if in doubt, don't use lead shot.'

Police Powers

The police are the only authority to enforce these Regulations. No specific police powers are contained in the Regulations, therefore police officers will have to use Common Law powers if there is a requirement to enter land, to search suspects or to seize items as productions.

The key purpose of the legislation is to stop lead shot falling into wetlands. Shooting behaviour must be modified to ensure this. A 12-bore shotgun shooting a normal cartridge has a maximum fall-out range of approximately 300 metres.

Where lead shot should not be used

The main factor when investigating alleged breaches of the Regulations is to be aware of which areas of water are affected by the Regulations. In summary, the habitats where lead shot must **not** be used are:

Marine and coastal wetlands
> Marine waters less than six metres deep at low tide and all areas between the mean upper and lower spring tide marks. This includes beaches, saltmarshes, estuarine intertidal areas and lagoons. Coastal areas above the high water mark, such as sand dunes where there is standing water (in dune slacks for example) are also included.

Inland wetlands
> Flowing water such as rivers, streams, either permanent, seasonal or intermittent are all included under the Regulations: a person cannot use lead shot on or over these habitats.
> Standing waters are also included; such as permanent or seasonal ponds, pools, lochs and lakes

Fens, marshes and swamps are covered by the Regulations if water is permanent or if they are flooded seasonally. These habitats can be recognised by the presence of vegetation like reed beds, sedge meadows or rushes. Peatlands, such as bogs and mires, *with visible standing water,* such as bog pools, lochans and dubh lochans are covered by the Regulations.

However, the Regulations do not cover all peatland: shrub or heath peatland or moorland, where standing open water only occurs on irregular occasions due to excessive hill run-off, are not covered by the Regulations and lead shot may continue to be used.

If a field is partly flooded (or if it is known to be flooded at certain times of year), or has wetland habitats or features, then non-lead shot should be used. This is not, however, intended to apply to tiny areas of water such as puddles on farm tracks after rain.

Artificial Wetlands

Water bodies such as canals, reservoirs, gravel pits, fishponds and flight-ponds are all covered by the Regulations. So are pools and ponds created as a result of farm works, irrigation, excavations, provision of water supply or wastewater treatment.

Farmland which is seasonally flooded on a regular basis is considered a wetland by the Regulations. For example lead shot must not therefore be used over winter flooding areas.

For a conviction, the shotgun used would require to be seized in order to prove that it is indeed a shotgun in terms of the Regulations. Cartridges and empty cartridge cases would need to be seized to prove that they contain – or originally contained – lead shot. In addition, any game, wildfowl or pescivorous birds (or even mammals, such as rabbits) which have been shot may be of evidential value in that lead shot may be able to be recovered from them.

Since some birds and mammals carry some lead shot as a consequence of being the subject of a non-fatal shooting, an examination by a veterinary pathologist may be required. Such an examination is likely to establish if the lead shot in the bird or animal had proved fatal. Proof of this would aid an investigation.

The principal organisation for advice or assistance in dealing with an investigation under these Regulations is the British Association for Shooting and Conservation (BASC) Trochry, Dunkeld, Perthshire, telephone 01350 723226, or email Scotland@basc.org.uk

15. Sites of Special Scientific Interest (SSSIs)

FORMERLY under Part II of the Wildlife and Countryside Act, 1981 and now under the Nature Conservation (Scotland) Act 2004, Scottish Natural Heritage has a duty to notify as sites of special scientific interest (SSSIs), land that it considers to be of special interest by way of its fauna, flora, geological or geomorphological natural features. The provisions of the 1981 Act, both to notify SSSIs and to ensure they are conserved, have been repealed and replaced with the stronger and broader provisions of the 2004 Act. The 2004 Act has been further amended by the Wildlife and Natural Environment (Scotland) Act 2011. Scottish Natural Heritage continues to be the lead agency in the implementation of the SSSI protection provisions.

The fact that police powers are written into the 2004 enforcement provisions is a clear indication that the intent of the Scottish Government is that police should be involved in the investigation of at least the more serious offences committed against the Act. A working protocol has been drawn up between police and SNH.

Offences in relation to SSSIs and unconsented operations
The 2004 Act introduced different arrangements for the owners and occupiers of land forming SSSIs and for public bodies. In fairly general terms, and without quoting sections of the Act, a non-public body owner or occupier of an SSSI must not carry out, or cause or permit to be carried out, an operation listed in the SSSI notification as an operation requiring consent, without written consent from SNH. To do so would be an offence. Subject to exceptions, a public body must not carry out or cause or permit to be carried out, on its own land, an operation likely to damage the protected natural features of an SSSI, whether that operation is on the SSSI or not, without SNH's written consent or in certain specified circumstances.

This is an area where SNH staff have the expertise and police officers need not concern themselves with the detail, but will expect guidance from SNH should the need arise.

Generally speaking the main offences which police officers would be expected to investigate are:

  • Intentionally or recklessly damaging any natural feature specified in

an SSSI notification. (s. 19(1))
- Without reasonable excuse, carrying out an operation without consent/ fail to restore. (s. 19(3))
- Carrying out, or causing or permitting to be carried out, a prohibited operation on any land to which a Nature Conservation Order relates. (s. 27(1)

  In general terms, where the Scottish Ministers consider that the carrying out of a listed operation on land within an SSSI, not within an SSSI but of special interest, or contiguous to, or associated with an SSSI, should be wholly or partly prohibited, they may make a Nature Conservation Order detailing the prohibition.
- Without reasonable excuse, disregarding a Land Management Order. (s. 36(1))

  In general terms, if SNH considers that work is necessary or expedient for the purpose of conserving, restoring or otherwise enhancing land which is part of, or contiguous to, an SSSI, they may propose to the Scottish Ministers that they make a Land Management Order. This order has effect where SNH has offered to enter into a management agreement in relation to the land and the relevant person has refused or failed to enter into such agreement. SNH may also propose a Land Management Order where it has been unable to identify or contact any owner or occupier of the land.
- Without reasonable excuse, carrying out or causing or permitting to be carried out, an excluded operation. (s. 36(2))
- Without reasonable excuse, breaching a restoration order. (s. 40)

  A court may order that a person convicted must carry out restoration work within a specified period to a protected natural feature damaged by his actions.
- Destruction of signs or notices. (s. 41(2))

  SNH may put up, maintain or remove signs on any land in respect of which an SSSI notification, nature conservation order or land management order relates, or in respect of which byelaws have been made, or take such other action as it considers appropriate for the purpose of providing information to the public.
- S. 47 creates provision for an individual as well as a body corporate, Scottish partnership or as the case may be, unincorporated association to be proceeded against and punished accordingly.

Police officers would expect to be advised on the technicalities of these offences by SNH, and given relevant assistance throughout every investigation. There are unlikely to be circumstances where the police and SNH do not work in tandem.

In some cases SNH may propose to give a Restoration Order under section 20A of the Act (which was introduced by the Wildlife and Natural Environment (Scotland) Act 2011). Though the whole of section 20A is the remit of SNH, it is worth noting that subsection 10 states that proceedings against the responsible person may not be commenced or continued for an offence in which the restoration notice has effect (even if the restoration notice is subsequently withdrawn).

Under section 20A(1) distinction should be made between the term 'proceedings' and the term 'investigation'. In most reports of operations being, or having been, carried out without consent on an SSSI, SNH will prefer restoration. Generally prosecution is only considered when the operations have been particularly destructive, previous experience has shown the suspect tends to disregard advice or legislation, or if a restoration notice has been offered and refused. SNH should be encouraged to notify the appropriate police wildlife crime officer in *all* breaches of the legislation. Even though the incident is not being reported as a crime at this stage, but as a 'heads up', this gives the officer an opportunity to advise that SHN staff, when they visit the site, should take photographs and/or video evidence of the damage *which is corroborated.* In that way, if things don't work out as SNH had hoped, and the matter is later reported as a crime, photographic evidence of the damage has already been secured and available to pass to the police.

Police powers and enforcement (s. 43) are identical to those under the Wildlife and Countryside Act 1981. (see p16)

16. Cruelty to Domestic and Captive Wild Animals

THERE IS a distinction between animal welfare and cruelty towards domestic animals. Animal welfare issues – normally guidance on keeping animals as either pets or livestock, or the rescue of animals in distress or injured – is the remit of animal welfare organisations. Police officers regularly investigate domestic animal cruelty, though these offences are also dealt with by the SSPCA. Many of these cases come direct to the police, sometimes linked with reports of other offences and very often related to violence, drink or drugs. It is therefore important that police officers, particularly wildlife crime officers, have a good working knowledge of their considerable powers.

For the purposes of Part 2 of the Animal Health and Welfare (Scotland) Act 2006, an animal is any vertebrate other than man. This includes all creatures which are mammals, birds, reptiles, amphibians and fish. Invertebrates such as insects, crustaceans, shellfish and cephalopods are *not* animals for the purposes of this part of the Act.

A 'protected animal' is – *of a kind which is commonly domesticated in the British Islands* (this would include sheep, dogs, goats and budgies;) *under the control of man on a permanent or temporary basis,* (this would include farmed deer or ostriches, penguins or lions in a zoo, or an animal caught in a trap set by man, such as a mink in a mink trap, a finch caught in a net to be ringed by an ornithologist or a crow caught in a cage trap;) *or not living in a wild state* (for example where a guinea pig or non-native snake escaped from captivity and, not being native to the British Isles, cannot be said to be living in a wild state even though it is temporarily living in the wild).

The welfare provisions of the Act distinguish between the duties owed towards an animal by the 'man in the street' and the duties owed to an animal by the person who has responsibility for it, with the latter naturally having the greater responsibility.

Responsibility for an animal is only intended to arise where a person can be said to have assumed responsibility for its day to day care, or for a specific purpose, or by virtue of owning it. The owner is always regarded as having a responsibility for an animal, but the owner's responsibility can be shared by another person who is *in charge* of the animal. This applies whether the person owns the animal or is in charge of the animal on a temporary or permanent basis. For example if a horse were to be stabled at a livery yard, both the horse owner and the operator of the livery yard would have responsibility for the welfare of the horse. The owner would have the responsibility to ensure that the livery yard was a suitable place to leave the horse. The livery yard would have the responsibility for the day to day welfare of the horse. Where a DIY livery arrangement had been made, the livery yard operator would *not* normally be expected to have responsibility for the day to day welfare of the animal. However he or she may have a responsibility for the welfare of a horse if the horse owner or the person contracted to take care of the animal failed to attend to it.

Causing an animal unnecessary suffering

The most common cruelty offence, causing an animal unnecessary suffering, can be caused in one of two ways: either by taking an action which causes unnecessary suffering, or by failing to take steps to prevent, or that result in, unnecessary suffering. The infliction of pain, even if extreme, is not in itself sufficient to constitute unnecessary suffering, as the pain may be caused for beneficial reasons, such as surgery or other medical treatment. Therefore consideration must be given as to whether the pain or suffering was necessary. Suffering includes mental as well as physical suffering. It is an offence to unnecessarily infuriate or terrify a protected animal as well as cause it physical pain.

It is an offence for any person, by an act, to cause unnecessary (physical or mental) suffering to a protected animal where the person committing the act knew or ought reasonably to have known that the act *would cause, or would be likely to cause,* suffering. (s.19(1) and (2)) In addition, where a person is responsible for an animal, an offence would be committed by that person if unnecessary suffering was being caused to the animal by another person and the person responsible for the animal, where that person knew or ought reasonably to have known that the act or omission would cause, or would be likely to cause, suffering failed to take preventative action. (s. 19(3)) It is not necessary to show that the person actually knew that his or her act or omission would cause suffering, but only that they *ought* to have known.

It should be noted that a person only commits an offence of causing unnecessary suffering by omitting to take some action *if that person is responsible for the animal.* As an example, a person does not commit an offence by failing to feed a stray cat if that person is not responsible for the animal.

The destruction of an animal in an appropriate and humane manner is not unnecessary suffering. However destruction must not cause suffering over and above that necessary. The term 'appropriate and humane' is not defined and it is for a court to interpret having regard to all the circumstances of the case.

Section 19 (4) provides a very important check list of considerations for the purpose of determining whether suffering is unnecessary. They are –
   (a) whether the suffering could reasonably have been avoided or reduced,
   (b) whether the conduct concerned was in compliance with any relevant enactment or any relevant provisions of a licence or code of practice issued under an enactment.
   (c) whether the conduct concerned was for a legitimate purpose, for example –
   (i) the purpose of benefiting the animal, or
   (ii) the purpose of protecting a person, property or other animal,
   (d) whether the suffering was proportionate to the conduct concerned,
   (e) whether the conduct concerned was in the circumstances that of a reasonably competent and humane person

Prohibited procedure – tail docking of dogs

It is an offence to carry out a prohibited procedure on a protected animal, or to cause that procedure to take place. This would include the docking of a dog's tail (s. 20). It is also an offence to take a dog or other protected animal from Scotland (or cause to be taken) for the purpose of having a prohibited procedure carried out on it outwith Scotland.

Animal fights

There are many offences that relate to animal fights. (s. 23) This is an occasion on which a protected animal is placed with an animal, or with a human, for the purposes of fighting, wrestling or baiting. With certain exemptions, these include:

- Keeping or training an animal for an animal fight
- Possessing, without lawful authority or reasonable excuse, any equipment which is designed or adapted for use at an animal fight
- Causing an animal fight to take place
- Arranging an animal fight,
- Participate in making, or carrying out, arrangements for an animal fight (including allowing premises to be used for, or charging admission to attend, an animal fight),
- Making or accepting a bet on the outcome of an animal fight or on the likelihood of anything occurring (or not occurring) in the course of an animal fight

- Being present at an animal fight
- Publishing, supplying or showing a video recording of an animal fight to another person,
- Possesses a video recording of an animal fight with the intention of supplying it to another person

Some of the offences listed can be committed without a fight having taken place. For example the offence of making arrangements for an animal fight would not depend on a fight actually taking place. An animal fight could be arranged which is later cancelled, but the offence would still have been committed.

An animal fight is defined as an occasion on which a protected animal is placed with an animal or human for the purpose of fighting, wrestling or baiting. This means that an animal fight will be deemed to have taken place even if both animals are wild animals, as the definition of protected animal includes any animal under the control of man. Dog fighting, cock fighting, bear and badger baiting are all prohibited as are bull fighting, kangaroo 'boxing' and certain rodeo events such as bull wrestling.

Allowing a cat to chase a mouse or a bird is not an animal fight as the cat (the protected animal) has not been placed with the mouse or the bird (the animal) for the purpose of fighting, wrestling or baiting. In a similar scenario, neither is it animal fighting to set a terrier in to a fox den to bolt a vixen or to kill the cubs after the vixen has bolted and been shot. This is a practice that is legitimate under the Protection of Wild Mammals (Scotland) Act 2002 if carried out by a landowner or with that person's permission.

No offence would be committed by a museum exhibiting cock fighting spurs, or police or an animal welfare organisation possessing animal fighting equipment for use as training aids.

The offences in the Act do not apply to broadcasting, anything done for law enforcement, and anything done in the course of any other lawful activity done in the public interest or with a view to the public interest being served. It would not be an offence for an undercover police officer to attend an animal fight to obtain evidence for a prosecution. Neither would an offence take place if a reporter was present at an animal fight if the intent was to write an article to expose the criminal activities.

No offence would be committed in showing a video of a bullfight that took place in Spain, a rodeo that took place in the USA or a video recording of an animal fight that took place before the date of the commencement of this Act on 11 July 2006.

Abandonment of animals

A person having responsibility for an animal commits an offence if, without reasonable excuse, he or she abandons it in circumstances likely to cause it unnecessary suffering. (s. 29(1)) It is also an offence for a person having responsibility for an animal, without reasonable excuse, to leave it and fail to make adequate provisions for its welfare. (s. 29(2))

Consideration must be taken of the kind of animal concerned and its age and state of health, the length of time for which it is, or has been, left, and what it reasonably requires by way of food, water, shelter and warmth. No time periods have been specified after which it can be assumed that an animal has been abandoned. This will vary according to individual circumstances.

An abandoned animal does not need to have suffered for an offence to have been committed. The offence would have been committed if the animal was abandoned in circumstances which were *likely* to cause it unnecessary suffering. An example might be a dog owner leaving his dog without food or water in a house while he goes on a week's holiday. That this is discovered the day after he left does not negate the offence. Conversely a small animal such as a hamster or a gerbil may be able to be left for a few days provided it has access to sufficient fresh food and water.

When introducing or re-introducing animals to the wild, care needs to be taken to ensure that they are able to survive and will not be in danger of suffering. This means that rescued injured animals should not be released until fit enough to fend for themselves and that animals being introduced to the wild for the first time, such as pheasants or fish, should be sufficiently mature to have a reasonable chance of survival. In the case of pheasants, it may be necessary for supplementary food to be provided for a short period until the birds learn to forage for themselves.

Seizing a suffering animal

A constable or an inspector under the Act may, if it appears that a protected animal is suffering, take, or arrange for the taking of, such steps as appear to be immediately necessary to alleviate the animals suffering. (s. 32 (1))

This can be done without the need to seek a vet's advice. Such action could include providing food or water for the animal or opening a gate or door to allow the animal out of an enclosed area. In more urgent cases it could include forcing entry to a car or breaking the window if an animal was suffering from heat stress. (s. 32 (4))

Police powers under the Act

Constables have nearly all of the powers of inspectors in relation to the commission of offences under the Act, plus the power of arrest. These are set out under **Schedule 1** of the Act (below), as introduced by section 49(7). Only the powers attributed to constables are listed. They have been left in the legislative format, with the addition of some notes that might help clarification:

Paragraph 2 – *Search warrant – urgent search without warrant – suffering – take possession/destroy animals*
Paragraph 2 (1) *A sheriff or justice of the peace may grant a warrant under this sub-paragraph if satisfied –*
(a) that there are reasonable grounds for believing that there is at the premises a protected animal which –
(i) is suffering, or
(ii) is likely to suffer if its circumstances do not change, and
(b) that paragraph 5 is complied with in relation to the premises

Paragraph 2 (2) *A warrant under sub-paragraph (1) authorises an inspector or a constable to enter and search the premises for the purpose of exercising any power conferred by sections 32 and 35 (taking possession of or destruction of animals)*

Paragraph 2 (3) *An inspector or a constable may –*
(a) enter and search premises for the purpose of exercising any power conferred by sections 32 and 35, and
(b) do so without a warrant under sub-paragraph (1) if it appears that immediate entry is appropriate in the interests of an animal

Paragraph 2 (4)
Sub-paragraph (3) does not apply in relation to domestic premises

NOTE: In a written judgement in a 2007 case (*PF Peebles v Andrew Crawford Struthers*) the court held that entry without warrant to alleviate the suffering of an animal is perfectly proper. However if during that process it appears that evidence should be gathered for a prosecution, a warrant should be sought before that is done. SSPCA inspectors had gone on to a farm after finding some dead sheep in a field. They took various photographs, called on the assistance of another inspector and plotted the position of carcasses on a rough plan. In all they took 66 photographs and seized three carcasses for post mortem examination. The sheriff's view was that the evidence was obtained illegally. There was no urgency, since they could have left someone watching over the evidence and obtained a warrant in the manner described at Paragraph 4.

While the search in this case was held to be unlawful, there will not always be a need to proceed straight to requesting a search warrant pre-emptively. In deciding whether or not to request one, the investigating officer should consider factors such as:

- will the occupier of the land permit access on request?
- if he declines, could (or is it likely that) evidence be interfered with or removed in the timescale within which a warrant may be obtained, for example, by the release of captive birds? This is likely to be less of an issue in the case of livestock for example.
- A warrant can only be granted if admission to the premises has been refused, or that it is reasonable to expect that admission will be refused; and that notice of the intention to seek a warrant has been given to the occupier of the premises, or that the giving of such notice would frustrate the purpose of the warrant. (See Paragraph 5) In most cases the investigating officer would have to give notice of his or her intention to seek a warrant, but this would not be necessary where, for example, it was suspected that an animal fight was about to take place. Giving notice of an intention to seek a warrant would simply warn the fight organisers of an impending law enforcement operation. Paragraph 4(3) (below) provides powers to enter and gather evidence without warrant in these circumstances.

Paragraph 4 – *Warrant – search for evidence – urgent search without warrant – unnecessary suffering/ mutilations/ cruel operations/ administering of poisons/ animal fighting/ abandonment/ disqualification*

Paragraph 4 (1) *A sheriff or a justice of the peace may grant a warrant under this sub-paragraph if satisfied –*

    (a) that there are reasonable grounds for believing –

        (i) that a relevant offence has been committed at premises, or

        (ii) that evidence of the commission of, or participation in, a relevant offence is to be found at premises, and

    (b) that paragraph 5 is complied with in relation to the premises

Paragraph 4 (2) *A warrant under sub-paragraph (1) authorises an inspector or a constable to*
(a) enter the premises, and
(b) search for, examine and seize any animal (including the carcass of an animal), equipment, document or other thing tending to provide evidence of the commission of, or participation in, a relevant offence

Paragraph 4 (3) *An inspector or a constable may –*
(a) enter premises and search for, examine and seize any animal (including the carcass of an animal), equipment, document or other thing tending to provide evidence of the commission of, or participation in a relevant offence, and
(b) do so without warrant under sub-paragraph (1), if it appears that delay would frustrate the purpose for which the search is to be carried out

Paragraph 4 (4) *Sub-paragraph (3) does not apply in relation to domestic premises*

Paragraph 4 (5) *In this paragraph, a 'relevant offence' is*
(a) an offence under sections 19 to 23 (causing unnecessary suffering; mutilations; cruel operations; administration of poisons; animal fights)
(b) an offence under section 24 (ensuring welfare of animals)
(c) an offence under section 29 (abandonment of animals)
(d) an offence under section 40(11) (breaching a disqualification order)

Note that the searches under the provisions of this paragraph, with or without warrant, are only available for the offences that are listed as 'relevant offences.'

In the case of an urgent search for evidence of the offence without warrant the terms of either sub-paragraph (2) or (3) of paragraph 5 must be met.

Paragraph 5 – *Conditions re paragraph 1 and paragraph 4*
Paragraph 5 (1)
This paragraph is complied with in relation to premises if either of the conditions specified in sub-paragraph (2) and (3) is met

Paragraph 5 (2)
The condition is –
(a) that
(i) admission to the premises has been refused, or

(ii) such a refusal may reasonably be expected, and

(b) that

(i) notice of the intention to seek a warrant has been given to the occupied of the premises, or

(ii) the giving of such notice would frustrate the purpose for which the warrant is sought

Paragraph 5 (3)

The condition is that the premises are unoccupied or the occupier is temporarily absent

Paragraph 6 – *Stopping or detaining vehicles or vessels*

Paragraph 6 (1)

A constable in uniform may stop and detain a vehicle or vessel for the purpose of the exercise of a relevant power

Paragraph 6 (2)

An inspector, if accompanied by a constable in uniform, may stop and detain a vehicle or vessel for the purpose of the exercise of a relevant power

Paragraph 6 (3)

A vehicle or vessel may be detained under sub-paragraph (1) or (2) for as long as is reasonably required for the exercise of the power concerned

Paragraph 6 (4)

The power concerned may be exercised at the place where the vehicle or vessel was first detained or nearby

Note that the search of the vehicle or vessel, or whatever power is to be exercised, must be carried out where the vehicle or vessel was first detained or nearby

Paragraph 7 – *Warrants – duration*

A warrant granted under a provision of this schedule remains in force for one month beginning with the date on which it is granted

Paragraph 8 – *Exercising powers*

Paragraph 8 (1)

A relevant power is exercisable only at a reasonable time

Paragraph 8 (2)
Sub-paragraph (1) does not apply if it appears that exercise of the power at a reasonable time would frustrate the purpose of exercising this power

Paragraph 9 – *Use of force*
Paragraph 9 (1)
A relevant power is exercisable, if necessary, using reasonable force

Paragraph 9 (2) Sub-paragraph (1) does not apply to a power conferred by paragraph 1 or 3
(Paragraphs 1 and 3 are not enforced by police officers)

Paragraph 10 – *Production of evidence of authority*
A person exercising a relevant power must, if required, produce evidence of the person's authority

Paragraph 11 – *Other persons and equipment to assist; sampling*
Paragraph 11 (1) *A relevant power includes power to take onto premises –*
 (a) such persons for assistance, and
 (b) such equipment as are required for the purpose of the exercise of the power

Paragraph 11 (2) *A relevant power includes power to secure the taking of any of the steps mentioned in sub-paragraph (3)*

Paragraph 11 (3) *Those steps are –*
 (a) carrying out tests on, and taking samples from
  (i) an animal (including a carcass of an animal),
  (ii) any equipment, substance or other thing
 (b) using a mark, microchip or another method of identifying an animal
As an example of the powers under this paragraph, a police officer may take other persons he or she thinks may be necessary to assist, or any equipment, substance or other thing necessary, which may be a vehicle, trailer or a JCB, may take samples, including, via a vet, blood samples, and may have a vet microchip the animal.

Paragraph 12 – *'Qualifying persons' – directions*
Paragraph 12 (1) *A qualifying person must –*
 (a) comply with any reasonable direction made by a person exercising a relevant power, and

(b) in particular, give that person such information and assistance as that person reasonably requires

Paragraph 12(2) *In sub-paragraph (1) a 'qualifying person' is –*
(a) the occupier of premises in relation to which a relevant power is being exercised,
and
(b) a person who appears to be responsible for animals at the premises
(c) a person who appears to be under the direction or control of a person referred to in paragraph (a) or (b)

Paragraph 13 *– Leaving premises secure*
A person exercising a relevant power in relation to unoccupied premises must leave the premises as effectively secured against entry as the person found them.

Paragraph 14 *– Qualifying persons – offences – obstruction*
(1) A person commits an offence if, without reasonable excuse, the person contravenes paragraph 12(1)
(2) A person commits an offence if the person intentionally obstructs a person in the exercise of a relevant power

Paragraph 15 *– Obstructions – taking possession of or destruction of animals – deprivation order – seizure*
Paragraph 15 (1) *A person commits an offence if the person intentionally obstructs a person in the exercise of a power conferred by –*
(a) section 32,
(b) an order under section 34(1)
(c) section 35

Paragraph 15(2) *A person commits an offence if the person intentionally obstructs a person in the carrying out of –*
(a) a deprivation order
(b) a seizure order
(c) an interim order under section 41(9) or 43(5)

Police powers of arrest:
Paragraph 16

A constable may arrest without warrant any person whom the constable
reasonably believes is committing or has committed an offence under
(a) sections 19 to 23, (unnecessary suffering, mutilations, cruel operations,
administration of poisons animal fights) or
(b) paragraphs 14 or 15 (obstructions)

Paragraph 17
The powers conferred on constables by this schedule are without prejudice to
any powers conferred on constables by law apart from this schedule

Paragraph 18
In this schedule, a 'relevant power' is a power –
  (a) conferred on an inspector by
    (i) a provision of this schedule, or
    (ii) a warrant granted under a provision of this schedule
  (b) conferred on a constable by –
    (i) a provision of this schedule except paragraph 16, or
    (ii) a warrant granted under a provision of this schedule

Detention – S. 14 Criminal Procedure (Scotland) Act 1995
All offences under this part of the Animal Health and Welfare (Scotland)
Act 2006 are punishable by imprisonment, therefore a police officer
would have power to detain a suspect.

In some incidents investigated by the police, the assistance of the SSPCA
or other wildlife rescue organisation, State Veterinary Service or local
authority animal health inspectors may be required for their experience of
animal welfare and animal handling. They may also in some cases be able to
re-home or rehabilitate animals.

Conversely, in some cases investigated by the State Veterinary Service,
local authority animal health inspectors or the SSPCA, the assistance of the
police will be requested, especially if forced entry needs to be made to premises
or a suspect may need to be detained.

By and large the State Veterinary Service, local authority animal health
inspectors or inspectors of the SSPCA investigate a high proportion of reports
of cruelty to *domestic* livestock, including farm livestock, while the police
investigate most cases of cruelty to *wild* animals, though often under other
legislation. In many cases of domestic livestock dealt with by the police they
are called because of other offences, very often related to drunkenness or

violence. Many cases of cruelty to domestic animals are investigated by the police as they have taken place in the late evening or at night when other organisations are not available. For these varied reasons, police officers must be aware of animal welfare legislation and their associated legislative and common law powers.

Dealing with allegations of cruelty can sometimes be complex, particularly in relation to the conditions in which animals are kept, and we must all guard against attributing anthropomorphic values to animals. Pet animals may be kept in conditions which we think are appalling and in which we would never consider keeping our own pet. An example may be a dog that is kept tied up outside for most of the day and gets little or no exercise, yet is well fed and has sufficient shelter. Under the almost completely repealed Protection of Animals (Scotland) Act 1912 this was unlikely to have been seen as an offence. Time will tell whether or not the courts consider this an offence under the 2006 Act but at least there is a starting point in that the officer could request the SSPCA to consider serving a care notice on the owner of the dog. If the dog's quality of life improves as a result the situation has been resolved. If the advice in the care notice is rejected then an offence may be committed.

In a similar vein, feeding young calves with nothing but milk to produce veal, despite the knowledge that this is extremely bad for their digestive system, or rearing chickens in sheds with crowded and dusty conditions and killing them for the poultry market at about 8 weeks of age may seem cruel to many of us, but these practices are deemed legal. Unless other specific cruelty issues emerge no offence has taken place.

Different people place different values on animals that they keep. While most of us who keep dogs may look on them as pets, some farmers and gamekeepers look on them as aids in carrying out their particular occupation. If a farmer or gamekeeper shoots his dog at the end of its working life, he may not think any less of the dog than the rest of us with our dogs but is probably being practical. He may not consider this any different to taking the dog to a vet to be put down. Provided the dog is destroyed in an appropriate and humane manner, he has not committed an offence. (*Patchett v MacDougall 1983*)

There is a fine line between what is unsatisfactory and what could be deemed as being cruel. Each case must be investigated on the strength of the evidence available and the interpretation of that evidence by veterinary surgeons or veterinary pathologists.

Having animals fight with each other, such as cock fighting, dog fighting or badger baiting are thankfully relatively uncommon in Scotland. These incidents, when they do occur, involve some of the most insidious forms of cruelty. Those who are involved take elaborate precautions to prevent detection and are very often criminals who diversify into several aspects of crime, particularly drugs and crimes of violence. To have success, enforcement action against them needs to be well planned and co-ordinated, and usually to be a joint operation between police and SSPCA. Every opportunity to gather and share intelligence on suspects, utilising the resources of the National Wildlife Crime Unit, must be taken. Police officers should be particularly alert, when visiting or searching houses for reasons other than cruelty issues, to the presence of dogs – or photographs of dogs – with old or fresh injuries, particularly to the face and lower jaw; suspicion that dogs are being used for fighting or baiting purposes should be discussed with the force wildlife crime officer.

Before taking possession of animals involved in a cruelty case, officers should consider if this is necessary or if there may be other options. Cases take a long time to come to court for a disposal and the animal(s) will have to be cared for during the intervening period. Costs may be substantial but this has to be balanced against whether or not the investigating officer intends requesting the court, under the provisions of the Act, to ban the accused from keeping animals. It would be unrealistic to consider leaving animals with the owner in such circumstances. In police investigations, consultation should be made with SSPCA, who may agree to look after cruelly-treated animals until the court case is completed.

In the case of captive wild animals, there will some circumstances when the animal should either be immediately released to the wild or taken for examination or treatment. In other circumstances, for example finch trapping, any birds recovered or seized should be kept until a clearance for release is given by the specialist wildlife prosecutor, though the shorter their period in captivity the better their chance of survival.

When investigating animal cruelty allegedly committed against a wild animal, be aware that even though the animal may be in very poor condition, it is up to the prosecution to prove that its condition was caused by the conditions of its captivity. Several very thin rabbits may be found caught in a rabbit box trap. If it can be proved that they are thin because the trap has not been checked for several days and the rabbits have had no food or water that is the essence of the case. Be aware, though, that in prolonged severe winters, many rabbits lose condition rapidly and are often reduced to eating bark from trees. Likewise a very thin fox in a snare or a very thin crow in a cage trap does not automatically mean it has been confined there for several days and has been starved. It may be newly caught and already in poor condition for some reason totally unrelated to its confinement. Officers should ensure that if someone is to be charged with a cruelty offence with thin captive wild animals, that the poor condition of the animals is the result of, and can be shown to be, the unlawful actions of that person.

It may be that this can be proved by the experience of the witnesses dealing with the investigation. If this is not the case and there is any doubt about what caused the animal or animals to be emaciated, the investigating officer should have them examined, if still alive, by a vet, and if dead, at a Scotland's Rural College (SRUC, formerly SAC) vet lab. (see Specialist Examinations – Veterinary Pathology p210) In the case of emaciation being due to a severe parasitic infection, some other clinical reason or because of an injury of some sort, establishing this before having someone charged with an offence he or she did not commit will save unnecessary stress on a suspect and prevent embarrassment for the investigating officer.

The investigating officer should consider that, in cases when distress is caused to an animal – such as a dog left in a car during a very hot day – the level of distress can sometimes be measured and demonstrated to a court to constitute cruelty. Dogs pant when they are hot, which is the equivalent of humans sweating. Panting means they are hot, but not necessarily distressed. It is the level of panting demonstrating distress which needs to be proved in court, but the evidence of lay persons may not be sufficient. Some cases are more easily proved if the animal is near death, but always bear in mind that a veterinary examination may be necessary.

Animals that are dead or have died should always be retained in case the defence requests to have them examined.

Lastly, officers should be aware of the correlation between cruelty to animals and domestic violence or child abuse. As part of First Strike Scotland, the SSPCA and Tayside Police worked in tandem to research past cases and this insidious link was frequently demonstrated. Police officers and SSPCA inspectors should bear in mind the need to exchange intelligence on cruelty via the National Wildlife Crime Unit, and on occasions consider bringing social services into the loop.

17. Dogs

IT IS unfortunate that, even with the Control of Dogs (Scotland) Act 2010, legislation to deal effectively with out of control and dangerous dogs is still woefully lacking. Attacks by dogs on people are all-too common, with many of those attacks involving dogs that are no more than a status symbol of the owner or a means of protection. Many of those dogs are cruelly treated and have in fact been encouraged to attack another domestic or wild animal, or even a human. Staffordshire terriers are regularly demonised because of the aggressive or indifferent nature of some of their owners, whereas the same breed of dog with a responsible owner is invariably good natured and friendly. There are complaints to the police of dangerous dogs on a daily basis and this short chapter is intended to provide a very basic guide as to which legislation is most suited to the circumstances.

Dogs worrying livestock

A dog unaccompanied in a public place can still be seized and dealt with by police or dog wardens as a stray, but this is the most minor of the offences. Some dogs worry livestock, and while it is often legitimate for the livestock owner to shoot the dog, there are limits on this offence by dint of the definition of 'worrying livestock.' This term, within the Dogs (Protection of Livestock) Act 1953, means attacking cattle, sheep, goats, swine, horses, asses, mules, domestic fowls, turkeys, geese or ducks; chasing livestock in such a way as may reasonably be expected to cause injury or suffering to the livestock or, in the case of females, abortion, or loss or diminution in their produce, or being at large (not on a lead or otherwise under close control) in a field or enclosure in which there are sheep. *The offence must have taken place on agricultural land*, which means land used as arable, meadow or grazing land, or for the purpose of poultry farming, pig farming, market gardens, allotments, nursery grounds or orchards. These offences would be dealt with by the police.

The definition above would not extend to a garden. A situation with a dog attacking poultry kept in a private garden would be excluded from the offence and would therefore require to be dealt with by the Local Authority under the Control of Dogs (Scotland) Act 2010, despite the fact that most calls reporting this type of incident would be made to the police.

Dangerous and annoying dogs

A dog that is dangerous or gives a person in a public place reasonable cause for alarm or annoyance can sometimes be dealt with under the Civic Government (Scotland) Act 1982. (s. 49(2) This Act is also suited to dealing with annoyance by noisy dogs (and other creatures, such as a noisy cockerel, pea fowl or guinea fowl). Section 49(2) may also be suitable, in some circumstances, for dealing with a dog which is continually chasing a neighbour's pet cat, or has attacked another dog.

The Dangerous Dogs Act 1991 was passed in response to a number of horrific attacks by specific types of dogs on members of the public and introduced strict controls on types of dogs which were specifically bred for fighting. This legislation was rushed and poorly drafted, and has failed to make the public much safer from dangerous dogs. The Act outlaws specific breeds of dog, but takes no account of the behaviour of dog owners.

Part of the Act applies to the breeding, selling or advertising for sale any dog of the type known as the pit bull terrier, any dog of the type known as the Japanese toza, the Dogo Argentino, the Fila Braziliero and any dog of any type designated by the Secretary of State. It also creates the offence of any of these dogs being in a public place without being muzzled, allowing such a dog to stray, or abandoning it. Dogs of these breeds or types must be registered on the Index of Exempted Dogs. (tel: 07000 783652)

This Act also creates the offence of a dog being dangerously out of control in *any* place (whether or not a public place.) If, while so out of control, it injures any person this is an aggravated offence. However the definition of the term 'dangerously out of control' limits the fear and concern for the dog's actions to injury *to humans as opposed to animals*. It may, therefore, be extremely difficult to get a prosecution against a person who allows their dog, while out of control, to chase and kill or injure a household pet. It appears that a dog that has attacked a household pet or possibly even a wild animal can only be dealt with under this Act if there is evidence that its actions instil fear and concern that a *person* might also be attacked. This might be the case where a pet owner is trying to save his or her pet from the attack, or trying to beat off a dog attacking, for instance, a roe deer fawn. Most of these incidents would be initially reported to the police, but in cases where the wording of the Act does not create an offence, would need then to be reported to the Local Authority dog wardens for them to deal with under the Control of Dogs (Scotland) Act 2010. Not the best situation for someone who has just had a pet savaged!

18. Specialist Examinations

AS IN any other sphere of investigation, police officers frequently need assistance from experts. We are extremely fortunate in Scotland in that much of the forensic, chemistry and pathology expertise required in wildlife investigations is funded by the Scottish Government. The cost of the examinations of dead animals, animal parts, toxic substances and certain wildlife crime scenes would be prohibitive and would simply not be possible within shrinking policing budgets. Inability through cost to have these examinations carried out would mean that many important prosecutions would not be possible. The absence of these prosecutions (and of course the immediate evaporation of their deterrent value) would be disastrous for wildlife and for conservation. The value, therefore, of the following schemes cannot be underestimated.

Science and Advice for Scottish Agriculture (SASA)
1. Suspected animal poisoning and Wildlife Incident Investigation Scheme (WIIS):

Services available: Under the Wildlife Incident Investigation Scheme (WIIS), the Pesticides and Wildlife branch at SASA undertakes analysis capable of detecting very low amounts of pesticide residues in animal tissues where poisoning is suspected.

Procedure: All samples relating to suspected poisoning incidents (e.g. carcasses, baits, vomit etc) should be collected in separate sealed bags with labels for chain of evidence. Keep samples in a cool place if there is a delay before samples are transferred to SASA. Any information indicating the possible use or abuse of a specific pesticide should be provided to the laboratory by the investigating officer along with details of the locations, including grid references, where the items were found.

Veterinary pathologists at the various Scottish Agricultural College veterinary laboratories can also take samples from suspected pesticide poisoning carcasses and baits and send them to SASA

Health and safety considerations: Always use gloves when handling carcases, suspected baits or other items for examination. The pesticides often associated with animal poisoning can be toxic by skin absorption or inhalation.

Contact details: Elizabeth Sharp or Laura Melton (0131 244 8874) or email elizabeth.sharp@sasa.gsi.gov.uk or laura.melton@sasa.gsi.gov.uk

2. Suspected illegal gassing

Services available: SASAs Wildlife Management staff members are able to safely investigate blocked animal tunnels in cases of suspected illegal gassing. Although legal products (Phostoxin and Talunex) are available for gassing of rabbits, moles and rats in outdoor burrows, they are not legal for gassing other mammals such as foxes or badgers. Cymag and Phostek have both lost approval for use.

Procedure: If blocked tunnels are found and illegal gassing is suspected, contact SASA staff for advice and investigative assistance. They will be able to safely open blocked holes and test residues for gassing agents. Although manufacturers claim that gas dispersal is generally complete within 48 hours of treatment, SASA staff have managed to obtain positive (reactive) samples several days after gassing treatment.

Health and safety considerations: Under no circumstances should any objects blocking the holes be removed or close examination of the hole made to look for signs of life. A dose of poison gas may be received which could be fatal.

Contact details: Dr Gill Hartley (0131 244 8804) or Steve Campbell (0131 244 8871)
or email gill.hartley@sasa.gsi.gov.uk or steve.campbell@sasa.gsi.gov.uk.

3. Analysis of animal DNA evidence

Services available: SASA's Wildlife DNA Forensic unit is available to analyse animal DNA evidence. Evidence collected from wildlife crimes often includes substances which may hold animal DNA. Examples include blood, hairs, tissue, saliva, bones, feathers, eggs, scales, and carcasses or even processed animal products (e.g. taxidermy specimens, bushmeat, powdered horn). This evidence can be used to identify the species, the sex of the animal and for individual matching in some cases.

Procedure: Officers should make contact by telephone or email as early as possible in the investigation in order to discuss the case and how the unit may be able to help. The unit can also give advice and training on collecting animal DNA evidence and storage.

Health and safety: Always use gloves when handling carcases, suspected baits or other items for examination. It is important for investigators to have some awareness of the potential for animals to transmit zoonotic diseases and to take appropriate precautions to minimise the risk of transmission (e.g. wear gloves and avoid inhalation of dust etc).

Contact: Dr Lucy Webster, telephone 07557197316
or email wildlifeforensics@sasa.gsi.gov.uk

Veterinary pathology
Organisations: Scotland's Rural College (SRUC, formerly SAC) (Veterinary Services Division), Glasgow and Edinburgh University Veterinary Schools and Veterinary Laboratories Agency (Lasswade).

Services available: In cases of unexplained death or injury to animals and birds, 'veterinary pathology' serves the same purpose as 'forensic pathology' of human cadavers in cases of unexpected or suspicious human deaths. The service provides the opportunity for impartial post-mortem examination of animals and birds. The reports should detail the cause of death, the nature and extent of injury or disease and, where possible, how it might have occurred. Appropriate samples for toxicology, ballistics or other procedures can be collected during the post-mortem examination. The pathologist may be able to comment on any suffering experienced by the animal or bird before death.

Procedure: Handling and appropriate storage of wildlife cases before delivery to the laboratory is important. Carcasses that are in a state of good preservation are, generally, the most useful. However, significant observations may also be made on cadavers in advanced stages of decomposition. For example, fractured bones, serious haemorrhages, bullets, trap injuries and some poisons may still be detectable.

Small animals and birds (e.g. most birds of prey, hares, pine martens etc) are relatively simple to store. If possible these corpses should be stored at domestic refrigerator temperature (5^0 C). It is less easy to find facilities to chill larger creatures such as swans, badgers and deer. In these latter cases, if the delay before delivery is likely to be 24 hours or less in summer or up to 2 days in winter, then keeping the body in a cool outbuilding is acceptable.

On occasion, for logistical or legal reasons, it may prove difficult to deliver the body within 1-2 days. Under these circumstances it may be necessary to freeze (-20⁰C) the body. However, freezing makes post-mortem examination less satisfactory as bruising and other subtle lesions may be lost and microscopic examination is often rendered impossible.

Carcasses should be labelled and bagged. Strong black bins liners are suitable. Labels should be attached by a length of string that allows the label to be kept outside the bag, so ensuring that the label does not become contaminated by blood or other fluids.

Any weapons, snares, ropes, dog leads or other paraphernalia should be bagged, labelled and submitted with the body. If snares/wires etc are attached or encircling any part of the cadaver, these should be left attached to the body.

Before despatch of the body to the laboratory, check that a pathologist will be able to examine the specimens.

Officers should not allow anyone to 'explore' or to 'examine superficially' any wound or lesions on the body before it is despatched to the laboratory. If any interference to the body has occurred before the investigator's involvement with the case, please inform the pathologist at the time of submission of the carcass.

Health and safety: Always use gloves when handling carcasses, suspected baits or other items for examination. It is important for investigators to have some awareness of the potential for animals to transmit zoonotic diseases and to take appropriate precautions to minimise the risk of transmission (e.g. wear gloves and avoid inhalation of dust etc).

Contact:
Scotland's Rural College Veterinary Services Division
Edinburgh – 0131 535 3130
Perth – 01738 629167
St Boswells – 01835 822456
Auchincruive – 01292 520318
Dumfries – 01387 267260
Aberdeen – 01224 711177
Thurso – 01847 892602

Inverness – 01463 243030
Edinburgh University Veterinary School,
Division of Veterinary Pathology,
Easter Bush Veterinary Centre,
Nr Roslin, Midlothian EH25 9RG.
Telephone; 0131 650 6265

Glasgow University Veterinary School,
Department of Veterinary Pathology,
Bearsden Road,
Bearsden,
Glasgow G61 1QH
Telephone (General Enquiries) 0141 330 6945

Veterinary Laboratories Agency (Lasswade),
Pentlands Science Park,
Bush Loan,
Penicuik, Midlothian EH26 0PZ.
Telephone 0131 445 6169.

APPENDIX A

ANNUAL GENERAL LICENCES

The list of 2012 general licences is as follows, though since they are continually evolving there will have been changes in 2013. For full details of current general licences and conditions see the Scottish Natural Heritage website at http://www.snh.gov.uk/protecting-scotlands-nature/species-licensing/birdlicensing/general/

SNH GL 01/2012	Licence to kill or take certain birds for the conservation of wild birds
SNH GL 02/2012	Licence to kill or take certain birds for the purpose of preventing serious damage to livestock, foodstuffs for livestock, crops, vegetables and fruit
SNH GL 03/2012	Licence to protect public health, public safety and prevent the spread of disease
SNH GL 04/2012	Licence to protect air safety
SNH GL 05/2012	Licence to keep certain wild birds for the purpose of rehabilitation
SNH GL 06/2012	Licence for veterinary surgeons and practitioners to keep certain birds
SNH GL 07/2012	Licence to take birds eggs for the purpose of removing unsuccessful eggs from nest boxes
SNH GL 08/2012	Licence to permit the sale of certain captive-bred species of bird
SNH GL 09/2012	Licence to permit the competitive showing of certain captive-bred live birds
SGGL 10/2011	Licence to allow the keeping of certain birds in show cages for training purposes
SNH GL 11/2012	Licence to take eggs of the mallard (Anas platyrhynchos) for incubation
SNH GL 12/2012	Licence to permit the incubation of schedule 4 chicks
SNH GL 13/2012	Licence to sell feathers and parts of certain dead wild birds
SNH GL 14/2012	Licence to sell dead birds

Scottish Natural Heritage General Licence No. 01/2012

Licensing Section
Scottish Natural Heritage
Great Glen House
Leachkin Road
Inverness IV3 8NW
01463 725000

LICENSING@snh.gov.uk

Scottish Natural Heritage General Licence No. 01/2012

WILDLIFE AND COUNTRYSIDE ACT 1981
LICENCE TO KILL OR TAKE CERTAIN BIRDS FOR THE
CONSERVATION OF WILD BIRDS

This licence is granted under Section 16(1)(c) of the Wildlife and Countryside Act 1981 by Scottish Natural Heritage and being convinced that there is no other satisfactory solution, it authorises the killing or taking of wild birds in accordance with the stated conditions, for the purpose of the conservation of wild birds. It also authorises attempts to kill certain birds, in line with the conditions of this licence, where the attempt results in injury to the bird concerned. It also authorises, for the purpose of the conservation of wild birds and subject to the stated conditions, the keeping or confinement of any bird listed in Condition 7 of this licence in a Larsen trap.

Failure to abide by anyone of the conditions may invalidate the licence and could lead to prosecution.

Only authorised persons may use this licence.

Please note that, in accordance with condition 3, no person convicted on or after 1 January 2008 of an offence to which this paragraph applies may use this licence unless, in respect of that offence, either (1) they were dismissed with an admonition, or (2) they are a rehabilitated person for the purposes of the Rehabilitation of Offenders Act 1974 and their conviction is treated as spent. A person may also use this licence where, in respect of such an offence, a court has made an order discharging them absolutely. This paragraph applies to offences under the Wildlife and Countryside Act 1981, the Conservation (Natural Habitats &c.) Regulations 1994, the Protection of Badgers Act 1992, the Protection of Wild Mammals (Scotland) Act 2002, the Animal Health and Welfare (Scotland) Act 2006 and the Protection of Animals (Scotland) Act

1912 (all as amended). Such a person may still, in spite of being debarred from the use of this General Licence, apply to Scottish Natural Heritage for a specific licence to control birds for the purpose of conserving wild birds. Any such application will be considered on its merits.

This licence is valid in Scotland, unless previously revoked, for the period 01 January 2012 to 31 December 2012.

CONDITIONS

1. This licence may only be used by authorised persons who have read and understood its conditions.

2. This licence can only be relied on in circumstances where the authorised person is satisfied that appropriate non-lethal methods of control such as scaring or proofing are either ineffective or impracticable.

3. No person convicted on or after 1 January 2008 of an offence to which this paragraph applies may use this licence unless, in respect of that offence, either (1) they were dismissed with an admonition, or (2) they are a rehabilitated person for the purposes of the Rehabilitation of Offenders Act 1974 and their conviction is treated as spent. A person may also use this licence where, in respect of such an offence, a court has made an order discharging them absolutely. This paragraph applies to offences under the Wildlife and Countryside Act 1981, the Conservation (Natural Habitats &c.) Regulations 1994, the Protection of Badgers Act 1992, the Protection of Wild Mammals (Scotland) Act 2002, the Animal Health and Welfare (Scotland) Act 2006 and the Protection of Animals (Scotland) Act 1912 (all as amended).

4. The methods of killing or taking which may be used under this licence, except where further restrictions, listed below in this licence, apply, are:
   - Pricking of eggs
   - Oiling of eggs with a product approved for use within Scotland
   - Destruction of eggs and nests
   - A Larsen trap
   - Any other crow cage trap
   - Shooting with any firearm, including semi-automatic firearms, shotguns or an weapons
   - Targeted falconry

5. Birds which may be taken or killed under this licence by the above methods are:

Great Black-backed Gull	*Larus marinus*
Carrion Crow	*Corvus corone*
Hooded Crow	*Corvus cornix*

Jackdaw	*Corvus monedula*
Jay	*Garrulus glandarius*
Magpie	*Pica pica*
Rook	*Corvus frugilegus*

Except where further restrictions apply as outlined below in these licence conditions.

TRAPS

6. For the purposes of this licence, a Larsen or crow cage trap is not required to satisfy the requirements of Section 8(1) of the Wildlife & Countryside Act 1981 with regard to the dimensions.

7. For the purposes of this licence birds other than the species listed in condition 5 should be released unharmed immediately on being found in a Larsen or a Cage Trap.

8. In the case of the Larsen trap, no bird may be confined in such a trap as a decoy except a bird of the following species:

Carrion Crow	*Corvus corone*
Hooded Crow	*Corvus cornix*
Magpie	*Pica pica*

9. In the case of other crow cage traps, only corvids included in condition 5 may be used as decoys. Raven (*Corvus corax*) and Chough (*Pyrrhocorax pyrrhocorax*) may not be used as decoys.

10. Except in the case where severe weather prohibits, any cage trap of any sort which is set under the terms of this licence shall be inspected by the authorised person, while it remains in use, at least once every day at intervals of no more than 24 hours.

11. Such an inspection must be sufficient to determine whether there are any live or dead birds in the trap.

12. Any dead or sickly decoy bird must be immediately removed from a trap.

13. In the case of the Larsen trap only one decoy bird may be used, and it must be removed from the trap when not in use. In the Larsen trap there must be a separate compartment for the decoy bird.

14. In the case of decoy birds, all relevant animal welfare legislation shall be complied with at all times, including the Animal Health and Welfare (Scotland) Act 2006. This includes providing decoy birds with adequate food, water and shelter and a suitable perch that does not cause discomfort to the birds' feet. Decoy birds shall also have adequate protection from the prevailing wind and rain.

15. When any cage trap is not in use it must be immobilised and rendered incapable of use in such a way that the immobilisation could not be reversed

without considerable forethought or considerable difficulty. Doors or panels of cage traps must be removed from the site or, if they are not removed from the site, they must be taken off the trap and secured by a locked padlock. When any Larsen trap is not in use, access doors must be secured with a padlock or the trap removed from the site and stored in such a manner as to prevent its accidental use.

16. Any cage trap or Larsen trap used under this licence shall carry a tag or sign that gives the number of the local police station or wildlife crime officer for the area. The tag or sign shall also carry a unique code that allows the owner to be identified by the police. The operator of the trap will contact their local wildlife crime officer to obtain this code in advance of use of traps. The operator may include other relevant material on the tag or sign.

GENERAL CONDITIONS

17. Any birds killed under the authority of this licence shall be destroyed humanely.
18. Any birds included in the list in Condition 5 which have become confined in a Larsen or cage trap and which are to be killed under this licence, must be killed in a quick and humane manner as soon as reasonably practicable after discovery.
19. This licence does not permit the use of any form of spring-over trap.

DEFINITIONS

21. In this licence 'authorised person' means:
* the owner or occupier, or any person authorised by the owner or occupier, of the landon which the action authorised is taken;
* any person authorised in writing by the local authority for the area within which the action authorised is taken;
* any person authorised in writing by any of the following bodies – Scottish Natural Heritage, a water authority or any other statutory water undertakers, a district board for a fishery district within the meaning of the Salmon Fisheries (Scotland) Act 1862 or the local Fisheries Regulation Act 1966.
* any person authorised in writing by a National Parks Authority established under the National Parks (Scotland) Act 2000 and the Loch Lomond and the Trossachs National Park Designation, Transitional and Consequential Provisions (Scotland) Order 2002.
22. 'Larsen trap' means a portable cage-trap which has a closed compartment for confining a live bird as a decoy and one or more spring activated trap-doors which are either top or side mounted.
23. For the purposes of this licence, 'humanely' means taking all reasonable

precautions to ensure that any killing of birds under this licence is carried out by a single, swift action.

24. For the purposes of this licence 'wild bird' means any bird of a species which is ordinarily resident in or is a visitor to any member State or the European territory of any member State in a wild state. 'Bird' includes all stages from chick to adult.

NOTES

1. Nothing in this licence exempts the licensee or any authorised person from complying with relevant firearms and public safety legislation.

ROBBIE KERNAHAN
Scottish Natural Heritage
Wildlife Operations Unit
Great Glen House
Leachkin Road
INVERNESS IV3 8NW
22 December 2011

Scottish Natural Heritage General Licence No. 02/2012

Licensing Section
Scottish Natural Heritage
Great Glen House
Leachkin Road
Inverness IV3 8NW
01463 725000

LICENSING@snh.gov.uk

Scottish Natural Heritage General Licence No. 02/2012

WILDLIFE AND COUNTRYSIDE ACT 1981
LICENCE TO KILL OR TAKE CERTAIN BIRDS FOR THE PURPOSE OF PREVENTING SERIOUS DAMAGE TO LIVESTOCK, FOODSTUFFS FOR LIVESTOCK, CROPS, VEGETABLES AND FRUIT

This licence is granted under Section 16(1)(k) of the Wildlife and Countryside Act 1981 by Scottish Natural Heritage, and being convinced that there is no other satisfactory solution, it authorises the killing or taking of wild birds in accordance with the stated conditions, for the purpose of the prevention of serious damage to livestock, foodstuffs for livestock, crops, vegetables and fruit. It also authorises attempts to kill certain birds, in line with the conditions of this licence, where the attempt results in injury to the bird concerned. It also authorises, for the purpose of the prevention of serious damage to livestock, foodstuffs for livestock, crops, vegetables and fruit, and subject to the stated conditions, the keeping or confinement of any bird listed in Condition 7 of this licence in a Larsen trap. Failure to abide by anyone of the conditions may invalidate the licence and could lead to prosecution. Only authorised persons may use this licence.

Please note that, in accordance with condition 3, no person convicted on or after 1 January 2008 of an offence to which this paragraph applies may use this licence unless, in respect of that offence, either (1) they were dismissed with an admonition, or (2) they are a rehabilitated person for the purposes of the Rehabilitation of Offenders Act 1974 and their conviction is treated as spent. A person may also use this licence where, in respect of such an offence, a court has made an order discharging them absolutely. This paragraph applies to offences under the Wildlife and Countryside Act 1981, the Conservation (Natural Habitats &c.) Regulations 1994, the Protection of Badgers Act 1992, the Protection of Wild Mammals (Scotland) Act 2002, the Animal Health and Welfare (Scotland) Act 2006 and the Protection of Animals (Scotland) Act 1912 (all as amended). Such a person may still, in spite of being debarred from the use of this General Licence, apply to Scottish Natural Heritage for a specific licence to control birds for the purpose of preventing serious damage to livestock, foodstuffs for livestock, crops, vegetables and fruit. Any such application will be considered on its merits.

This licence is valid in Scotland, unless previously revoked, for the period 01 January 2012 to 31 December 2012.

CONDITIONS

1. This licence may only be used by authorised persons who have read and understood its conditions.

2. This licence can only be relied on in circumstances where the authorised person is satisfied that appropriate non-lethal methods of control such as scaring or proofing are either ineffective or impracticable.

3. No person convicted on or after 1 January 2008 of an offence to which this paragraph applies may use this licence unless, in respect of that offence, either (I) they were dismissed with an admonition, or (2) they are a rehabilitated person for the purposes of the Rehabilitation of Offenders Act 1974 and their conviction is treated as spent. A person may also use this licence where, in respect of such an offence, a court has made an order discharging them absolutely. This paragraph applies to offences under the Wildlife and Countryside Act 1981, the Conservation (Natural Habitats &c.) Regulations 1994, the Protection of Badgers Act 1992, the Protection of Wild Mammals (Scotland) Act 2002, the Animal Health and Welfare (Scotland) Act 2006 and the Protection of Animals (Scotland) Act 1912 (all as amended).

4. The methods of killing or taking which may be used under this licence, except where further restrictions, listed below in this licence, apply, are:
* Pricking of eggs
* Oiling of eggs with a product approved for use within Scotland
* Destruction of eggs and nests
* A Larsen trap
* Any other crow cage trap
* Shooting with any firearm, including semi-automatic firearms, shotguns or air weapons
* In the case of Feral Pigeon, *Columba livia*, shooting with the aid of any device for illuminating a target or any device for night shooting
* Targeted falconry

5. Bird species which may be taken or killed by the above methods for the purpose outlined in paragraph 1 are:

Great Black-backed	*Gull Larus marinus*
Collared Dove	*Streptopelia decaocto*
Feral Pigeon	*Columba livia*
Woodpigeon	*Columba palumbus*
Carrion Crow	*Corvus corone*
Hooded Crow	*Corvus cornix*
Jackdaw	*Corvus monedula*
Magpie	*Pica pica*

Rook	*Corvus frugilegus*

Except where further restrictions apply as outlined below in these licence conditions.

TRAPS

6. For the purposes of this licence birds other than the species listed in condition 5 should be released unharmed immediately on being found in a Larsen or a Cage Trap.

7. In the case of the Larsen trap, no bird may be confined in such a trap as a decoy except a bird of the following species:

Carrion Crow	*Corvus corone*
Hooded Crow	*Corvus cornix*
Jackdaw	*Corvus monedula*
Magpie	*Pica pica*

8. For the purposes of this licence, a Larsen or crow cage trap is not required to satisfy the requirements of Section 8(1) of the Wildlife & Countryside Act 1981 with regard to the dimensions.

9. In the case of other cage traps, only corvids included in condition 5 may be used as decoys. Raven (*Corvus corax*) and Chough (*Pyrrhocorax pyrrhocorax*) may not be used as decoys.

10. Except in the case where severe weather prohibits, any cage trap of any sort which is set under the terms of this licence shall be inspected by the authorised person, while it remains in use, at least once every day at intervals of no more than 24 hours.

11. Such an inspection must be sufficient to determine whether there are any live or dead birds in the trap.

12. Any dead or sickly decoy bird must be immediately removed from a trap.

13. In the case of the Larsen trap only one decoy bird may be used, and it must be removed from the trap when not in use. In the Larsen trap there must be a separate compartment for the decoy bird.

14. In the case of decoy birds, all relevant animal welfare legislation shall be complied with at all times, including the Animal Health and Welfare (Scotland) Act 2006. This includes providing decoy birds with adequate food, water and shelter and a suitable perch that does not cause discomfort to the birds' feet. Decoy birds shall also have adequate protection from the prevailing wind and rain.

15. When any cage trap is not in use it must be immobilised and rendered incapable of use in such a way that the immobilisation could not be reversed without considerable forethought or considerable difficulty. Doors or panels of cage traps must be removed from the site or, if they are not removed from

the site, they must be taken off the trap and secured by a locked padlock. When any Larsen trap is not in use, access doors must be secured with a padlock or the trap removed from site and stored in such a manner as to prevent its accidental use.

16. Any cage trap or Larsen trap used under this licence shall carry a tag or sign that gives the number of the local police station or wildlife crime officer for the area. The tag or sign shall also carry a unique code that allows the owner to be identified by the police. The operator of the trap will contact their local wildlife crime officer to obtain this code in advance of use of traps. The operator may include other relevant material on the tag or sign.

GENERAL CONDITIONS

17. Any birds killed under the authority of this licence shall be destroyed humanely.

18. Any birds included in the list in Condition 5 which have become confined in a Larsen or cage trap and which are to be killed under this licence, must be killed in a quick and humane manner as soon as reasonably practicable after discovery.

19. This licence does not permit the use of any form of spring-over trap.

DEFINITIONS

20. In this licence 'authorised person' means:
   * the owner or occupier, or any person authorised by the owner or occupier, of the land on which the action authorised is taken;
   * any person authorised in writing by the local authority for the area within which the action authorised is taken;
   * any person authorised in writing by any of the following bodies – Scottish Natural Heritage, a water authority or any other statutory water undertakers, a district board for a fishery district within the meaning of the Salmon Fisheries (Scotland) Act 1862 or the local Fisheries Regulation Act 1966.
   * any person authorised in writing by a National Parks Authority established under the National Parks (Scotland) Act 2000 and the Loch Lomond and the Trossachs National Park Designation, Transitional and Consequential Provisions (Scotland) Order 2002.

21. 'Larsen trap' means a portable cage-trap which has a closed compartment for confining a live bird as a decoy and one or more spring activated trap-doors which are either top or side mounted.

22. For the purposes of this licence, 'humanely' means taking all reasonable precautions to ensure that any killing of birds under this licence is carried

out by a single, swift action.

23. For the purposes of this licence 'wild bird' means any bird of a species which is ordinarily resident in or is a visitor to any member State or the European territory of any Member State in a wild state. 'Bird' includes all stages from chick to adult.

NOTES

I. Nothing in this licence exempts the licensee or any authorised person from complying with relevant firearms and public safety legislation.

2. For the purposes of this licence, *Columba livia* does not include specimens of wild Rock Dove.

ROBBIE KERNAHAN
Scottish Natural Heritage
Wildlife Operations Unit
Great Glen House
Leachkin Road
INVERNESS
IV3 8NW
22 December 2011

Scottish Natural Heritage General Licence No. 03/2012

Licensing Section
Scottish Natural Heritage
Great Glen House
Leachkin Road
Inverness
IV3 8NW
01463 725000

LICENSING@snh.gov.uk

Scottish Natural Heritage General Licence No. 03/2012

WILDLIFE AND COUNTRYSIDE ACT 1981
LICENCE TO PROTECT PUBLIC HEALTH, PUBLIC SAFETY AND PREVENT THE SPREAD OF DISEASE

This licence is granted under Section 16(1)(i)&(i) of the Wildlife and Countryside Act 1981 by Scottish Natural Heritage and being convinced that there is no other satisfactory solution, it authorises the killing or taking of wild birds in accordance with the stated conditions, for the purpose of preserving public health and safety and for the purpose of preventing the spread of disease. This licence also authorises attempts to kill certain birds, in line with the conditions of this licence, where the attempt results only in injury to the bird concerned, rather than immediate death. It also authorises, for the purpose of preserving public health and safety and for the purpose of preventing the spread of disease, and subject to the stated conditions, the keeping or confinement of any bird listed in Condition 7 of this licence in a Larsen trap Failure to abide by anyone of the conditions may invalidate the licence and could lead to prosecution. Only authorised persons may use this licence. Please note that, in accordance with condition 3, no person convicted on or after 1 January 2008 of an offence to which this paragraph applies may use this licence unless, in respect of that offence, either (1) they were dismissed with an admonition, or (2) they are a rehabilitated person for the purposes of the Rehabilitation of Offenders Act 1974 and their conviction is treated as spent. A person may also use this licence where, in respect of such an offence, a court has made an order discharging them absolutely. This paragraph applies to offences under the Wildlife and Countryside Act 1981, the Conservation (Natural Habitats &c.) Regulations 1994, the Protection of Badgers Act 1992, the Protection of Wild Mammals (Scotland) Act 2002, the Animal Health and Welfare (Scotland) Act 2006 and the Protection of Animals (Scotland) Act 1912 (all as amended). Such a person may still, in spite of being debarred from the use of this General Licence, apply to Scottish Natural Heritage for a specific licence to control birds for the purpose of preserving public health and safety and for the purpose of preventing the spread of disease. Any such application will be considered on its merits.

A separate licence, Scottish Natural Heritage General Licence No. 04/2012, is available for the purpose of protecting air safety. This licence is valid in Scotland, unless previously revoked, for the period 01 January 2012 to 31 December 2012.

CONDITIONS

1. This licence may only be used by authorised persons who have read and understood its conditions.

2. This licence can only be relied on in circumstances where the authorised person is satisfied that appropriate non-lethal methods of control such as scaring or proofing are either ineffective or impracticable.

3. No person convicted on or after 1 January 2008 of an offence to which this paragraph applies may use this licence unless, in respect of that offence, either (1) they were dismissed with an admonition, or (2) they are a rehabilitated person for the purposes of the Rehabilitation of Offenders Act 1974 and their conviction is treated as spent. A person may also use this licence where, in respect of such an offence, a court has made an order discharging them absolutely. This paragraph applies to offences under the Wildlife and Countryside Act 1981, the Conservation (Natural Habitats &c.) Regulations 1994, the Protection of Badgers Act 1992, the Protection of Wild Mammals (Scotland) Act 2002, the Animal Health and Welfare (Scotland) Act 2006 and the Protection of Animals (Scotland) Act 1912 (all as amended).

4. The methods of killing or taking which may be used under this licence, except where further restrictions, listed below in this licence, apply, are:
    * Pricking of eggs
    * Oiling of eggs with a product approved for use within Scotland
    * Destruction of eggs and nests
    * A Larsen trap
    * Any other crow cage trap
    * Shooting with any firearm, including semi-automatic firearms, shotguns or air weapons
    * In the case of Feral Pigeon, *Columba livia*, shooting with the aid of any device for illuminating a target or any device for night shooting
    * Targeted falconry

5. Birds which may be taken or killed under this licence are:

Great Black-backedGull	*Larus marinus*
Herring Gull	*Larus argentatus*
Lesser Black-backed	*Gull Larus fuscus*
Collared Dove	*Streptopelia decaocto*
Feral Pigeon	*Columba livia*
Woodpigeon	*Columba palumbus*
Carrion Crow	*Corvus corone*
Hooded Crow	*Corvus cornix*
Jackdaw	*Corvus monedula*
Magpie	*Pica pica*
Rook	*Corvus frugilegus*

TRAPS

6. For the purposes of this licence birds other than the species listed in condition 5 should be released unharmed immediately on being found in a Larsen or a crow cage trap.

7. In the case of the Larsen trap, no bird may be confined in such a trap as a decoy except a bird of the following species:

Carrion Crow	*Corvus corone*
Hooded Crow	*Corvus cornix*
Magpie	*Pica pica*

8. For the purposes of this licence, a Larsen or crow cage trap is not required to satisfy the requirements of Section 8(1) of the Wildlife & Countryside Act 1981 with regard to the dimensions.

9. In the case of other crow cage traps, only corvids included in condition 5 may be used as decoys. Raven (*Corvus corax*) and Chough (*Pyrrhocorax pyrrhocorax*) may not be used as decoys.

10. Except in the case where severe weather prohibits, any cage trap of any sort which is set under the terms of this licence shall be inspected by the authorised person, while it remains in use, at least once every day at intervals of no more than 24 hours.

11. Such an inspection must be sufficient to determine whether there are any live or dead birds in the trap.

12. Any dead or sickly decoy bird must be immediately removed from a trap.

13. In the case of the Larsen trap only one decoy bird may be used, and it must be removed from the trap when not in use. In the Larsen trap there must be a separate compartment for the decoy bird.

14. In the case of decoy birds, all relevant animal welfare legislation shall be complied with at all times, including the Animal Health and Welfare (Scotland) Act 2006. This includes providing decoy birds with adequate food, water and shelter and a suitable perch that does not cause discomfort to the birds' feet. Decoy birds shall also have adequate protection from the prevailing wind and rain.

15. When any cage trap is not in use it must be immobilised and rendered incapable of use in such a way that the immobilisation could not be reversed without considerable forethought or considerable difficulty. Doors or panels of cage traps must be removed from the site or, if they are not removed from the site, they must be taken off the trap and secured by a locked padlock. When any Larsen trap is not in use, access doors must be secured with a padlock or the trap removed from site and stored in such a manner as to prevent its accidental use.

16. Any cage trap or Larsen trap used under this licence shall carry a tag or sign that gives the number of the local police station or wildlife crime officer for the area. The tag or sign shall also carry a unique code that allows the owner to be identified by the police. The operator of the trap will contact their local wildlife crime officer to obtain this code in advance of use of traps. The operator may include other relevant material on the tag or sign.

GENERAL CONDITIONS
17. Any birds killed under the authority of this licence shall be destroyed humanely.

18. Any birds included in the list in Condition 5 which have become confined in a Larsen or cage trap and which are to be killed under this licence, must be killed in a quick and humane manner as soon as reasonably practicable after discovery.

19. This licence does not permit the use of any form of spring-over trap.

REPORTING AND RECORDING REQUIREMENTS FOR BIRDS OF AMBER OR RED CONSERVATION CONCERN
20. Where any action is taken against Lesser Black-backed Gull, *Larus fuscus*, or Herring Gull, *Larus argentatus* under this licence, the licensee shall, as soon as the action is completed or by 31 January 2013 at the latest, submit to Scottish Natural Heritage, Licensing Team, Great Glen House, Leachkin Road, Inverness, IV3 8NW, a report detailing the number of such birds, or their eggs, killed, taken or destroyed in each month and the reason why such action was taken in each month. The methods of control used against these birds in each month, and the locations of any such actions shall also be detailed.

DEFINITIONS

22. In this licence 'authorised person' means:

* the owner or occupier, or any person authorised by the owner or occupier, of the land on which the action authorised is taken;

* any person authorised in writing by the local authority for the area within which the action authorised is taken;

* any person authorised in writing by any of the following bodies – Scottish Natural Heritage, a water authority or any other statutory water undertakers, a district board for a fishery district within the meaning of the Salmon Fisheries (Scotland) Act 1862 or the local Fisheries Regulation Act 1966.

* any person authorised in writing by a National Parks Authority established under the National Parks (Scotland) Act 2000 and the Loch Lomond and the Trossachs National Park Designation, Transitional and Consequential Provisions (Scotland) Order 2002.

23. 'Larsen trap' means a portable cage-trap which has a closed compartment for confining a live bird as a decoy and one or more spring activated trap-doors which are either top or side mounted.

24. For the purposes of this licence, 'humanely' means taking all reasonable precautions to ensure that any killing of birds under this licence is carried out by a single, swift action.

25. For the purposes of this licence 'wild bird' means any bird of a species which is ordinarily resident in or is a visitor to any member State or the European territory of any member State in a wild state. 'Bird' includes all stages from chick to adult.

NOTES

1. Nothing in this licence exempts the licensee or any authorised person from complying with relevant firearms and public safety legislation.

2. For the purposes of this licence, *Columba livia* does not include specimens of wild Rock Dove.

ROBBIE KERNAHAN
Scottish Natural Heritage
Wildlife Operations Unit
Great Glen House

Leachkin Road
INVERNESS
IV3 8NW
22 December 2011

Scottish Natural Heritage General Licence No. 04/2012

Licensing Section
Scottish Natural Heritage
Great Glen House
Leachkin Road
Inverness
IV3 8NW
01463 725000

LICENSING@snh.gov.uk
Scottish Natural Heritage General Licence No. 04/2012

WILDLIFE AND COUNTRYSIDE ACT 1981
LICENCE TO PROTECT AIR SAFETY

This licence is granted under Section 16(1)(i) of the Wildlife and Countryside Act 1981 by Scottish Natural Heritage and being convinced that there is no other satisfactory solution, it is granted for the purpose of preserving air safety and may be used for no other purpose. This licence permits certain methods, subject to strict conditions, to be used to that effect, including the keeping or confinement of any bird listed in Condition 7 of this licence in a Larsen trap. Only authorised persons may use this licence.

This licence is valid in Scotland, unless previously revoked, for the period 01 January 2012 to 31 December 2012.

CONDITIONS

1. This licence is granted for the purpose of controlling birds to protect air safety, and may only be used by owners or managers of airports and aerodromes or persons authorised by them or their deputies.

2. The methods which may be used under this licence, except where further restrictions apply, are:
    * Pricking of eggs

* Oiling of eggs with a product approved by the Pesticide Safety Directorate
* Destruction of eggs and nests
* A Larsen cage trap
* A crow cage trap
* Shooting with any firearm, including semi-automatic firearms, shotguns or air weapons and, where necessary for the preservation of air safety, shooting from a moving vehicle
* Shooting with the aid of any device for illuminating a target or any device for night shooting
* Targeted falconry

3. Birds which may be taken or killed, within or without the perimeter of the aerodrome under this licence are:

Greylag Goose	*Anser anser*
Canada goose	*Branta canadensis*
Mallard	*Anas platyrhynchos*
Eurasian Curlew	*Numenius arquata*
Eurasian Oystercatcher	*Haematopus ostralegus*
Northern Lapwing	*Vanellus vanellus*
Black headed Gull	*Larus ridibundus*
Common or Mew Gull	*Larus canus*
Great Black-backed Gull	*Larus marinus*
Herring Gull	*Larus argentatus*
Lesser Black-backed Gull	*Larus fuscus*
Feral Pigeon	*Columba livia*
Woodpigeon	*Columba palumbas*
Stock Dove	*Columba oenas*
Carrion Crow	*Corvus corone*
Hooded Crow	*Corvus cornix*
Jackdaw	*Corvus monedula*
Magpie	*Pica pica*
Rook	*Corvus frugilegus*
Starling	*Sturnus vulgaris*

4. This licence only applies to airports that adhere to the guidelines set out in the Civil Aviation Authority document CAP 772.

REPORTING REQUIREMENTS

5. Aerodrome Managers using this licence shall submit a report to Scottish Natural Heritage by 31 January 2013, detailing the name of the airport and the numbers of birds of each species taken or killed under this licence.

TRAPS

6. Birds other than the species listed in condition 3 should be released unharmed immediately on being found in a Larsen or other Cage Trap.

7. In the case of the Larsen trap, no bird may be confined in such a trap as a decoy except a bird of the following species:

Carrion Crow	*Corvus corone*
Hooded Crow	*Corvus cornix*
Magpie	*Pica pica*

8. For the purposes of this licence, a Larsen or crow cage trap is not required to satisfy the requirements of Section 8(1) of the Wildlife & Countryside Act 1981 with regard to the dimensions.

9. In the case of other cage traps, only corvids may be used as decoys. Raven (*Corvus corax*) and Chough (*Pyrrhocorax pyrrhocorax*) may not be used as decoys.

10. Except in the case where severe weather prohibits, any cage trap of any sort which is set under the terms of this licence shall be inspected by the authorised person, while it remains in use, at least once every day at intervals of no more than 24 hours.

11. Such an inspection must be sufficient to determine whether there are any live or dead birds in the trap.

12. Any dead or sickly decoy bird must be immediately removed from a trap.

13. In the case of the Larsen trap only one decoy bird may be used, and it must be removed from the trap when not in use. In the Larsen trap there must be a separate compartment for the decoy bird.

14. In the case of decoy birds, all relevant animal welfare legislation shall be complied with at all times, including the Animal Health and Welfare (Scotland) Act 2006. This includes providing decoy birds with adequate food, water and shelter and a suitable perch that does not cause discomfort

to the birds' feet. Decoy birds shall also have adequate protection from the prevailing wind and rain.

15. When any cage trap is not in use it must be immobilised and rendered incapable of use in such a way that the immobilisation could not be reversed without considerable forethought or considerable difficulty. Doors or panels of cage traps must be removed from the site or, if they are not removed from the site, they must be taken off the trap and secured by a locked padlock. When any Larsen trap is not in use, access doors must be secured with a padlock or the trap removed from site and stored in such a manner as to prevent its accidental use.

16. Any cage trap or Larsen trap which is sited outwith the perimeter of the airport, shall carry a tag or sign that gives the number of the local police station or wildlife crime officer for the area. The tag or sign shall also carry a unique code that allows the owner to be identified by the police. The operator of the trap will contact their local wildlife crime officer to obtain this code in advance of use of traps. The operator may include other relevant material on the tag or sign.

GENERAL CONDITIONS

17. Any birds killed under the authority of this licence shall be destroyed humanely as possible.

18. Any birds included in the list in Condition 3 which have become confined in a Larsen or cage trap and which are to be killed under this licence, must be killed in a quick and humane manner as soon as reasonably practicable after discovery.

19. This licence does not permit the use of any form of spring-over trap.

DEFINITIONS

20. The term feral pigeon for the purposes of this licence includes racing pigeons which have settled or become resident in or around an airport, but does not include wild Rock Dove, *Columba livia*.

21. For the purposes of this licence 'wild bird' means any bird of a species which is ordinarily resident in or is a visitor to any member State or the European territory of any member State in a wild state. 'Bird' includes all stages from chick to adult.

NOTES
1. Nothing in this licence exempts the licensee or any authorised person from complying with relevant firearms and public safety legislation.

ROBBIE KERNAHAN
Scottish Natural Heritage
Wildlife Operations Unit
Great Glen House
Leachkin Road
INVERNESS
IV3 8NW
22 December 2011

Scottish Natural Heritage General Licence No. 05/2012

Licensing Section
Scottish Natural Heritage
Great Glen House
Leachkin Road
Inverness
IV3 8NW
01463 725000

LICENSING@snh.gov.uk
Scottish Natural Heritage General Licence No. 05/2012

WILDLIFE AND COUNTRYSIDE ACT 1981
LICENCE TO KEEP CERTAIN WILD BIRDS FOR THE PURPOSE OF REHABILITATION

Scottish Natural Heritage, in exercise of the powers conferred by Section 16(1)(c) and 16(5) of the Wildlife and Countryside Act (WCA) 1981, hereby grants this licence for the purpose of the rehabilitation of disabled wild birds, but always subject to the following conditions.

CONDITIONS
1. Section 7(1)-(2) of the WCA (including the regulations made under it) shall not apply in respect of an authorised person keeping or having in his

possession or under his control a disabled wild-bred Schedule 4 bird for the purpose described above.

2. This licence only has effect in respect of the period of 15 days commencing with the day on which the authorised person takes into his possession or control the disabled wild-bred Schedule 4 bird.

3. The Licence shall not apply to any person who would be guilty of an offence under Section 7(3) by having in his possession or control a bird on Schedule 4.

4. The authorised person shall, within 4 days commencing with the day on which he takes into his control a disabled wild-bred Schedule 4 bird, notify that fact in writing to Scottish Natural Heritage.

5. The authorised person shall keep a record of each such disabled bird coming into his possession or control. That record shall contain the following information:
    * The species of bird, and the date on which it was taken into possession or control by the authorised person.
    * The name and address of the person from whom the bird was received (if applicable), and the time and place the bird was taken.
    * The injuries sustained by the bird at the time the authorised person took it into possession or control.
    * The cause of those injuries (if known).
    * The date and place that the bird was released back into the wild (if applicable).

6. The record shall be kept for a period of 2 years from the date the bird came into the possession or control of the authorised person.

7. Within four months of the date on which an authorised person takes into possession or control a disabled wild-bred Schedule 4 bird, that person shall send to Scottish Natural Heritage, Licensing Section a copy of the record maintained in accordance with paragraph 6 above.

8. If so required in writing by Scottish Natural Heritage, the authorised person shall produce the record to a person authorised in writing by Scottish Natural Heritage.

9. The transfer by an authorised person to any other person of any disabled wild-bred Schedule 4 bird held in accordance with the terms of this licence is not permitted, except when urgent medical attention is required.

10. Any disabled wild-bred Schedule 4 bird held in excess of the 15 days mentioned in paragraph 3 of the licence shall be registered in accordance with Section 7(1)-(2) of the 1981 Act and the regulations made under it. In such a case, Scottish Natural Heritage may require, with the application for registration, a certificate by a qualified veterinary surgeon or veterinary practitioner that it is not possible to return the bird to the wild within the 15 days because of its injuries or illness.

11. Every effort must be made to ensure that any disabled wild bird falling within the terms of this licence does not become imprinted or otherwise rendered unfit, as a consequence of being in captivity, for subsequent release back into the wild.

DEFINITIONS

12. In this licence 'authorised person' means any person who:
    a. Is a full time official of the RSPB (Royal Society for Protection of Birds)
    or
    b. Is an inspector or animal welfare staff member of the SSPCA (Scottish Society for Prevention of Cruelty to Animals), or a person being trained by such a person
    or
    c. A person employed by a wildlife sanctuary or other such place which is officially approved by SSPCA for the purpose of caring for Schedule 4 birds.
    or
    d. has previously been accepted within the Department of the Environment Licensed Rehabilitation Keeper (LRK) scheme or who was permitted to keep birds for rehabilitation under the terms of DOE licence WLF100099, which replaced the LRK scheme.
    or
    e. has been a registered keeper of three disabled wild-bred Schedule 4 birds
    pursuant to Section 7(1)-(2) of the Act and the regulations made under it, and who has subsequently notified the Scottish Ministers that such birds have been successfully released into the wild; or
    or

f. a constable or employee of a police force.

13. In this licence 'a wild-bred Schedule 4 bird' means a wild bird included in Schedule 4 to the Wildlife and Countryside Act 1981 other than a bird treated as bred in captivity within the meaning of Section 27(2) of the Act. Reference to regulations made under the Act in regard to registration and ringing provisions shall have regard to the Wildlife and Countryside Act (Registration and Ringing of Certain Captive Birds) Regulations 1982, SI 1982/1221 as amended by SI 1991/478 and SI 1994/1151.

14. This licence is valid in Scotland, unless previously revoked, for the period 01 January 2012 to 31 December 2012.

ROBBIE KERNAHAN
Scottish Natural Heritage
Wildlife Operations Unit
Great Glen House
Leachkin Road
INVERNESS
IV3 8NW
22 December 2011

Scottish Natural Heritage General Licence No. 06/2011

Licensing Section
Scottish Natural Heritage
Great Glen House
Leachkin Road
Inverness
IV3 8NW
01463 725000

LICENSING@snh.gov.uk
Scottish Natural Heritage General Licence No. 06/2011

WILDLIFE AND COUNTRYSIDE ACT 1981
LICENCE FOR VETERINARY SURGEONS AND PRACTITIONERS TO KEEP CERTAIN BIRDS

This licence is granted by Scottish Natural Heritage under Section 16(1)(c) of the Wildlife and Countryside Act 1981, being satisfied that there is no other satisfactory solution. The purpose of this licence is to allow Veterinary surgeons and Veterinary practitioners to keep specimens of certain species of birds for the purposes of treatment. These are birds listed on Schedule 4 of the Wildlife and Countryside Act 1981, notwithstanding the provisions of Section 7 of that Act and the Wildlife and Countryside (Registration and Ringing of Certain Captive Birds) Regulations 1982 – SI 1981 No.1221, as amended by SI 1991 No.478 and SI 1994 No.1 152.

CONDITIONS

1. This licence only applies to qualified Veterinary practitioners and Veterinary surgeons in the course of their duties and in accordance with this licence for treating Schedule 4 birds.

2. A bird receiving treatment may be kept under the terms of this licence for a period not exceeding 6 weeks.

3. The Veterinary practitioner or Veterinary surgeon shall keep a record of each bird kept.

4. Any bird kept under the provisions of this licence may be kept only for the purpose of receiving professional veterinary treatment.

5. If a veterinary practitioner suspects that a bird has been incapacitated through illegal activity this must be reported to the police.

6. This licence is valid in Scotland, unless previously revoked, for the period 01 January 2012 to 31 December 2012.

NOTE

This licence allows authorised persons to keep specimens of species listed on Schedule 4 which are receiving professional treatment, for a period not exceeding six weeks, without the requirement to register the bird.

ROBBIE KERNAHAN
Scottish Natural Heritage
Wildlife Operations Unit
Great Glen House
Leachkin Road
INVERNESS
IV3 8NW
22 December 2011

Scottish Natural Heritage General Licence No. 07/2012

Licensing Section
Scottish Natural Heritage
Great Glen House
Leachkin Road
Inverness
IV3 8NW
01463 725000

LICENSING@snh.gov.uk
Scottish Natural Heritage General Licence No. 07/2012

WILDLIFE AND COUNTRYSIDE ACT 1981
LICENCE TO TAKE BIRDS EGGS FOR THE PURPOSE OF REMOVING
UNSUCCESSFUL EGGS FROM NEST BOXES

This licence is granted by Scottish Natural Heritage under Section 16(1)(c) of the Wildlife and Countryside Act 1981, being satisfied that there is no other satisfactory solution. It authorises the taking and destroying of the eggs of wild birds, or any part of such an egg, for the sole purpose of allowing the removal and prompt destruction of abandoned and unsuccessful eggs from nest boxes before the commencement of the next breeding season.

CONDITIONS

1. This licence only applies to the taking by hand and destroying of eggs of wild birds, or any part of such eggs, from nest boxes in Scotland not currently in use by birds, during the period 01 August to 31 January, and is issued solely in order to permit the removal of abandoned or unsuccessful eggs from nest boxes before the next breeding season.

2. No unauthorised person shall remove eggs from another person's nest box, that is a person not authorised by the owner or occupier, of the land on which the action is taken.

3. Eggs removed from nest boxes shall either be destroyed immediately or sent to an authorised authority (e.g. Royal Museum of Scotland). If a person intends to give the eggs to an authorised authority, they must do so within three days of taking the eggs from the nest box.

4. Nothing in this licence permits the sale, hire, barter or exchange of any egg of a wild bird or any part of such an egg.

5. This licence is valid in Scotland, unless previously revoked, for the period 01 January 2012 to 31 December 2012.

ROBBIE KERNAHAN
Scottish Natural Heritage
Wildlife Operations Unit
Great Glen House
Leachkin Road
INVERNESS
IV3 8NW
22 December 2011

Scottish Natural Heritage General Licence No. 08/2012

Licensing Section
Scottish Natural Heritage
Great Glen House
Leachkin Road
Inverness
IV3 8NW
01463 725000

LICENSING@snh.gov.uk
Scottish Natural Heritage General Licence No. 08/2012

WILDLIFE AND COUNTRYSIDE ACT 1981
LICENCE TO PERMIT THE SALE OF CERTAIN CAPTIVE-BRED SPECIES OF BIRD

This licence is granted by Scottish Natural Heritage under Section 16(4)(a) of the Wildlife and Countryside Act 1981, being satisfied that there is no other satisfactory solution. Subject to the conditions below, this licence authorises:

(a) the sale, hire, barter or exchange;

(b) the offering or exposure for sale, hire, barter or exchange;

(c) the possession or transport for the purpose of sale, hire, barter or exchange;

(d) the publication, or the causing to be published, of any advertisement likely to be understood as conveying the intention to buy, sell, hire, barter or exchange of any captive-bred live bird of a species which is NOT listed in

(i) Appendix 1 of the Convention on International Trade in Endangered Species of Wild Fauna and Flora (CITES) and Part 1 of Annex C of EC Regulation 338/97

or

(ii) Schedule 3 Part 1 to the Wildlife and Countryside Act 1981

or

(iii) The following species in the Anatidae family:

Common Scoter	*Melanitta nigra*
Egyptian Goose	*Alopochen aegyptiacus*
Ferruginous Duck	*Aythya nyroca*
Garganey	*Anas querquedula*
Goldeneye	*Bucephala clangula*
Goosander	*Mergus merganser*
Long-tailed Duck	*Clangula hyemalis*
Mute Swan	*Cygnus olor*
Red-breasted Merganser	*Mergus serrator*
Ruddy Duck	*Oxyura jamaicensis*
Velvet Scoter	*Melanitta fusca*

CONDITIONS

1. Any bird sold, hired, bartered or exchanged under the terms of this licence must have been bred in captivity. A bird shall not be treated as having been bred in captivity unless its parents were lawfully in captivity when the egg from which it hatched was laid. Documentary evidence of captive breeding must accompany any sale, hire, barter or exchange.

2. Any bird sold, hired, bartered or exchanged under the terms of this licence which is not on Schedule 4 to the Wildlife and Countryside Act 1981 must be ringed with a legible individually numbered metal close ring, which is a ring or band in a continuous circle (without any break, join, or any sign of tampering since it was manufactured) and which cannot be removed from the bird when its leg is fully grown.

3. Any bird sold, hired, bartered or exchanged under the terms of this licence which is on Schedule 4 to the Wildlife and Countryside Act 1981 must be registered and ringed with a close ring issued by the Department of the Environment, Food and Rural Affairs (or, where authorised, a cable tie or Swiss/Hess ring issued by the said Department) in accordance with Section 7 of the Wildlife and Countryside Act 1981 and the Wildlife and Countryside (Registration and Ringing of Certain Captive Birds) Regulations 1982 SI 1982/1221.

4. The owner or keeper of any bird sold, hired, bartered or exchanged under the terms of this licence must if requested by an official of Scottish Natural Heritage or the Department of the Environment, Food and Rural Affairs or a Police Officer make the bird available for a sample of blood to be taken. The blood sample will be taken by a qualified veterinary surgeon. Such a sample may be used to establish the ancestry of the bird. Likewise, any request to take a feather or swab from the bird, for DNA analysis, must be met with by the owner or keeper of the bird.

5. This licence is valid in Scotland, unless previously revoked, for the period 01 January 2012 to 31 December 2012.

NOTES
1. Section 6(1) of the Wildlife and Countryside Act 1981 provides that it shall be an offence if any person a) sells, offers or exposes for sale, or has in his possession or transports for the purpose of sale, any live wild bird other than a bird included in Part I of Schedule 3, or an egg of a wild bird or any part of such an egg; or b) publishes or causes to be published any advertisement likely to be understood as conveying that he buys or sells, or intends to buy or sell, any of those things. Section 16(4)(a) provides that Section 6(1) does not apply to anything done under and in accordance with the terms of a licence granted by the appropriate authority.

2. 'Wild bird' is defined in Section 27 of the Act as 'any bird of a species which is ordinarily resident in or is a visitor to any member State or the European territory of any member State in a wild state but does not include poultry or, except in sections 5 and 16 of the Act, any game bird.

ROBBIE KERNAHAN
Scottish Natural Heritage
Wildlife Operations Unit
Great Glen House
Leachkin Road
INVERNESS
IV3 8NW
22 December 2011

Scottish Natural Heritage General Licence No. 09/2012

Licensing Section
Scottish Natural Heritage
Great Glen House
Leachkin Road
Inverness
IV3 8NW
01463 725000

LICENSING@snh.gov.uk
Scottish Natural Heritage General Licence No. 09/2012

WILDLIFE AND COUNTRYSIDE ACT 1981
LICENCE TO PERMIT THE COMPETITIVE SHOWING OF CERTAIN CAPTIVE-BRED LIVE BIRDS

This licence is granted by Scottish Natural Heritage under Section 16(1)(f) of the Wildlife and Countryside Act 1981, being satisfied that there is no other satisfactory solution. It allows the showing for competitive purposes of any captive-bred live bird (as defined below), other than any bird of the species listed on the on Schedule 3 Part I to the Wildlife and Countryside Act 1981.

CONDITIONS
1. Any bird shown under the terms of this licence must have been bred in

captivity. A bird shall not be treated as having been bred in captivity unless its parents were lawfully in captivity when the egg from which it hatched was laid. Documentary evidence of captive breeding must accompany any bird shown under the terms of this licence.

2. Any bird shown under the terms of this licence which is not on Schedule 4 to the Wildlife and Countryside Act 1981 must be ringed with a legible individually numbered metal close ring, which is a ring or a band in a continuous circle (without any break, join, or any sign of tampering since it was manufactured) and which cannot be removed from the bird when its leg is fully grown.

3. Any bird shown under the terms of this licence which is on Schedule 4 to the Wildlife and Countryside Act 1981 must be registered and ringed with a close ring issued by the Department of the Environment, Food and Rural Affairs (or, where authorised, a cable tie or Swiss/Hess ring issued by the said Department) in accordance with Section 7 of the Wildlife and Countryside Act 1981 and the Wildlife and Countryside (Registration and Ringing of Certain Captive Birds) Regulations 1982 SI 1982/1221, as amended by SI 1991/478 and SI 1994/1552.

4. The owner or keeper of any bird shown under the terms of this licence must, if requested by an official of Scottish Natural Heritage, the Department of the Environment, Food and Rural Affairs or a Police Officer, make the bird available for a sample of blood to be taken. The blood sample will be taken by a qualified veterinary surgeon. Such a sample may be used to establish the ancestry of the bird. Likewise, any request from such an official or officer to take a feather or swab from the bird, for DNA analysis, must be met with by the owner or keeper of the bird.

NOTES

1. Section 6(3) of the Wildlife and Countryside Act 1981 provides that it shall be an offence if any person shows or causes or permits to be shown for the purposes of any competition or in any premises in which a competition is being held – a) any live wild bird other than a bird included in Part I of Schedule 3; or b) any live bird one of whose parents was such a wild bird. Section 16(1)(t) provides that Section 6(3) does not apply to anything done, for the purposes of any public exhibition or competition, under and in accordance with the terms of a licence granted by the appropriate authority.

2. 'Wild bird' is defined in Section 27 of the Act as 'any bird of a species which is ordinarily resident in or is a visitor to any member State or the European territory of any member State in a wild state but does not include poultry or, except in sections 5 and 16 of the Act, any game bird'.

3. Birds listed on Part I of Schedule 3 are covered by ringing requirements under Section 6(5) of the Act and SI 1982/1221.

4. This licence is valid in Scotland, unless previously revoked, for the period 01 January 2012 to 31 December 2012.

ROBBIE KERNAHAN
Scottish Natural Heritage
Wildlife Operations Unit
Great Glen House
Leachkin Road
INVERNESS
IV3 8NW
22 December 2011

Scottish Natural Heritage General Licence No.10/2012

Licensing Section
Scottish Natural Heritage
Great Glen House
Leachkin Road
Inverness
IV3 8NW
01463 725000

LICENSING@snh.gov.uk
Scottish Natural Heritage General Licence No.10/2012

WILDLIFE AND COUNTRYSIDE ACT 1981
LICENCE TO ALLOW THE KEEPING OF CERTAIN BIRDS IN SHOW CAGES FOR TRAINING PURPOSES

This licence is granted by Scottish Natural Heritage under Section 16(1)(f) of the Wildlife and Countryside Act (WCA) 1981, being convinced that there is no other satisfactory solution. The purpose of this licence is to allow the keeping or confining of any bird in a show cage the dimensions of which do not satisfy the requirements of Section 8(1) of the above Act, for the purpose of training birds for any public exhibition or competition.

CONDITIONS

1. No bird shall be kept or confined in such a cage for longer than one hour in any period of 24 hours.

2. The minimum dimensions of the cage in which the bird is kept shall be:
> Height 24.13cms
> Breadth 25.4 cms
> Depth 11.43 cms

3. This licence shall only apply to those birds whose showing for the purposes of any public exhibition or competition is not otherwise specifically prohibited by the Act.

4. This licence is valid in Scotland, unless previously revoked, for the period 01 January 2012 to 31 December 2012.

ROBBIE KERNAHAN
Scottish Natural Heritage
Wildlife Operations Unit
Great Glen House
Leachkin Road
INVERNESS
IV3 8NW
22 December 2011

Scottish Natural Heritage General Licence No. 11/2012

Licensing Section
Scottish Natural Heritage

Great Glen House
Leachkin Road
Inverness
IV3 8NW
01463 725000

LICENSING@snh.gov.uk
Scottish Natural Heritage General Licence No. 11/2012

WILDLIFE AND COUNTRYSIDE ACT 1981
LICENCE TO TAKE EGGS OF THE MALLARD (*ANAS PLATYRHYNCHOS*) FOR INCUBATION

This licence is granted by Scottish Natural Heritage under Section 16(1)(c) of the Wildlife and Countryside Act 1981 and being satisfied that there is no other satisfactory solution. The purpose of this licence is to allow the eggs of Mallard to be taken and incubated, in order to replenish stocks of Mallard for wildfowl collections when the natural renewal of those stocks is threatened by severe weather conditions. It permits:

a) any authorised person to take eggs of the Mallard (*Anas platyrhynchos*), before 31 March, for the purpose of incubation, to assist in the successful rearing of birds which otherwise would have been unlikely to withstand adverse weather conditions;

b) any authorised person to have in their possession such an egg and any bird hatched from such an egg, to assist in the successful rearing of birds which otherwise would have been unlikely to withstand adverse weather conditions.

CONDITIONS
1. Eggs may only be taken by hand.
2. No eggs shall be taken after 31 March in any year.
3. Any live bird hatched from an egg taken under this licence, unless it is disabled or has died, shall be released to the wild not later than the 31 July in the year in which the egg was taken.
4. Every effort must be made to ensure that any bird hatched from an egg taken and incubated under the terms of this licence does not become imprinted or otherwise rendered unfit, as a consequence of being in captivity, for subsequent release back into the wild.
5. Neither the eggs, nor any birds hatched from the eggs, taken under the provisions of this licence, may be sold, hired, bartered or exchanged.

6. This licence is valid in Scotland, unless previously revoked, for the period 01 January 2012 to 31 December 2012.

DEFINITION

In this licence 'authorised person' means:

* the owner or occupier, or any person authorised by the owner or occupier, of the land on which the action authorised is taken;
* any person authorised in writing by the local authority for the area within which the action authorised is taken;
* any person authorised in writing by any of the following bodies – Scottish Natural Heritage, a water authority or any other statutory water undertakers, a district board for a fishery district within the meaning of the Salmon Fisheries (Scotland) Act 1862 or a local Fisheries Regulation Act 1966.
* any person authorised in writing by a National Parks Authority established under the National Parks (Scotland) Act 2000 and the Loch Lomond and the Trossachs National Park Designation, Transitional and Consequential Provisions (Scotland) Order 2002.

ROBBIE KERNAHAN
Scottish Natural Heritage
Wildlife Operations Unit
Great Glen House
Leachkin Road
INVERNESS
IV3 8NW
22 December 2011

Scottish Natural Heritage General Licence No. 12/2012

Licensing Section
Scottish Natural Heritage
Great Glen House
Leachkin Road
Inverness
IV3 8NW
01463 725000
LICENSING@snh.gov.uk
Scottish Natural Heritage General Licence No. 12/2012

WILDLIFE AND COUNTRYSIDE ACT 1981
LICENCE TO PERMIT THE INCUBATION OF SCHEDULE 4 CHICKS

This licence is issued by Scottish Natural Heritage under Section 16(1)(e) of the Wildlife and Countryside Act 1981 and being satisfied that there is no other satisfactory solution. It authorises the keeping of Schedule 4 birds without registration for a maximum of seven days after hatching, by the end of which time they should be ringed and registered.

CONDITIONS

1. Any bird incubated under this licence must have been bred in captivity. A bird shall not be treated as bred in captivity unless its parents were lawfully in captivity when the egg from which it hatched was laid. Documentary evidence of captive breeding must accompany any temporary transfer for incubation purposes.

2. A person incubating Schedule 4 eggs shall keep a record of all live chicks hatched. The record shall contain the following information;
   (a) the date and place where the egg was hatched;
   (b) if the person incubating the egg is not the owner, then the name and address of the owner of the hatched chick must also be included.

3. Any person incubating and hatching live chicks of Schedule 4 birds must send a copy of the record collated, within three months, to Scottish Natural Heritage, Licensing Section, Great Glen House, Leachkin Road, Inverness, IV3 8NW.

4. The person incubating any Schedule 4 bird shall if requested by an Officer of Scottish Natural Heritage or a Police Officer, produce the completed record as required by condition 2.

5. The person incubating any Schedule 4 bird shall at any reasonable time permit an Officer of Scottish Natural Heritage, or a Police Officer, to enter any premises used for the purposes of;
   (a) inspecting the premises where the chick is kept; and
   (b) inspecting the chick.

6. This licence is valid in Scotland, unless previously revoked, from 01 January 2012 to 31 December 2012.

NOTE

This licence allows the incubation of any egg of a Schedule 4 bird which produces live young, without requirement to register hatchlings with Scottish Natural Heritage for a maximum of seven days, after the chick has hatched.

ROBBIE KERNAHAN
Scottish Natural Heritage
Wildlife Operations Unit
Great Glen House
Leachkin Road
INVERNESS
IV3 8NW
22 December 2011

Scottish Natural Heritage General Licence No. 13/2012

Licensing Section
Scottish Natural Heritage
Great Glen House
Leachkin Road
Inverness
IV3 8NW
01463 725000

LICENSING@snh.gov.uk
Scottish Natural Heritage General Licence No. 13/2012

WILDLIFE AND COUNTRYSIDE ACT 1981
LICENCE TO SELL FEATHERS AND PARTS OF CERTAIN DEAD WILD BIRDS

This licence is granted by Scottish Natural Heritage under Section 16(4)(a) of the Wildlife and Countryside Act (WCA) 1981, being convinced that there is no other satisfactory solution. It authorises, subject to further conditions;

(i) the sale, offer or exposure for sale, possession or transport for the purpose of sale, and

(ii) the publication or the causing to be published of any advertisement likely to be understood as conveying the intention of buying or selling, of feathers, feathered wings or pieces of feathered skin or anything manufactured, or deriving from, such items from any bird, formerly included in Schedule 3 Part III of the WCA (now included on Schedule 2 Part I) during the period from 01 March 2012 to 31 August 2012 (The WCA permits the sale, possession and transportation for sale of dead former Schedule 3 Part III birds during the period between 1 September and 28 February) namely:

Mallard	*Anas platyrhynchos*
Pintail	*Anas acuta*
Pochard	*Anas ferina*
Shoveler	*Anas clypeata*
Teal	*Anas crecca*
Tufted Duck	*Aythya fuligula*
Wigeon	*Anas penelope*
Common Snipe	*Gallinago gallinago*
Golden Plover	*Pluvialis apricaria*
Woodcock	*Scolopax rusticola*
Coot	*Fulica atra*

CONDITIONS

1. This licence only applies to the sale of any part or product of a small number of dead birds that were:

   (a) bred in captivity. A bird shall not be treated as being bred in captivity unless its parents were lawfully in captivity when the egg from which it hatched was laid. Documentary evidence of captive breeding must accompany any sale, or

   (b) removed from the natural state within the United Kingdom under legal provisions in force in the United Kingdom. Documentary evidence that the bird was lawfully removed from the natural state must accompany the sale.

2. Any person who sells a part or product of such a dead bird, under this licence ('the seller') shall keep a record ('the record'), for a minimum of two years from such sale. The record shall contain details of;

   (a) the person from whom the seller acquired the bird or part or product of such a bird;

   (b) the person to whom the part or product of such a bird was sold; and

   (c) the species of the bird sold, the cause of death (if known) and the age of the bird.

3. The seller must certify the record as accurate.

4. The seller shall, on being given reasonable notice in writing by Scottish Natural Heritage, produce the record to a person authorised in writing by Scottish Natural Heritage and the seller shall also permit such authorised person to inspect the record.

5. The seller shall submit to Scottish Natural Heritage by 31 December of each year a report giving details of any sale by him in that year of any part or product of such a dead bird which in either case has not previously been sold. The report shall also:
(a) state how the seller acquired each such bird or part or products of such a bird; and
(b) list the type and number of each species sold.

ROBBIE KERNAHAN
Scottish Natural Heritage
Wildlife Operations Unit
Great Glen House
Leachkin Road
INVERNESS
IV3 8NW
22 December 2011

Scottish Natural Heritage General Licence No.14/2012

Licensing Section
Scottish Natural Heritage
Great Glen House
Leachkin Road
Inverness
IV3 8NW
01463 725000

LICENSING@snh.gov.uk
Scottish Natural Heritage General Licence No.14/2012

WILDLIFE AND COUNTRYSIDE ACT 1981
LICENCE TO SELL DEAD BIRDS

This licence is granted by Scottish Natural Heritage under Section 16(4)(a) of the Wildlife and Countryside Act (WCA) 1981, being convinced that there is no other satisfactory solution. It authorises, subject to further conditions;

(a) the sale of, offering for sale, exposure for sale, or possession or transporting for the purpose of sale; and

(b) the publishing of, or causing to be published, any advertisement likely to be understood as conveying that any person to whom this licence applies buys or sells or intends to buy or sell, any dead wild bird, or any part of, or anything derived from such a dead wild bird, other than a wild bird of the following species:

(1) those species included in Part 1 of Schedule 2, to the 1981 Act (Schedule 2 Part I includes all those species formerly contained on Schedule 3 Part III of the WCA). A separate General Licence, 13/2012 is available to allow the sale of parts of dead birds formerly on Schedule 3 Part III outside the closed season for such sale); and

(2) the barnacle and white-fronted goose, except in the case of those specimens where there is proof that they were bred in captivity.

CONDITIONS

1. This licence applies only to the sale of dead birds, or any part or product of such dead birds, that:

(a) were bred in captivity. A bird shall not be treated as being bred in captivity unless its parents were lawfully in captivity when the egg from which it hatched was laid. Documentary evidence of captive breeding must accompany any sale, hire, barter or exchange; or

(b) originated from a Member State of the European Union and were lawfully removed from the natural state under legal provisions in force in that Member State or with the approval of competent authorities of that Member State.

Documentary evidence that the bird was lawfully removed from the natural state must accompany any sale, hire, barter or exchange.

2. The vendor of, any dead bird, parts of, or anything derived from such a dead bird, to be sold under this licence shall keep a record of all sales. This record must contain details of:

(a) the person(s) from whom the birds were acquired, and the person(s) to whom they were sold;

(b) the species of the birds sold, the cause of death (if known), and the age of the specimen (if the specimen is over 30 years old this should be noted), and the date of acquisition.

3. The vendor must certify that the record is accurate.

4. The vendor shall submit to Scottish Natural Heritage by 31 December of each year a report giving details of any sale by him in that year of any dead bird, or part or product of such a dead bird which in either case has not previously been sold. The report should also:
   (a) state how the seller acquired each such bird or part or product of such a bird;
   and
   (b) list the type and number of each species sold.

5. The vendor shall, on being given reasonable notice in writing, produce the record to a person authorised in writing by Scottish Natural Heritage and the vendor shall also permit such an authorised person to inspect the record.

6. This licence is valid from 01 January 2012 to 31 December 2012.

ROBBIE KERNAHAN
Scottish Natural Heritage
Wildlife Operations Unit
Great Glen House
Leachkin Road
INVERNESS
IV3 8NW
22 December 2011

GENERAL AUTHORISATION FOR SHOOTING DEER
Scottish Natural Heritage *Dualchas Nàdair na h-Alba*
All of nature for all of Scotland *Nàdar air fad airson Alba air fad*

DEER (SCOTLAND) ACT 1996

General Authorisation under Section 5(6) (a) for the taking or killing of deer during close season.

We, Scottish Natural Heritage (SNH), in exercise of the powers conferred by Section 5(6) (a) of the Deer (Scotland) Act 1996 (as amended by the Public Services Reform (Scotland) Act 2010) and the Wildlife and Natural Environment (Scotland) Act 2011, being satisfied:

1)

    (a) that the taking or killing of deer is necessary:

        (i) to prevent damage to any crops, pasture or human or animal foodstuffs on any agricultural land which forms part of that land; or

        (ii) to prevent damage to any enclosed woodland which forms part of that land;

    and,

    (b) that no other means of control which might reasonably be adopted in the circumstances would be adequate, hereby authorise:

2)

(a) the occupier suffering damage to those interests outlined in subsection 1(a) above and; if duly authorised in writing by the occupier suffering damage for the purpose, any or all of;

(b) the owner in person;

(c) the owner's employees;

(d) the occupier's employees, or any other person normally resident, on the land;

(e) any other person approved in writing by SNH as a fit and competent person for the purpose to take or kill:

3)

(a) Male deer and juveniles (up to 12 months old) of any species, during the period of any statutory close season; and/or

(b) Female deer of any species during the period of any statutory close season, but not including the period 1st April to 31 st August;

Only during daylight hours, as may be necessary to prevent damage to the aforementioned interests on:

4)

(a) arable land, improved permanent pasture (other than moorland) and land which has been regenerated so as to be able to make a significant contribution to the productivity of a holding which forms part of that agricultural land; or

(b) enclosed woodland

This general authorisation will remain in force from 01-04-2012 until 31-03-2013.

FEMALE DEER OVER 12 MONTHS OLD MAY NOT BE KILLED under this general authorisation during the period 1 April to 31 August.

This authorisation will remain in force until the expiry date, or the authorised person ceases to be so authorised and is subject to the following conditions:

1. No person convicted on or after 18 November 1996 of an offence under the Deer (Scotland) Act 1996 (as amended) may use this authorisation unless, in respect of that offence, either (1) they were dismissed with an admonition, or (2) they are a rehabilitated person for the purposes of the Rehabilitation of Offenders Act 1974 and their conviction is treated as spent. A person may also use this authorisation where, in respect of such an offence, a court has made an order discharging them absolutely. Such a person may apply for a specific authorisation from Scottish Natural Heritage.

2. SNH may withdraw this authorisation at any time, in whole or in part.

3. The authorised person must comply with The Deer (Firearms etc.) (Scotland) Order 1985, the Deer (Scotland) Act 1996 (as amended) and Best Practice as published by the Wild Deer Best Practice Partnership and available on the Best Practice website www.bestpracticeguides.orQ.uk.

4. SNH reserves the right to accompany controllers operating under this authorisation.

5. Occupiers should be able to demonstrate that other appropriate means of control, including liaison with others who control deer on the land and on

adjacent lands or, where appropriate, the local deer management group, have been explored before undertaking control under this authorisation.

6. The safe use of firearms is the responsibility of the nominated controller(s).

7. Occupiers must provide details of deer killed under this general authorisation to the owner of the land.

Wildlife Operations Unit, Scottish Natural Heritage

Notes:
1. This general authorisation applies only to the land types and classes of persons specified.
2. For the avoidance of doubt, this general authorisation allows for the shooting of female deer during the following periods (dates inclusive):
   a. Red deer from 16 February to 31 March and 1September to 20 October
   b. Sika deer from 16 February to 31 March and 1September to 20 October
   c. Fallow deer from 16 February to 31 March and 1September to 20 October
   d. Red/Sika hybrids from 16 February to 31 March and 1September to 20 October
   e. Roe deer from 1September to 20 October
3. Any requirement to shoot adult female deer for the prevention of damage to the classes of land specified, outwith the period of this general authorisation will require a specific authorisation from SNH.
4, Any requirement for out of season shooting to prevent damage to:
   a. unenclosed woodland; or
   b. the natural heritage; or
   c. in the interests of public safety;
   will require a specific authorisation from SNH.
5. This general authorisation does not place any requirement on the occupier; the owner, the owner's employees, the occupier's employees, or any other person normally resident, on the land to be on the SNH Fit & Competent Register.
6. Any reference to deer means deer as specified by Section 45 of the Deer (Scotland) Act 1996 (as amended).

Definitions:
The following definitions from the Deer (Scotland) Act 1996 are of relevance:
'agricultural land' has the meaning given by the Agricultural Holdings (Scotland) Act 1991;

'enclosed' means enclosed by a stock-proof fence or other barrier, and 'unenclosed' shall be construed accordingly;

'occupier' in relation to any land includes any tenant or sub-tenant, whether in actual occupation of the land or not;

'owner' in relation to any land includes any person who under the Land Clauses Acts would be enabled to sell and convey the land to promoters of an undertaking;

'woodland' means land on which trees are grown, whether or not commercially, and includes any such trees and any vegetation planted or growing naturally among such trees on that land.

WILDLIFE AND COUNTRYSIDE ACT 1981 SCHEDULES

SCHEDULE 1
BIRDS WHICH ARE PROTECTED BY SPECIAL PENALTIES
Sections 1, 2, 4, 6, 19 and 22
PART I
AT ALL TIMES

Common Name	Scientific name
Avocet	*Recurvirostra avosetta*
Bee-eater	*Merops apiaster*
Bittern	*Botaurus stellaris*
Bittern, Little	*Ixobrychus minutes*
Bluethroat	*Luscinia svecica*
Brambling	*Fringilla montifringilla*
Bunting, Cirl	*Emberiza cirlus*
Bunting, Lapland	*Calcarius lapponicus*
Bunting, Snow	*Plectrophenax, nivalis*
Buzzard, Honey	*Pernis apivorus*
Capercaillie	*Tetrao urogallus*
Chough	*Pyrrhocorax pyrrhocorax*
Corncrake	*Crex crex*
Crake, Spotted	*Porzana porzana*
Crossbills (all species)	*Loxia*
Curlew, Stone	*Burhinus oedicnemus*
Divers (all species)	*Gavia*
Dotterel	*Charadrius morinellus*
Duck, Long-tailed	*Clangula hyemalis*
Eagle, Golden	*Aquila chrysaetos*
Eagle, White-tailed	*Haliaetus albicilla*
Falcon, Gyr	*Falco rusticolus*
Fieldfare	*Turdus pilaris*
Firecrest	*Regulus ignicapillus*
Garganey	*Anas querquedula*
Godwit, Black-tailed	*Limosa limosa*

Goshawk	*Accipiter gentiles*
Grebe, Black-necked	*Podiceps nigricollis*
Grebe, Slavonian	*Podiceps auritus*
Greenshank	*Tringa nebularia*
Gull, Little	*Larus minutes*
Gull, Mediterranean	*Larus melanocephalus*
Harriers (all species)	*Circus*
Heron, Purple	*Ardea purpurea*
Hobby	*Falco subbuteo*
Hoopoe	*Upupa epops*
Kingfisher	*Alcedo atthis*
Kite, Red	*Milvus milvus*
Merlin	*Falco columbarius*
Oriole, Golden	*Oriolus oriolus*
Osprey	*Pandion haliaetus*
Owl, Barn	*Tyto alba*
Owl, Snowy	*Nyctea scandiaca*
Peregrine	*Falco peregrinus*
Petrel, Leach's	*Oceanodroma leucorhoa*
Phalorope, Red-necked	*Phalaropus lobatus*
Plover, Kentish	*Charadrius alexandrinus*
Plover, Little Ringed	*Charadrius dubius*
Quail, Common	*Coturnix coturnix*
Redstart, Black	*Phoenicurus ochruros*
Redwing	*Turdus iliacus*
Rosefinch, Scarlet	*Carpodacus erythrinus*
Ruff	*Philomachus pugnax*
Sandpiper, Green	*Tringa ochropus*
Sandpiper, Purple	*Calidris maritime*
Sandpiper, Wood	*Tringa glareola*
Scaup	*Aythya marila*
Scoter, Common	*Melanitta nigra*
Scoter, Velvet	*Melanitta fusca*
Serin	*Serinus serinus*
Shorelark	*Eremophila alpestris*
Shrike, Red-backed	*Lanius collurio*
Spoonbill	*Platalea leucorodia*
Stilt, Black-winged	*Himantopus himantopus*
Stint, Temminck's	*Calidris temminchkii*
Swan, Bewick's	*Cygnus Bewickii*

Swan, Whooper	*Cygnus Cygnus*
Tern, Black	*Chlidonia niger*
Tern, Little	*Sterna albifrons*
Tern, Roseate	*Sterna dougallii*
Tit, Bearded	*Panurus biarmicus*
Tit, Crested	*Parus cristatus*
Treecreeper, Short-toed	*Certhia brachydactyla*
Warbler, Cetti's	*Cettia cetti*
Warbler, Dartford	*Sylvia undata*
Warbler, Marsh	*Acrocephalus palustris*
Warbler, Savi's	*Locustella luscinioides*
Whimbrel	*Numenius phaeopus*
Woodlark	*Lullula arborea*
Wryneck	*Jynx torquilla*

PART II
BIRDS WHICH ARE PROTECTED BY SPECIAL PENALTIES
DURING THE CLOSE SEASON

Common name	Scientific name
Goldeneye	*Bucephala clangula*
Goose, Greylag (in Outer Hebrides, Caithness, Sutherland and Wester Ross only)	*Anser anser*
Pintail	*Anas acuta*

SCHEDULE 1A
BIRDS WHICH ARE PROTECTED FROM HARASSMENT

Common name	Scientific name
Eagle, White-tailed	*Haliaetus albicilla*

SCHEDULE A1
PROTECTED NESTS AND NEST SITES: BIRDS

Common name Scientific name

Eagle, White-tailed	*Haliaetus albicilla*

SCHEDULE 2
BIRDS WHICH MAY BE KILLED OR TAKEN
PART I BIRDS WHICH MAY BE KILLED OR TAKEN
OUTSIDE THE CLOSE SEASON

Common name	Scientific name
Coot	*Fulica atra*
Duck, Tufted	*Aythya fuligula*
Gadwall	*Anas strepera*
Goldeneye	*Bucephala clangula*
Goose, Canada	*Branta canadensis*
Goose, Greylag	*Anser anser*
Goose, Pink-footed	*Anser brachyrhynchus*
Goose, White-fronted (in England and Wales only)	*Anser albifrons*
Grouse, Black	*Tetrao tetrix*
Grouse, Red	*Lagopus lagopus scoticus*
Mallard	*Anas platyrhynchos*
Moorhen	*Gallinula chloropus*
Partridge, Grey	*Perdix perdix*
Partridge, Red-legged	*Alectoris rufa*
Pheasant, Common	*Phasianus colchicus*
Pintail	*Anas acuta*
Plover, Golden	*Pluvialis apricaria*
Pochard	*Aythya farina*
Ptarmigan	*Lagopus mutus*
Shoveler	*Anas clypeata*
Snipe, Common	*Gallinago gallinago*
Teal	*Anas crecca*
Wigeon	*Anas Penelope*
Woodcock	*Scolopax rusticola*

PART IA
EXCEPTION: BIRDS INCLUDED IN PART I WHICH MAY NOT BE
KILLED OR TAKEN ON SUNDAYS OR CHRISTMAS DAY

Common name	Scientific name
Coot	*Fulica atra*
Duck, Tufted	*Aythya fuligula*
Gadwall	*Anas strepera*
Goldeneye	*Bucephala clangula*
Goose, Canada	*Branta Canadensis*

Goose, Greylag	*Anser anser*
Goose, Pink-footed	*Anser brachyrhynchus*
Mallard *Anas*	*platyrhynchos*
Moorhen	*Gallinula chloropus*
Pintail	*Anas acuta*
Plover, Golden	*Pluvialis apricaria*
Pochard	*Aythya farina*
Shoveler	*Anas clypeata*
Snipe, Common	*Gallinago gallinago*
Teal	*Anas crecca*
Wigeon	*Anas Penelope*
Woodcock	*Scolopax rusticola*

SCHEDULE 3
BIRDS WHICH MAY BE SOLD
Sections 6 and 22
PART I
BIRDS WHICH MAY BE SOLD ALIVE AT ALL TIMES IF RINGED AND
BRED IN CAPTIVITY

Common name	Scientific name
Blackbird	*Turdus merula*
Brambling	*Fringilla montifringilla*
Bullfinch	*Pyrrhula pyrrhula*
Bunting, Reed	*Emberiza schoeniclus*
Chaffinch	*Fringilla coelebs*
Dunnock	*Prunella modularis*
Goldfinch	*Carduelis carduelis*
Greenfinch	*Carduelis chloris*
Jackdaw	*Corvus monedula*
Jay	*Garrulus glandarius*
Linnet	*Carduelis cannabina*
Magpie	*Pica pica*
Owl, Barn	*Tyto alba*
Redpoll	*Carduelis flammea*
Siskin	*Carduelis spinus*
Starling	*Sturnus vulgaris*
Thrush, Song	*Turdus philomelos*
Twite	*Carduelis flavirostris*
Yellowhammer	*Emberiza citrinella*

PART IA
BIRDS WHICH MAY BE SOLD ALIVE IF TAKEN IN CAPTIVITY OR BY CERTAIN PERSONS OUTSIDE CLOSE SEASON OR DURING FIRST 28 DAYS OF CLOSE SEASON

Common name	Scientific name
Grouse, Red	*Lagopus lagopus scoticus*
Mallard	*Anas platyrhynchos*
Partridge, Grey	*Perdix perdix*
Partridge, Red-legged	*Alectoris rufa*
Pheasant, Common	*Phasianus colchicus*

PART II
BIRDS WHICH MAY BE SOLD DEAD AT ALL TIMES

Common name	Scientific name
Woodpigeon	*Columba palumbus*

PART IIA
BIRDS WHICH MAY BE SOLD DEAD IF KILLED OUTSIDE CLOSE SEASON BY CERTAIN PERSONS

Common name	Scientific name
Coot	*Fulica atra*
Duck, Tufted	*Aythya fuligula*
Grouse, Black	*Tetrao tetrix*
Grouse, Red	*Lagopus lagopus scoticus*
Mallard	*Anas platyrhynchos*
Partridge, Grey	*Perdix perdix*
Partridge, Red-legged	*Alectoris rufa*
Pheasant, Common	*Phasianus colchicus*
Pintail	*Anas acuta*
Plover, Golden	*Pluvialis apricaria*
Pochard	*Aythya farina*
Ptarmigan	*Lagopus mutus*
Shoveler	*Anas clypeata*
Snipe, Common	*Gallinago gallinago*
Teal	*Anas crecca*
Wigeon	*Anas Penelope*
Woodcock	*Scolopax rusticola*

SCHEDULE 4
BIRDS WHICH MUST BE REGISTERED AND RINGED IF KEPT IN CAPTIVITY
Section 7 and 22

Common name	Scientific name
Buzzard, Honey	*Pernis apivorus*
Eagle, Golden	*Aquila chrysaetos*
Eagle, White-tailed	*Haliaeetus albicilla*
Falcon, Peregrine	*Falco peregrinus*
Goshawk	*Accipiter gentilis*
Harrier, Marsh	*Circus aeruginosus*
Harrier, Montagu	*Circus pygargus*
Merlin	*Falco columbarius*
Osprey	*Pandion haliaetus*

SCHEDULE 5
ANIMALS WHICH ARE PROTECTED UNDER SECTION 9
Sections 9, 10, 22 and 24

To assist with this schedule, the subsections of the WCA referred to are:

9(1) – intentionally or recklessly kill, injure or take

9(2) – possess or control, live, dead, parts or anything derived from animal

9(4) (a) – intentionally or recklessly damage or destroy or obstruct place of shelter

9(4) (b) – disturb when occupying place of shelter

9(5) – sell, offer, expose or transport for sale live or dead animal, or publish advert relating to buying or selling.

As examples, the adder is only protected against being intentionally or reckless killed or injured, or any action relating to its sale. The Ivell's sea anemone is protected against all of these subsections.

Common name	Scientific name
Adder	*Vipera berus*

(in respect of section 9(5) & section 9(1)
so far as it relates to killing and injuring)

Anemone, Ivell's Sea	*Edwardsia ivelli*
Anemone, Startlet Sea	*Nematosella vectensis*
Apus	*Triops cancriformis*
Atlantic Stream Crayfish	*Austropotamobius pallipes*

(in relation to section 9(1)
(so far as it relates to taking) and in respect of section 9(5))

Beetle, Rainbow Leaf	*Chrysolina cerealis*

Beetle, Violet Click	*Limoniscus violaceus*
Burbot	*Lota lota*
Butterfly, Heath Fritillary	*Mellicta athalia* (otherwise known as *Melitaea athalia*)
Butterfly, Northern Brown Argus (in respect of section 9(5) only)	*Aricia artaxerxes*
Butterfly, Adonis Blue (in respect of section 9(5) only)	*Lysandra bellargus*
Butterfly, Chalkhill Blue (in respect of section 9(5) only)	*Lysandra coridon*
Butterfly, Silver-studded Blue (in respect of section 9(5) only)	*Plebejus argus*
Butterfly, Small Blue (in respect of section 9(5) only)	*Cupido minimus*
Butterfly, Large Copper	*Lycaena dispar*
Butterfly, Purple Emperor (in respect of section 9(5) only)	*Apatura iris*
Butterfly, Duke of Burgandy Fritillary (in respect of section 9(5) only)	*Hamearis lucina*
Butterfly, Glanville Fritillary (in respect of section 9(5) only)	*Melitaea cinxia*
Butterfly, High Brown Fritillary	*Argynnis adippe*
Butterfly, Marsh Fritillary	*Eurodryas aurinia*
Butterfly, Pearl-bordered Fritillary (in respect of section 9(5) only)	*Boloria euphrosyne*
Butterfly, Black Hairstreak (in respect of section 9(5) only)	*Strymonidia pruni*
Butterfly, Brown Hairstreak (in respect of section 9(5) only)	*Thecla betulae*
Butterfly, White Letter Hairstreak (in respect of section 9(5) only)	*Stymonida w-album*
Butterfly, Large Heath (in respect of section 9(5) only)	*Coenonympha tullia*
Butterfly, Mountain Ringlet (in respect of section 9(5) only)	*Erebia epiphron*
Butterfly, Chequered Skipper (in respect of section 9(5) only)	*Carterocephalus palaemon*
Butterfly, Lulworth Skipper (in respect of section 9(5) only)	*Thymelicus action*
Butterfly, Silver Spotted Skipper	*Hesperia comma*

(in respect of section 9(5) only)	
Butterfly, Swallowtail	*Papilio machaon*
Butterfly, Large tortoiseshell	*Nymphalis polychloros*
(in respect of section 9(5) only)	
Butterfly, Wood White	*Leptidea sinapis*
(in respect of section 9(5) only)	
Cicada, New Forest	*Cicadetta Montana*
Cricket, Field	*Gryllus campestris*
Cricket, Mole	*Gryllotalpa gryllotalpa*
Dragonfly, Norfolk Aeshna	*Aeshna isosceles*
Frog, Common	*Rana temporaria*
(in respect of section 9(5) only)	
Grasshopper, Wart-biter	*Decticus verrucivorus*
Leech, Medicinal	*Hirudo medicinalis*
Lizard, Viviparous	*Lacerta vivipara*
(in respect of section 9(5) and	
section 9(1) so far as it relates to killing and injuring)	
Marten, Pine	*Martes martes*
Mat, Trembling Sea	*Victorella pavida*
Moth, Barberry Carpet	*Pareulype berberata*
Moth, Black-veined	*Siona lineata (otherwise known as Idaea lineata)*
Moth, Essex Emerald	*Thetidia smaragdaria*
Moth, New Forest Burnet	*Zygaena viciae*
Moth, Reddish Buff	*Acosmetia caliginosa*
Newt, Palmate	*Triturus helveticus*
(in respect of section 9(5) only)	
Newt, Smooth	*Triturus vulgaris*
(in respect of section 9(5) only)	
Sandworm, Lagoon	*Armandia cirrhosa*
Shrimp, Fairy	*Chirocephalus diaphanous*
Shrimp, Lagoon Sand	*Gammarus insensiblis*
Slow-worm (in respect of section 9(5) only and section 9(1) so far as it relates to killing or injuring)	*Anguis fragilis*
Snail, Glutinous	*Myxas glutinosa*
Snail, Sandbowl	*Catinella arenaria*
Snake, Grass (in respect of section 9(5) and section 9(1) so far as it relates to killing and injuring)	*Natrix helvetica (also known as Natrix natrix)*

Spider, Fen Raft	*Dolomedes plantarius*
Spider, Ladybird	*Eresus niger*
Squirrel, Red	*Sciurus vulgaris*
Toad, Common	*Bufo bufo*
(in respect of section 9(5) only	
Vendace	*Coregonus albula*
Walrus	*Odebenus rosmarus*
Whitefish	*Coregonus lavaretus*
Allis Shad	*Alosa alosa*
(in respect of section 9(1) and (4)(a) only)	
Mussel, Freshwater Pearl	*Margaritifera margaritifera*
Beetle	*Graphoderus zonatus*
Beetle	*Hypebaeus flavipes*
Beetle	*Parcymus aeneus*
Beetle, Lesser Silver Water	*Hydrochara caraboides*
Beetle, Mire Pill	*Curimopsis nigrita*
(in respect of section 9(4)(a) only)	
Hatchet Shell, Northern	*Thyasira gouldi*
Lagoon Snail	*Paludinella littorina*
Lagoon Snail, De Folin's	*Caecum armoricum*
Lagoon Worm, Tentacled	*Alkmaria romijni*
Moth, Sussex Emerald	*Thalera fimbrialis*
Sea Fan, Pink	*Eunicella verrucosa*
(in respect of section 9(1), 9(2) and 9(5) only	
Sea Slug, Lagoon	*Tenellia adspersa*
Beetle, Stag	*Lucanus Cervus*
(in respect of section 9(5) only)	
Dameselfly, Southern	*Coenagrion mercuriale*
Goby, Couch's	*Gobius couchii*
Goby, Giant	*Gobius cobitis*
Hydroid, Marine	*Clavopsella navis*
Moth, Fiery Clearwing	*Bembecia chrysidiformis*
Moth, Fisher's Estuarine	*Gortyna borelii*
Mussel, Fan	*Atrina fragilis*
(in respect of section 9(1), (2) and (5) only)	
Shad, Twaite	*Alosa fallax*
(in respect of section 9(4)(a) only)	
Shark, Basking	*Cetorhinus maximus*
Vole, Water	*Arvicola terrestris*
(in respect of section 9(4) only)	

SCHEDULE 5A
(introduced by sections 10A and 22)
ANIMALS WHICH ARE PROTECTED
UNDER SECTION 10A IN THEIR CLOSE SEASON

Common name	Scientific name
Hare, mountain	*Lepus timidus*
Hare, brown	*Lepus europaeus*

SCHEDULE 6
ANIMALS WHICH MAY NOT BE KILLED OR TAKEN BY CERTAIN METHODS
Section 19 of the Wildlife and Natural Environment (Scotland) Act 20011 amends Schedule 6 of the 1981 Act to remove duplication in relation to species which are also protected by the Conservation (Natural Habitats &c.) Regulations 1994

Sections 11 and 22

Common name	Scientific name
Badger	*Meles meles*
Hedgehog	*Erinaceus europaeus*
Shrews (all species)	*Soricidae*
Squirrel, Red	*Sciurus vulgaris*

SCHEDULE 6A
(introduced by sections 11E and 22)
ANIMALS NOT TO BE POACHED

Common name	Scientific name
Hare, mountain	*Lepus timidus*
Hare, brown	*Lepus europaeus*
Rabbit	*Oryctolagus cuniculus*

SCHEDULE 7
AMENDMENT OF ACTS IN RELATION TO NIGHT
SHOOTING OF HARES AND RABBITS
Section 12YA
The Ground Game Act 1880
1.

    (1) Notwithstanding the provisions of section 6 of the Ground Game Act 1880, it shall not be unlawful for the occupier of any land himself, or one other person authorised by him under section 1 of that Act, to use firearms

for the purpose of killing ground game thereon between the expiration of the first hour after sunset and the commencement of the last hour before sunrise if (except where he has exclusive right) the occupier has the written authority of the other person or one of the other persons entitled to kill and take the ground game on the land.

(2) In this paragraph 'ground game' means hares and rabbits.

The Agriculture (Scotland) Act 1948

2.

(1) Notwithstanding the provisions of section 50(1)(a) of the Agriculture (Scotland) Act 1948, it shall not be unlawful for the owner of the shooting rights on any land or any person holding those rights from him, or subject to sub-paragraph (2) below the occupier of any land, to use a firearm for the purpose of killing ground game thereon between the expiration of the first hour after sunset and the commencement of the last hour before sunrise.

(2) The occupier of any land shall not use a firearm as mentioned in sub-paragraph (1) above unless (except where he has the exclusive right) he has first obtained the written authority of the other person or one of the other persons entitled to kill and take the ground game on the land.

(3) An occupier who is entitled, in terms of this paragraph, to use a firearm for the purpose of killing ground game may, subject to the provisions of section 1 of the Ground Game Act 1880, authorise one other person so to use a firearm.

(4) In this paragraph 'ground game' means hares and rabbits.

SCHEDULE 8
PLANTS WHICH ARE PROTECTED
Section 13,22 and 24

Common name	Scientific name
Adder's-tongue, Least	*Ophioglossum lusitanicum*
Alison, Small	*Alyssum alyssoides*
Anomodon, Long-leaved	*Anomodon longifolius*
Beech-lichen, New Forest	*Enterographa elaborate*
Blackwort	*Southbya nigrella*
Bluebell	*Hyacinthoides non-scripta*
(in respect of section 13(2) only)	
Bolete, Royal	*Boletus regius*
Bright Green Cave	*Cyclodictyon laetevirens*
Broomrape, Bedstraw	*Orobanche caryophyllacea*

Broomrape, Oxtongue	*Orobanche loricata*
Broomrape, Thistle	*Orobanche reticulate*
Cabbage, Lundy	*Rhynchosinapis wrightii*
Calamint, Wood	*Calamintha sylvatica*
Caloplaca, Snow	*Caloplaca nivalis*
Catapyrenium, Tree	*Catapyrenium psoromoides*
Catchfly, Alpine	*Lychnis alpina*
Catillaria, Laurer's	*Catellaria laurei*
Centaury, Slender	*Centaurium tenuiflorum*
Cinquefoil, Rock	*Potentilla rupestris*
Cladonia, Convoluted	*Cladonia convoluta*
Cladonia, Upright Mountain	*Cladonia stricta*
Clary, Meadow	*Salvia pratensis*
Club-rush, Triangular	*Scirpus triquetrus*
Colt's-foot, Purple	*Homogyne alpina*
Cotoneaster, Wild	*Cotoneaster integerrimus*
Cottongrass, Slender	*Eriophorum gracile*
Cow-wheat, Field	*Melampyrum arvense*
Crocus, Sand	*Romulea columnae*
Crystalwort, Lizard	*Riccia bifurca*
Cudweed, Broad-leaved	*Filago pryamidata*
Cudweed, Jersey	*Gnaphalium luteoalbum*
Cudweed, Red-tipped	*Filago lutescens*
Cut-grass	*Leersia oryzoides*
Deptford Pink	*Dianthus armeria*
(in respect of England and Wales only)	
Diapensia	*Diapensia lapponica*
Earwort, Marsh	*Jamesoniella undulifolia*
Eryngo, Field	*Eryngium campestre*
Feather-moss, Polar	*Hygrohypnum polare*
Fern, Dickie's Bladder	*Cystopteris dickieana*
Flapwort, Norfolk	*Leiocolea rutheana*
Fleabane, Alpine	*Erigeron borealis*
Fleabane, Small	*Pulicaria vulgaris*
Frostwort, Pointed	*Gymnomitrion apiculatum*
Fungus, Hedgehog	*Hericium erinaceum*
Galingale, Brown	*Cyperus fuscus*
Gentian, Alpine	*Gentiana nivalis*
Gentian, Dune	*Gentianella uliginosa*
Gentian, Fringed	*Gentianella ciliata*

Gentian, Spring	*Gentiana verna*
Germander, Cut-leaved	*Teucrium botrys*
Germander, Water	*Teucrium scordium*
Gladiolus, Wild	*Gladiolus illyricus*
Goblin Lights	*Catolechia wahlenbergii*
Goosefoot, Stinking	*Chenopodium vulvaria*
Grass-poly	*Lythrum hyssopifolia*
Grimmia, Blunt-leaved	*Grimmia unicolor*
Gyalecta, Elm	*Gyalecta ulmi*
Hare's-ear, Sickle-leaved	*Bupleurum falcatum*
Hare's-ear, Small	*Bupleurum baldense*
Hawk's-beard, Stinking	*Crepis foetida*
Hawkweed, Northroe	*Hieracium northroense*
Hawkweed, Shetland	*Hieracium zetlandicum*
Hawkweed, Weak-leaved	*Hieracium attenuatifolium*
Heath, Blue	*Phyllodoce caerulea*
Helleborine, Red	*Cephalanthera rubra*
Helleborine, Young's	*Epipactis youngiana*
Horsetail, Branched	*Equisetum ramosissimum*
Hound's-tongue, Green	*Cynoglossum germanicum*
Knawel, Perennial	*Scleranthus perennis*
Knotgrass, Sea	*Polygonum maritimum*
Lecanactis, Churchyard	*Lecanactis hemisphaerica*
Lecanora, Tarn	*Lecanora archariana*
Lecidea, Copper	*Lecidea inops*
Leek, Round-headed	*Allium sphaerocephalon*
Lettuce, Least	*Lactuca saligna*
Lichen, Arctic Kidney	*Nephroma arcticum*
Lichen, Ciliate Strap	*Heterodermia leucomelos*
Lichen, Coralloid Rosette	*Heterodermia propagulifera*
Lichen, Ear-lobed Dog	Peltigera lepidophora
Lichen, Forked Hair	*Bryoria furcellata*
Lichen, Golden Hair	*Teloschistes flavicans*
Lichen, Orange Fruited Elm	*Caloplaca luteoalba*
Lichen, River Jelly	*Collema dichotomum*
Lichen, Scaly Breck	*Squamarina lentigera*
Lichen, Stary Breck	*Buellia asterella*
Lily, Snowdon	*Lloydia serotina*
Liverwort	*Petallophyllum ralfsi*
Liverwort, Lindenberg's Leafy	*Adelanthus lindenbergianus*

Marsh-mallow, Rough	*Althaea hirsuta*
Milk-parsley, Cambridge	*Selinum carvifolia*
Moss	*Drepanocladius vernicosus*
Moss Large Yellow Feather	*Scorpidium turgescens*
Moss, Alpine Copper	*Mielichoferia mielichoferi*
Moss, Baltic Bog	*Sphagnum balticum*
Moss, Blue Dew	*Saelania glaucescens*
Moss, Blunt-leaved Bristle	*Orthotrichum obtusifolium*
Moss, Cordate Beard	*Barbula cordata*
Moss, Cornish Path	*Ditrichum cornubicum*
Moss, Derbyshire Feather	*Thamnobryum angustifolium*
Moss, Dune Thread	*Bryum mamillatum*
Moss, Flamingo	*Desmatodon cernuus*
Moss, Glaucous Beard	*Barbula glauca*
Moss, Green Shield	*Buxbaumia viridis*
Moss, Hair Silk	*Plagiothecium piliferum*
Moss, Knothole	*Zygodon forsteri*
Moss, Millimetre	*Micromitrium tenerum*
Moss, Multifruited River	*Cryphaea lamyana*
Moss, Nowell's Limestone	*Zygodon gracilis*
Moss, Rigid Apple	*Bartramia stricta*
Moss, Round-leaved Feather	*Rhynocostegium rotundifolium*
Moss, Schleicher's Thread	*Bryum schleicheri*
Moss, Triangular Pygmy	*Acaulon triquetrum*
Moss, Vaucher's Feather	*Hypnum vaucheri*
Mudwort, Welsh	*Limosella australis*
Naiad, Holly-leaved	*Najas marina*
Orache, Stalked	*Halimione pedunculata*
Orchid, Early Spider	*Ophryas sphegodes*
Orchid, Ghost	*Epipogium aphyllum*
Orchid, Lapland Marsh	*Dactylorhiza lapponica*
Orchid, Late Spider	*Ophrys fuciflora*
Orchid, Lizard	*Himantoglossum hircinum*
Orchid, Military	*Orchis militaris*
Orchid, Monkey	*Orchis simian*
Pannaria, Caledonia	*Pannaria ignobilis*
Parmelia, New Forest	*Parmelia minarum*
Parmentaria, Oil Stain	*Parmentaria chilensis*
Pear, Plymouth	*Pyrus cordata*
Penny-cress, Perfoliate	*Thlaspi perfoliatum*

Pennyroyal	*Mentha pulegium*
Pertusaria, Alpine Moss	*Pertusaria bryontha*
Physcia, Southern Grey	*Physcia tribacioides*
Pigmyweed	*Crassula aquatica*
Pine, Ground	*Ajuga chamaepitys*
Pink, Cheddar	*Dianthus gratianopolitanus*
Pink, Childling	*Petroraghia nanteuilii*
Polypore, Oak	*Buglossoporus pulvinus*
Pseudocyphellaria, Ragged	*Pseudocyphellaria lacerate*
Psora, Rusty Alpine	*Psora rubiformis*
Puffball, Sandy Stilt	*Battarraea phalloides*
Ragwort, Fen	*Senecio paludosus*
Ramping-fumitory, Martin's	*Fumaria martini*
Rampion, Spiked	*Phyteuma spicatum*
Restharrow, Small	*Ononis reclinata*
Rock-cress, Alpine	*Arabis alpine*
Rock-cress, Bristol	*Arenaria norvegica*
Rustworth, Western	*Marsupella profunda*
Sandwort, Norwegian	*Arabis stricta*
Sandwort, Teesdale	*Minuartia stricta*
Saxifrage, Drooping	*Saxifraga cernua*
Saxifrage, Tufted	*Saxifraga cespitosa*
Solenopsora, Serpentine	*Solenopsora liparina*
Solomon's-seal, Whorled	*Polygonatum verticillatum*
Sow-thistle, Alpine	*Cicerbita alpine*
Spearwort, Adder's-tongue	*Ranunculus ophioglossifolius*
Speedwell, Fingered	*Veronica triphyllos*
Speedwell, Spiked	*Veronica spicata*
Spike-rush, Dwarf	*Eleocharis parvula*
Stack Fleawort, South	*Tephroseris integrifolia (ssp maritima)*
Starfruit	*Damasonium alisma*
Star-of-Bethlehem, Early	*Gagea bohemica*
Stonewort, Bearded	*Chara canescens*
Stonewort, Foxtail	*Lamprothamnium papulosum*
Strapwort	*Corrigiola litoralis*
Sulphur-tresses, Alpine	*Alectoria ochroleuca*
Threadmoss, Long-leaved	*Bryum neodamense*
Turpswort	*Geocalyx graveolens*
Violet, Fen	*Viola persicifolia*
Viper's-grass	*Scorzonera humilis*

Water-plantain, Ribbon leaved	*Alisma gramineum*
Wood-sedge, Starved	*Carex depauperata*
Woodsia, Alpine	*Woodsia alpina*
Woodsia, Oblong	*Woodsia ilvensis*
Wormwood, Field	*Artemisia campestris*
Woundwort, Downy	*Stachys germanica*
Woundwort, Limestone	*Stachys alpina*
Yellow-rattle, Greater	*Rhinanthus serotinus*

APPENDIX D

CONSERVATION (NATURAL HABITATS ETC) REGULATIONS 1994
SCHEDULES

SCHEDULE 2 – EUROPEAN PROTECTED SPECIES OF ANIMALS

Bats, Horseshoe (all species)	*Rhinolophidae*
Bats, Typical (all species)	*Vespertilionidae*
Butterfly, Large Blue	*Maculinea arion*
Cat, Wild	*Felis silvestris*
Dolphins, porpoises and whales (all species)	*Cetacea*
Dormouse	*Muscardinus avellanarius*
Lizard, Sand	*Lacertas agilis*
Newt, Great Crested	*Triturus cristatus*
Otter, Common	*Lutra lutra*
Snail, Little (or Lesser) Whirlpool Ramshorn	*Anisus vorticulus*
Snake, Smooth	*Coronella austriaca*
Sturgeon	*Acipenser sturio*
Toad, Natterjack	*Bufo calamita*
Turtles, Marine	*Caretta caretta*
	Chelonia mydas
	Lepidochelys kempii
	Eretmochelys imbricata
	Dermochelys coriacea

SCHEDULE 2A – EXCLUDED POPULATIONS OF CERTAIN SPECIES

Beaver, Eurasian	*Castor fiber* Estonia, Finland, Latvia, Lithuania, Poland and Sweden
Hamster, Common	*Cricetus cricetus* Hungary (or black bellied)
Wolf, Grey	*Canis Lupus* Estonia, Greece north of the 39th parallel, Latvia, Lithuania, Poland, Slovakia, Spain north of the

Duerno, and the reindeer
management area in Finland as
defined in Para 2 of the Finnish Act
No. 848/90 of 14/0990 on reindeer
management

Lynx, Eurasian	*Lynx lynx*	Estonia
Viper, Seoane's	*Vipera seoanni*	Spain

SCHEDULE 3 – ANIMALS WHICH MAY NOT BE TAKEN OR KILLED IN CERTAIN WAYS

Barbel	*Barbus barbus*
Grayling	*Thymallus thymallus*
Hare, Mountain	*Lepus timidus*
Lamprey, River	*Lampetra fluviatilis*
Marten, Pine	*Martes martes*
Polecat	*Mustela putorius*
Salmon, Atlantic	*Salmo salar*
Seal, Bearded	*Erignathus barbatus*
Seal, Common	*Phoca vitulina*
Seal, Grey	*Halichoerus grypus*
Seal, Harp	*Phoca groenlandica*
Seal, Hooded	*Cystophora cristata*
Seal, Ringed	*Phoca hispida*
Shad, Allis	*Alosa alosa*
Shad, Twaite	*Alosa fallax*
Vendace	*Coregonus albula*
Whitefish	*Coregonus lavaretus*

SCHEDULE 4 – EUROPEAN PROTECTED SPECIES OF PLANTS

Dock, Shore	*Rumex rupestris*
Fern, Killarney	*Trichomanes speciosum*
Gentian, Early	*Gentianella alnglica*
Lady's-slipper	*Cypripedium calceolus*
Marshwort, Creeping	*Apium repens*
Naiad, slender	*Najas flexilis*
Orchid, Fen	*Liparis loeselii*
Plantain, Floating-leaved water	*Luronium natans*
Saxifrage, Yellow Marsh	*Saxifraga hirculus*

THE WILDLIFE AND COUNTRYSIDE ACT 1981 (KEEPING AND RELEASE AND NOTIFICATION REQUIREMENTS) (SCOTLAND) ORDER 2012, SCHEDULE 1

PART 1 Types of animals specified for the purposes of section 14(1)(a)(ii) of the 1981 Act (types of animal which it is an offence for a person to release or allow to escape from captivity)

Deer	All species of the genus Cervus	Outer Hebrides and the islands of Arran (including Holy Island) Islay, Jura and Rum

PART 2 Types of invasive animals specified for the purposes of section 14ZC(1)(a) of the 1981 Act (types of animal which it is an offence for a person to keep, have in their possession or have under their control)

Asp	*Aspius aspius*
Barbel	species of the genus *Barbus* (excluding *Barbus barbus*) Bass (excluding sea bass *Mircopterus salmoides; Mircopterus dolmieu; Ambloplites rupestris Dicentrarchus labrax*) and species of the genus *Morone*
Bighead carp	*Hypophthalmichthys nobilis*
Blacknose dace	*Rhinichthys atratulus*
Blageon	*Leuciscus souffia*
Blue bream	*Ballerus ballerus*
Blue sucker	*Cycleptus elongatus*
Burbot	*Lota lota*
Catfish	species of the genera *Ictalurus, Ameiurus and Silurus*
Char	species of the genus *Salvelinus* (excluding *Salvelinus alpinus*)
Chinese black or snail-eating carp	*Mylopharyngodon piceus*
Chinese sucker (also known as Zebra hi fin, banded shark/sucker)	*Myxocyprinus asiaticus*

Coho salmon	*Oncorhychus kisutch*
Common white sucker	*Catostomus commersoni*
Coypu	*Myocastor coypus*
Crayfish	freshwater decapod crustacean of the Families *Astacidae, cambaridae* or *Parastacidae* (excluding *Austropotamobius pallipes*)
Danubiab bleak	*Chalcalbumus chalcoides*
Danubian salmon and Taimen	species of the genus *Hucho*
Eastern mudminnow	*Umbra pygmaea*
European bitterling	*Rhodeus sericeus*
European mudminnow	*Umbra krameri*
Fathead minnow (or Roseyreds)	*Pimephales promelas*
Freshwater minnow, Dragon fish or Pale chub	*Zacco platypus*
Grass carp	*Ctenopharyngodon idella*
Grey squirrel	*Sciurus carolinensis*
Landlocked salmon	non anaddromous varieties of the species *Salmo salar*
Marbled trout	*Salmo marmoratus*
Mink	*Mustela vison*
Muntjac	species of the genus *Muniacus*
Muskrat	*Ondatra zibethica*
Nase	*Chondrostoma nasus*
Northern redbelly dace (common minnow)	*Phoxinus/Chrosomus eos*
Pacific salmon and trout	species of the genus *Oncorhynchus* (excluding *Oncorhynchus mykiss* and *Oncorhynchus kisutch*)
Paddlefish	species of the genus *Polyondon* and *Psephurus*
Perch s	pecies of the genus *Perca* (excluding *Perca fluviatilis*)
Pike	species of the genus *Esox* (excluding *Esox lucius*)
Pikeperch	species of the genus *Stizostedion lucioperca*
Rabbit	(excluding European species of the genera *Bunolagus, Brachylagus, Nesolagus, Pentalagus,* rabbit) *Poelagus, Romerolagus* and *Syvilagus*
Red shiner	*Cyprinella/Notrois lutrensis*
Ruffe	*Gymnocephalus Cernuss*

Schneider	*Albornoides bipunctatus*
Silver carp	*Hypophthalmichthys molitrix*
Snakehead	species of the genus *Channa*
Southern redbelly dace (common minnow)	*Phoxinus/Chrosomus erythrogaster*
Sturgeon or Sterlet	species of the genera *Acipenser, Huso, Pseudoscaphirhynchus and Scaphirhynchus*
Sunbleak (Sundace) also known as Belica or Motherless minnow	*Leucaspius delineatus*
Sunfish, including pumpkinseed (also Basses, Crappies and Bluegills)	species of the genus *Lepomis*
Topmouth gudgeon *Pseudorasbora parva*	
Toxostrome (or French nase) *Chondostroma toxostroma*	
Vimba	*Vimba vimba*
Weatherfish	*Misgurnus fossilis*
Whitefish	species of the genus *Coregonus* (excluding *Coregonus lavaretus* and *Coregonus albula*)

PART 3 Types of invasive animals which require notification under article 4 of this Order

Coypu	*Myocastor coypus*
Muntjac species of the genus	*Muniacus*
Muskrat	*Ondatra zibethica*
Rabbit	*Poelagus, Romerolagus* and *Syvilagus*

(excluding European species of the genera *Bunolagus, Brachylagus, Nesolagus, Pentalagus,* rabbit)

NOTE: The common name or names given in Column (1) of the tables in Parts 1, 2 and 3 of this Schedule are included by way of guidance only; in the event of any dispute or proceedings, the common name or names shall not be taken into account.

THE WILDLIFE AND COUNTRYSIDE ACT 1981 (EXCEPTIONS TO SECTION 14) (SCOTLAND) ORDER 2012, SCHEDULE

PART 1 Type of animal specified for the purposes of section 14(2B)(a) of the 1981 Act (types of animal to which section 14(1)(a)(i) does not apply) –
a fish caught by rod and line, but only where the release takes place:
(a) at the same location where the fish was caught; and
(b) on the same day that the fish was caught.

PART 2 Types of plants specified for the purposes of section 14(2B)(b) of the 1981 Act (types of plants to which section 14(2) does not apply) –

Common name	Latin name	Extent
Ash	*Fraxinus excelsior*	All Scotland
Atlas cedar	*Cedrus atlantica*	"
Austrian pine	*Pinus nigra ssp, nigra*	"
Bay willow	*Salix pentandra*	"
Beech	*Fagus sylvatica*	"
Birch, specific hybrid	*Betula pendulax x pubescens (B x aurata) hybrid birch*	"
Bird cherry	*Prunus padus*	"
Bishop pine	*Pinus muratica*	"
Black currant	*Ribes nigrum*	"
Black poplar	*Populus nigra all ssp.*	"
Blackthorn	*Prunus spinosa*	"
Bugloss	*Anchusa arvensis*	"
Cedar of Lebanon	*Cedrus libani*	"
Charlock	*Sinapis arvensis*	"
Coastal redwood	*Sequoia sempervirens*	"
Common alder	*Alnus glutinosa*	"
Common elder	*Sambucus nigra*	"
Common frumitory	*Fumaria officinalis*	"
Common hawthorn	*Crataegus monogyna*	"
Common poppy	*Papaver rhoeas*	"
Cornflower	*Centaurea cyanus*	Mainland, Orkney and Shetland
Corn marigold	*Glebionis segetum*	All Scotland

Corn Spurrey	*Spregula arvensis*	"
Corsican pine	*Pinus nigra ssp, larico*	"
Crab apple	*Malus sylvestris ssp. sylvestris*	"
Crack willow	*Salix fragilis*	"
Cut leaves crane's bill	*Geranium dissectum*	"
Dark leaved willow	*Salix myrsinifolia*	"
Deodar	*Cedrus deadara*	"
Dog rose	*Rosa canina*	"
Douglas fir	*Pseudotsuga menziesii*	"
Dwarf birch	*Betula nana*	"
Eastern hemlock	*Tsuga canadensis*	"
European larch	*Larix decidua*	"
European	silver fir *Abies alba*	"
Field forget-me-not	*Myosatis arvensis*	"
Field maple	*Acer campestre*	Mainland only
Field pansy	*Viola arvensis*	All Scotland
Field woundwort	*Strachys arvensis*	Mainland, Orkney and Hebrides
Gean	*Prunus avium*	All Scotland
Glaucus dog rose	*Rosa caesia ssp. glauca*	"
Boat willow	*Salix caprea*	"
(Pussy willow or Great sallow)		
Gooseberry	*Ribes uva-crispa*	"
Grand fir	*Abies grandis*	"
Grey alder	*Alnus incana*	"
Grey poplar	*Populus x canescens*	"
Guelder rose	*Viburnum opulus*	"
Hairy dog rose	*Rosa caesia ssp. caesia*	"
Hedge mustard	*Sisymbrium officinale*	"
Holly	*Ilex aquifolium*	"
Hornbeam	*Carpinus betulus*	Mainland only
Horse chestnut	*Aesculus hippocastanum*	All Scotland
Hybrid aspen	*Populus tremula x Populus tremuloides*	"
Hybrid black poplar	*Populus x canadensis*	"
Hybrid larch	*Larix x marschlinsii/Laris x eurolepis*	"
Japanese larch	*Larix kaempferi*	"
Japanese red cedar	*Cryptomeria japonica*	"
Large hemp nettle	*Galeopsis speciosa*	"
Large-leaved lime	*Tilia platyphyllos*	"
Lawson cypress	*Chamaecyparis lawsoniana*	"

Leyland cypress X	*Cupressocyparis leylandii*	"
Lime	*Tilia platyphyllos and Tilia x europea*	"
	(Tilia cordata x Tilia platyphyllos)	
Lodgepole pine	*Pinus contorta var latifolia*	"
Long-headed poppy	*Papaver dubium*	"
Macedonian pine	*Pinus peuce*	"
Mountain pine	*Pinus mugo*	"
Noble fir	*Abies procera*	"
Nootka cypress	*Chamaecyparis nootkatensis*	"
Norway maple	*Acer platanoides*	"
Norway spruce	*Picea abies*	"
Oak, specific hybrid	*Ouercus petraea x*	"
	Ouercus robur (ouercus x rosacea) hybrid oak	
Omorika spruce	*Picea omorika*	"
Osier willow	*Salix viminalis*	"
Pacific silver fir	*Abies amabilis*	"
Pedunculate oak	*Ouercus robur*	"
Petty spurge	*Euphorbia peplius*	"
Purple willow	*Salix pupurea*	"
Rauli beech	*Nothofagus nervosa (=procera)*	"
Red alder	*Alnus rubra*	"
Red oak	*Ouercus rubra*	"
Roble beech	*Nothofagus obliqua*	"
Scentless mayweed	*Tripleurospermum inodorum*	"
Scots pine	*Pinus sylvestris*	"
Sessile oak	*Ouercus petraea*	"
Sherards downy rose	*Rosa sherardii*	"
Silver birch	*Betula pendula*	"
Sitka spruce	*Picea sitchensis*	"
Small-leaved lime	*Tilia cordata*	"
Soft downy rose	*Rosa mollis*	"
Spindle	*Euonymus europaeus*	"
Sun spurge	*Euphorbia helioscopia*	"
Sweet briar	*Rosa rubignosa*	"
Sweet chestnut	*Castanea sativa*	"
Sycamore	*Acer pseudoplatanus*	"
Tea-leaved willow	*Salix phylicifolia*	"
Walnut	species of the genus *Juglans*	"
Weld *Reseda*	*luteola*	Mainland only
Wellingtonia	*Sequoiadendron giganteum*	All Scotland

Western hemlock	*Tsuga heterophylla*	"
Western red cedar	*Thuja plicata*	"
White campion	*Silene latifolia*	"
White poplar	*Populus alba*	"
White willow	*Salix alba*	"
Whitebeam	*Sorbus aria sesu lato*	Mainland only
Wych elm	*Ulmus glabra*	All Scotland
Yew *T*	*axus baccata*	"

NOTE: The common name or names given in column (1) of the table are included by way of guidance only; in the event of any dispute or proceedings, the common name or names shall not be taken into account.

INDEX

A

Agriculture (Scotland) Act 1948 13, 46, 48, 49, 65, 269

air safety 5, 38, 213, 224, 229, 230

Anderson v Laverock 1976 (retaining productions) 94, 165

Animal Health, Defra 98, 158, 167, 168, 172

Animal Health wildlife inspector 83, 168

antiques 172, 174, 175

Aquaculture and Fisheries (Scotland) Act 2007 21, 171

Article 10 (certificate of licence) 79, 80, 137, 138, 145, 148, 149, 150, 151, 153, 154, 155, 157, 159, 161

artificial light source 84, 104, 134, 180

B

badger
    – dog as a production 98

badger guard hair 98

badger sett definition 97, 98

ballistics 64, 106, 210

barn owl 145

bat 89, 95, 108, 109, 110, 117, 135, 165
    – rabies 109

beaver 125, 131

bird lime 78

bird ringer 41

birds, captive 34, 83, 180, 203, 236, 237, 241, 243

bluebell 123, 124, 126, 152

British Association for Shooting and Conservation 53, 187

British Bird Council 79

British Trust for Ornithology 41

butterflies 11, 41, 42, 86, 118, 133

buzzard 12, 38, 40, 42, 63, 66, 67, 69, 137, 143, 144, 149

C

cat , feral 43

cause or permit 88, 89, 137, 188

certificate, specimen-specific 148, 153

certificate, transaction 153, 158

cetaceans 89, 112, 113, 133, 135

chicks, dependent 39

chough 39, 216, 221, 226, 231

Civic Government (Scotland) Act 1982 207

Conservation (Natural Habitats etc) Amendment (Scotland) Regulations 2002 21, 133

Conservation (Natural Habitats etc) Regulations 1994 8, 13, 20, 35, 60, 89, 108, 133, 146, 155, 275

Conservation of Salmon (Prohibition of Sale) (Scotland) Regulations 2002 20, 171

conservation of wild birds 214

contaminants
    – Cyphermark 168
    – Smartwater 168
    – ultra-violet paste 168

Control of Dogs (Scotland) Act 2010 206, 207

Control of Trade in Endangered Species (Enforcement) Regulations 1997 136

crayfish, signal 122

Criminal Justice (Scotland) Act 2003 17, 20

Criminal Justice Act 2003 20, 141, 142

crow, carrion and hooded 32, 33, 34, 35, 36, 37, 38, 39, 40, 41, 43, 65, 69, 143, 191, 203, 204, 215, 216, 220, 221, 225, 226, 230, 231

Crown Office and Procurator Fiscal Service (COPFS) 14, 21

Customs and Excise Management Act 1979 136

Cymag 169, 177, 209